Lickety-Split Diabetic Meals

Save Time

Eat Smart

Lose Weight

by *Zonya Foco*, RD, CHFI, CSP

American Diabetes Association®

Cure • Care • Commitment®

Director, Book Publishing, Robert Anthony; Managing Editor, Book Publishing, Abe Ogden; Editor, Rebekah Renshaw; Production Manager, Melissa Sprott; Composition, ADA; Cover Design, Jennifer Sage; Printer, Worzalla Publishing

Printed in the United States of America
1 3 5 7 9 10 8 6 4 2

The suggestions and information contained in this publication are generally consistent with the Clinical Practice Recommendations and other policies of the American Diabetes Association, but they do not represent the policy or position of the Association or any of its boards or committees. Reasonable steps have been taken to ensure the accuracy of the information presented. However, the American Diabetes Association and Zonya Foco cannot ensure the safety or efficacy of any product or service described in this publication. Individuals are advised to consult a physician or other appropriate health care professional before undertaking any diet or exercise program or taking any medication referred to in this publication. Professionals must use and apply their own professional judgment, experience, and training and should not rely solely on the information contained in this publication before prescribing any diet, exercise, or medication. Zonya Foco and the American Diabetes Association—its officers, directors, employees, volunteers, and members—assumes no responsibility or liability for personal or other injury, loss, or damage that may result from the suggestions or information in this publication.

The paper in this publication meets the requirements of the ANSI Standard Z39.48-1992 (permanence of paper).

ADA titles may be purchased for business or promotional use or for special sales. To purchase more than 50 copies of this book at a discount, or for custom editions of this book with your logo, contact the American Diabetes Association at the address below, at booksales@diabetes.org, or by calling 703-299-2046.

American Diabetes Association
1701 North Beauregard Street
Alexandria, Virginia 22311

Library of Congress Cataloging-in-Publication Data

Foco, Zonya.
Lickety-split diabetic meals / Zonya Foco.
    p. cm.
Includes index.
ISBN 978-1-58040-288-0 (alk. paper)
1. Diabetes--Diet therapy--Recipes. I. Title.

RC662.F66 2008
641.5'6314--dc22

                        2008023399

Dedicated to –

All families and individuals seeking healthy meals
and regular exercise, despite limited time.

May this book help you, once and for all …

make your good intentions come true!

Acknowledgements

My husband and soul-mate, Scott Foco, who forever encourages me in our work together and everything we do. Those of you who know him, know what a very, very lucky wife I am!

My parents, Grace Owens and Don Edwards, who, along with everything else, provided me with fine formal and informal educations. Without your unconditional love and support, I never would have acquired the expertise for this passion, which truly fulfills me.

My brothers, Clif and Mark Edwards, who helped teach me the value of fitness at an early age.

My Director of Marketing and Operations, Deb Wise. Talk about an angel! This updated edition was completely orchestrated by Deb, and done so well. All on the heels of publishing our companion weight-loss novel, Water with Lemon, which words cannot express how she has impacted that book. Everyday, I'm amazed at how her crystal-clear thinking moves our projects and this company continually forward in the most positive and professional way.
Thank you, Deb!

My partnering dietitian, Robin Shear, RD. I call her "Rockin' Robin." From research, to recipe testing, to recipe analysis, she's my right-hand nutrition pro, making this new edition truly exceptional. Thanks so much, Robin. I can't wait to do the next book with you!

My marketing firm, Market Arts. Talk about a talented duo. Jan Welborn-Nichols is "Word Girl Extraordinaire" and Susan Bachman is the most patient and talented "Art Girl" around. Thank you both for the fabulously fresh look and message to this new edition (as well as my Web site, product packaging and everything else my face and name are on)! Deb and I both thank you for all your hard work.

My recipe contributors, testers and faithful supporters: Lisa Back, Connie & Rich Bloom, Tom & Jean Cellantani, Barbara Christenson, Suzy Crossley, Gloria Edwards, Jo Edwards, Barb Filler, Trista Foco, Karen Hettel, Lori Hunt, Jay Johnson, Deb Norbotten, Grace Owens, Karen Pender, Virginia Pender, Diane Petersen, Lori Poi, Stacy Rafalko, Robin Shear, Eric & Ann Tooley, Elizabeth Wagner and Deb Wise.

My professional mentors and peers who continue to guide me in so many ways: Carol Brickenden, Barbara Christenson, Sheila Feigelson, PhD, Barbara Kopasz, Celeste Kukla, Bethany Thayer, RD, and Rob Pasick, PhD.

My former colleagues at NutriCare of St. Joseph Mercy Health System in Ann Arbor, Michigan, who helped me "apply book knowledge" to successful weight and cholesterol control during the 9 years I had the honor of working with such a fantastic group of dedicated professionals. I'm indebted to you for practical application of lifestyle change and client counseling, and for helping me with my own weight-control issues.

All the delightful clients and loyal followers (you know who you are), who have taught me over the past 20 years about the obstacles to weight loss. From you, I've learned what is needed to make "good intentions come true," and exactly what was needed to make this book work.
Thank you all!!

Zonya

Contents

Contents

Contents

Introduction

Lickety-Split Diabetic Meals: How the seed was planted

The cook without a clue

I will never forget the summer I was 16 years old. I was working 40 hours a week for $1.85 per hour. Every dime I made went to support my new (to me) pride and joy, a Datsun 280z. I was thoroughly enjoying my independence and steps toward adulthood. Like most parents of a 16 year old, Mom and Dad still saw to it that I had house chores to do. "In addition to working 40 hours a week?" I moaned.

"Welcome to adulthood," they said.

One night while I was begrudgingly doing the dishes, Mom offered a deal that I could not believe.

"You want to get out of doing dishes?" she asked.

"Well, yeah," I muttered.

"Since you have your own car now, why don't you get the groceries and make the meals?" Hungry for more grown-up independence, I liked the sound of this.

"I'll make arrangements at the bank and the IGA store so you can sign my checks," Mom explained. "You can buy however many groceries you think we need, no limits. Plan the meals, cook them, and I'll do the dishes."

"You'll do the dishes?" Well, this idea sounded really good to me. Cooking was definitely more fun than doing dishes. Then her deal got even better.

"I'll also pay you for it," she said.

"Pay me?" I'd been trying to get them to pay me for doing chores for some time.

Lickety-Split Diabetic Meals: How the seed was planted

"Yes. How does $40 a week sound?"

I did not need to think about this one!

I knew it took me 25 hours to bring home that much money from my other job. Had Mom lost her mind? I knew I'd better jump on this before she came to her senses. I made her shake on it, right then and there.

The right ingredients

Fortunately, Mom agreed to help me my first week. We glanced through her *Betty Crocker Cookbook* and her trusty recipe box. I already knew how to make five dinners, we decided. We agreed that for my first week I could make those five dinners, and we would have soup and sandwiches for the other two nights. No need to learn new meals the first week. "Why is she being so nice?" I wondered.

Then it was off to the grocery store. She quickly taught me her "no list" method of shopping. You walk up and down the aisles, glancing at everything. If you think we might need it, buy it. And always include a 4-pack of toilet paper.

"That's all you need to know," she said. I was trained and ready. This was going to be a piece of cake. Forty dollars a week and no dishes. I couldn't wait!

The first week of grocery shopping, I arrived home with $120 worth of groceries. Mom would have only spent $80. Did she say anything? No. She didn't even discourage me. She knew better than to throw in the economics lesson. That could

Needless to say, a lot of food spoiled. Again, no criticism. One night, while making dinner, I discovered that the can of tomatoes I had was 14 ounces and the recipe called for 28 ounces. The store was 15 minutes away. That's okay; I loved to drive my car. It's a good thing Mom never said that dinner had to be on time.

Fast, easy, and on-time

I managed to spend less the second week (only $75), but my cooking got worse. All new recipes! I really struggled getting a whole meal on the table at the same time. Why is it, that after slaving through a recipe, I would read, "Serve with hot cooked noodles and a tossed salad?" So when were you supposed to boil those darn noodles and make that tossed salad?

I turned to books for help. Shouldn't there be a book out there that instructs people on how to put an entire meal on the table? The only one I found was too gourmet and definitely over my head. I wanted simple, everyday meals that my family would eat. I wanted recipes that were fast and easy to follow. I also needed a list of groceries to buy. Did I have to make a special list each week? Mom never did!

The vision for this book

And that's how the seed was planted for *Lickety-Split Diabetic Meals*. After six years of college, nine years of marriage, and eight years as a registered dietitian working with clients who

inspired me, I created the complete countertop coach cookbook that I had never found. The initial idea quickly grew into the form of three books in one: a collection of easy-to-follow recipes that included directions for getting an entire meal on the table; a complete grocery list with advice on stocking your pantry; and a powerful collection of inspiring tips and useful nutrition information for losing weight and gaining health.

The story continues

After completing these projects, I decided to rework *Lickety Split Diabetic Meals* to aid those with diabetes in their quest for a healthier, happier life. Through the inclusion of diabetes-related tips and with the addition of the new American Diabetes Association's *Choose Your Foods* Exchange/Choices lists, I have created a complete list of recipes that will help those with diabetes thrive. All of the recipes included in this book meet the ADA's guidelines for nutrition. Along with the recipes, I have included tips for surviving the holidays, ways to work exercise and physical activity into your life, and other tips that will revitalize you and aid you in your quest to lead the fullest, happiest life imaginable. It is my sincerest wish that *Lickety-Split Diabetic Meals* will show you how easy it can be to eat healthy, delicious meals while saving time and keeping your diabetes under control.

Why Lickety-Split Diabetic Meals is Unique

Lickety-Split Diabetic Meals has recipes like a cookbook, healthy eating and exercise tips like a diet book, nutrition information like a health book, plus time-management and kitchen-organization strategies like a personal transformation book. You get all of these book plus a master grocery list in one package.

Recipes that fit your time limits

With your busy schedule, how much time do you have to prepare a meal? One minute, five, 15, or 30? Would you like to put something in the oven, exercise, and then eat? This book is categorized according to **YOUR** specific time demands.

Recipes that help you get a complete meal on the table

Just glance at a recipe and you'll see how easy it is to get an entire meal on the table. You will be instructed when to boil water, when to add the noodles, and when to make the salad, so the meal is hot and ready when it's time to eat.

Recipes that taste great and satisfy your entire family

Lickety-Split Diabetic Meals features tried and true family favorites. The menus are colorful, flavorful, and well balanced. You will find that for nearly all the menus, there is either a serving of fruit or a dessert suggested. By ending your meal with a hint of sweetness, you will feel satisfied, thereby ending any tendency to roam the kitchen all night!

Recipes that are healthful and list complete nutrition facts

These recipes are designed for today's health-minded family. It seems everyone wants to have more energy, ward off aging, and raise healthy children with positive eating habits. *Lickety-Split Diabetic Meals* is perfect for people wanting to:

- Lose weight
- Lower cholesterol
- Control diabetes
- Reduce the risk of cancer
- Increase their energy level
- Perform well in sports
- Slow the aging process

With so many different health recommendations making news headlines, you will be reassured to know that these recipes are:

- Low in total fat
- Low in saturated and trans fats
- Low in cholesterol
- Low in calories
- High in fiber
- Moderately low in carbohydrates
- Low in sodium
- High in phytochemicals (anti-cancer and anti-aging compounds)

A complete time-saving grocery shopping list

Shop from the grocery list, and you'll **ALWAYS** have **EVERYTHING** you need. Check the items you run out of and your next list will always be ready. (See pages 322 and 323 for more information about this kitchen stocking system!)

A built-in weekly menu planner

The next time you hear that dreaded question, "What's for dinner?" you will now know the answer. By following the basic menu planner provided on the inside front cover, you'll save time while serving plenty of variety week after week. Here's how it works: Determine who in the family will be the cook for each night; have the cook select a recipe from the category listed for that night; and use a wipe-erase marker to record the week's selections. In minutes you have your menu planned for the week! With *Lickety-Split Diabetic Meals*, I have also given you over 170 health tips so you can develop great eating and exercise habits for winning the war on obesity, diabetes, heart disease, and cancer. Knowledge is power and we have choices. So read the tips, gain the knowledge, and make your choices. I have had more than one *Lickety-Split Diabetic Meals* reader tell me that they have lost weight by following the tips alone. Just imagine what happened when they started using the recipes!

How to Read Lickety-Split Diabetic Meals' Nutrition Facts

Nutrition facts are great to know, but only if you understand what they mean. I've listed the nutrition information for each recipe with the recommended per-meal ranges, taking into account recommendations from the American Diabetes Association. All of the recipes in this book meet the nutrition guidelines of the ADA, which have been specifically designed to support people with diabetes who strive for improved blood glucose management.

Nutrition information for 1 cup (main course serving) From recipe, White Beans with Tomato, Basil & Parmesan

| Calories | 250 | Fat | 7 g | Fiber | 11 g | Sodium | 501 mg | Total Carbohydrate | 32 g |
| Calories from Fat | 25% | Saturated Fat | 2 g | Cholesterol | 9 mg | Protein | 14 g | Sugars | 0 g |

Calories—Per-meal calorie requirements range from 300–500 for weight loss and 500–700 for weight maintenance. Generally, recipe and serving size were designed with weight loss in mind.* Adjust portion size accordingly as well as the side dishes you add to the meal. A registered dietitian can help you determine your specific calorie needs based on factors such as your current calorie intake, your level of blood glucose control, and your activity level.

Calories from Fat—Goal is 30% or less for the entire meal. Some foods, like some salads and desserts, may be higher; that's okay as long as the meal is balanced to total not more than 30%.

Fat—Goal is 10–20 grams per meal for weight loss and 16–22 grams for weight maintenance. Recipes are designed to have 6–12 grams of fat per meal.* Remember, fat plays an important role in appetite satisfaction so zero is not our goal, but a moderate amount of "good" fats is. Some good tips for including good fats in your diet are: choosing lean cuts of meat, trimming fat off meat before preparing it, and grilling or broiling to decrease fat content. Using only low-fat or fat-free milk and other dairy products is another way to cut some unneccessary fat from your diet.

Saturated Fat—The lower, the better, and these recipes are very low. The American Diabetes Association recommends consuming foods with less than 2 g saturated fat; however, 3–7 grams per meal is an acceptable range based on calorie needs. People with diabetes should keep their intake of saturated fats to no more than 10% of their total calories. Saturated fats come mainly from animal prducts, such as meat, poultry, butter, and whole milk.

Fiber—The American Diabetes Association recommends that we all include a variety of fiber-containing foods such as whole grains, fruits, and vegetables in our meal plans because they provide vitamins, minerals, fiber, and other substances important for good health. Fiber can improve blood fat levels and lower the risk of heart disease, an important consideration for people with diabetes. The goal is at least 7–10 grams per meal. Recipes are designed to be high in fiber. Recipes with less fiber are accompanied by high-fiber side dishes in the menu to meet this goal. Refer to the Index to find more great tips on fiber.

Cholesterol—Cholesterol is a fat-like substance found in foods of animal origin; therefore, vegetables, fruits, beans, peas, grains, and seeds are always cholesterol free. Limiting cholesterol intake is important because a diet high in dietary cholesterol is one factor that can elevate blood cholesterol levels for some people. 200–300 mg per day is acceptable, and this can be spread out any way you wish throughout the day. Refer to the Index to find more great tips on cholesterol.

Sodium—We require a certain amount of sodium in our diet; however, excess sodium intake is linked to hypertension (high blood pressure), particularly in people with type 2 diabetes who may be more sodium sensitive than the general population. An acceptable range is

400–800 mg per meal, and the lower the better. Most recipes have less than 600 mg of sodium per entrée. An occasional entrée higher in sodium is not a problem for most people. I refer to my recipes as "salt to taste." Everyone's salt acuity is different, and my goal is to help you lower your level for salt preference. Refer to the Index to find more great tips on sodium.

Protein—The body uses protein for energy if not enough fat and carbohydrates are available. Meat, poultry, fish, eggs, milk, cheese, yogurt, soy, legumes, seeds, and nuts are the main sources of protein in our diet. Because people with diabetes are at risk for kidney disease, protein intake is often of special concern. A registered dietitian can help keep you up to date on the latest research on protein and work with you to develop an individualized meal plan. Based on daily calorie requirements, 18–35 grams per meal are needed. A healthy balance of protein, carbohydrate, and fat at every meal helps keep your energy and blood sugar stable between meals. Recipes with less protein have higher-protein side dishes recommended in the menu for proper balance.

Total Carbohydrate—Carbohydrate is the primary nutrient in food that causes blood glucose to rise. Almost 90% of the carbohydrate we eat appears in the blood as glucose within two hours after we eat it. Therefore, carbohydrate counting is helpful for people trying to control their diabetes, hypoglycemia, and weight. Sound goals are 45–70 grams per meal for weight loss and 70–90 grams per meal for weight maintenance. Remember, one super-size Coke has 113 grams of carbohydrates! Refer to the Index to find more great tips on carbohydrates.

Sugars—The best tip for people with diabetes when thinking about sugar: choose beverages and foods to moderate your intake of sugar. A good goal is less than one-third of total carbohydrates from sugars (roughly 15–30 grams per meal). This book opts to use fruit for sweetening plus sugar in moderation instead of artificial sweeteners. Refer to the Index to find more great tips on sugar.

Choose Your Foods: Exchange Lists for Diabetes—Included above the nutrition label of every recipe in this book are the exchanges from the new American Diabetes Association's *Choose Your Foods: Exchange Lists for Diabetes*. Each recipe contains the Exchange/ Choices information, which provide the Starch, Fruit, Milk, Carbohydrates, Vegetable, Meat, and Fat content of each serving. You should work with a registered dietitian to figure out how many servings of Exchange/ Choices you should consume daily.

In this recipe—White Beans with Tomato, Basil & Parmesan; wiggle room has been left to serve with raw veggies and dip, cornbread, and sorbet too for those people with higher per-meal reference goals.

Frequently Asked Questions

Is this a diet book?

Yes and no. Even though there is no official diet outlined for you to follow in *Lickety-Split Diabetic Meals*, this book IS the solution to what puts weight on you. You know what the experts say, "Don't diet, just change your lifestyle." And right now, in your hot little hands is your healthy lifestyle kitchen countertop coach. You CAN, once and for all, lose weight, lower your cholesterol, and control diabetes, all WITHOUT dieting. It's easy to do and healthy for the whole family!

Is This a low-fat, low-carb, or low-calorie cookbook?

Actually, it's all of the above. These recipes are certainly lower in fat, carbohydrates, and calories than typical North American fare, but not so unrealistically low that you can't live with them for the rest of your life. What this book does bring you is the **right** fats and the **right** carbohydrates in the guaranteed **right** amounts. In other words: BALANCE and MODERATION.

What about carbohydrates?

Restricting yourself to only 50 carbohydrates all day is an effective short-term route to "tricking" yourself into eating fewer calories. But for how long will you be able to do this? Never have pizza, popcorn, bread, desserts? And at what cost to your health? You will lose weight initially, but will you be able to stick with it? What about the rest of your life? You know deep down that it wasn't the carbohydrate in the apples or

oranges, or small baked potato or half-cup of rice that caused your weight gain. The question you must answer is: How can I lose the bad sugar carbohydrates, and how much is the right amount of good carbohydrates at each meal?

When it comes to carbohydrates, the two points you must understand are "smart carbohydrates" and "smart amounts." For instance, choosing brown rice and whole-grain pasta instead of white, and eating 1/2 cup instead of two or three. For desserts, when I use sugar and honey, they're used in half the amounts typically called for, combined with whole-grain flour or oats plus a controlled amount of fat from nuts or oil, all working together to slow the release of sugar into the bloodstream.

What about portion control?

Yes HOW MUCH you eat is as important as WHAT you eat, so always heed my recommended portion size. If the recipe says it serves 12, make sure your portion is exactly that. So go ahead, eat the right foods, in the right amounts. And *Lickety-Split Diabetic Meals* helps you do exactly that!

What about fats?

To get your fats straight, just remember: "the good, the bad and the ugly." First, the "good" unsaturated and omega-3 fats come from foods like nuts and salmon, and oils like olive and canola. Our body needs some of these good fats every day, but the secret is to know how much is not too much. Never fear, the recipes in

Lickety-Split Diabetic Meals use these good fats almost exclusively and always in the right amounts. As for the "bad" saturated fats, these come mostly from animals and their by-products like beef, pork, poultry, eggs, and whole dairy products. We definitely want to reduce the bad fats to as low as possible by choosing low-fat dairy products and lean meats. Again, *Lickety-Split Diabetic Meals* has you covered! The last fat, the "ugly" trans fats, is partially hydrogenated fats made through a manufacturing process and have been found to be worse than saturated animal fats. These trans fats are found in most restaurant fried foods, doughnuts and pastries, some shortenings, margarines, cookies, and crackers. The best way to avoid these ugly fats is to become a no-fried-foods person when eating out, avoid doughnuts and pastries like the plague, and clear your pantry of nearly every food product listing "partially hydrogenated" in the ingredients.

What's the perfect balance?

With *Lickety-Split Diabetic Meals*, you can rest assured that each meal is perfectly balanced with approximately 50 grams of carbohydrates per meal (roughly 150 grams per day) and 6–12 grams of fat per meal. Both carbohydrates and fats are equally important to control for effective weight loss. And most importantly, it's the good-for-you carbohydrates and good fats that are used in the book, with the appropriate portion size noted with every recipe!

Getting Started with Lickety-Split Diabetic Meals

"Speedisize" your kitchen

Are you really ready to take this system to the max and save yourself up to five hours each week? Then say YES to investing the time you need to get your kitchen "speedisized"! Minutes spent now will save you hours of time in the future. (And how are you going to spend those five extra hours a week, you ask? Exercising, of course!)

Some people will have no problem at all turning out one of my 15-minute meals in 15 minutes. Others will swear it takes 40 minutes. The magic is in a properly equipped and organized kitchen!

1. Clean and organize your cupboards.
Still looking for that can of tomatoes? Let me help. Group together canned fruits, vegetables, meats, tomato products, etc. Label your shelves, so that everyone putting groceries away can easily place items on their proper shelf.

2. Clean and organize your refrigerator/freezer.
Say goodbye to wasting minutes searching for a green pepper on every shelf and in every drawer. Designate specific areas for your common items and don't forget a special shelf for leftovers. You will now be able to find things in seconds flat. Now, put on some gloves and tackle your freezer.

3. Inspect your spice rack.
How old are your herbs and spices? Did you get those as a wedding present? If so, and you've celebrated five or more anniversaries, then it's time to spice up your life. The rule of thumb is after five years, throw those old spices out! But hang on to the containers. With your Lickety-Split spice list in hand, head out to your local bulk food store, health food store, or co-op, where you can purchase spices by the ounce. (The staff will show you how.) You can purchase as little as 1 tablespoon, if that's all you want to try.

4. Organize your utensil drawer
You're only a spoon away from a completely "speedisized" kitchen! Now it's time to untangle that jammed utensil drawer. It should only take two seconds to grab just the right spatula, measuring spoon, measuring cup, or ladle. HANG in there! If you have the wall space, hang your frequently used utensils, including your strainer.

Getting equipped

To achieve the Lickety-Split time requirements, you will need the following:
- Microwave
- Food processor
- Electric can opener
- Slow cooker or crock-pot
- Plastic spatula and serving spoons (appropriate for nonstick cookware)
- Sharp knives (and I do mean sharp!)
- Sharp vegetable peeler (yes, there is such a thing)
- Hot-air popcorn popper (optional, but recommended)

Recommended Ingredients That Pass the Test of Time, Taste, and Health

Minced/chopped garlic in a jar

If you want to make things Lickety-Split, you won't have time to peel and chop or mince fresh garlic cloves. Thus, welcome to the convenience of chopped or minced garlic in a jar (look in the produce section to find your choice.) Either works in all my recipes. Garlic powder can also be quickly and conveniently substituted as well.

Here's the conversion:

     1 garlic clove = 1/2 tsp chopped garlic
                    = 1/4 tsp garlic powder

Fresh ground pepper

I highly recommend using a pepper mill. If you have one, you know why! If you don't, simply substitute "10 grinds of fresh ground pepper" with "10 dashes of pepper." And go shopping, eh?

Nuts

Nuts contain many wonderful trace minerals, along with fiber and the "good" kinds of fat. As long as nuts are consumed in moderation, they are a fine addition to a healthy diet. (It is perfectly acceptable to use 1/2 cup of nuts in a recipe that serves six.)

Light or fat-free cream cheese?

If you are currently using full-fat cream cheese, please start using light in all my recipes as

a temporary step-down. If you are currently using light, I suggest it's time to come on down to fat-free. I would like to think that going to light is "good enough," but in our fight against heart disease, the facts are that it's necessary to keep saturated fats as low as possible, allowing for good monounsaturated fats from nuts, oils, and fatty fish. For the recipes, I have tested and analyzed them using fat-free, except for Creamy Frosted Carrot Cake.

Light or fat-free sour cream?

Similar to my message about light and fat-free cream cheese, if you are currently using full-fat sour cream, please start using light sour cream in all my recipes as a temporary step-down. If you are currently using light, I suggest it's time to come on down to fat-free. I used to think that "fat-free" products contained more "questionable" ingredients for flavor enhancers, etc., but this is not always the case. And fat-free sour cream is absolutely delicious in all my recipes, and is therefore what I call for.

Nonfat plain yogurt

This is a cooking and baking gem that I call for quite a bit. Yogurt is a nutrition dynamo, loaded with calcium, potassium, protein, and other important nutrients. It works great on baked potatoes, in a cream sauce, or in baking. Quite often I will have you mix it 50–50 with Miracle Whip Light to keep calories and fat grams down, while simultaneously adding valuable nutrients.

You can easily transform plain nonfat yogurt into any other flavor you desire. For instance:

Vanilla = 1 cup plain yogurt plus 1 tsp vanilla extract and 1-1/2 T sugar

Lemon = 1 cup plain yogurt plus 1/2 tsp lemon extract and 1-1/2 T sugar

Fruit = 1 cup plain yogurt plus 2 to 3 T jam or preserves

Cheese

Mix fat-free cheese with reduced-fat for great tasting low-fat cheese! The ideal is to use fat-free cheese. But what about the taste? There are good-tasting low-fat cheeses available, but they run 5 to 7 grams of fat per ounce, which is TOO MUCH. So, when it comes to shredded cheese, I mix fat-free with the reduced-fat for a great compromise! I do this with both shredded cheddar and mozzarella cheeses. This produces a wonderful, tasty, and evenly melting cheese with only 3 grams of fat per ounce. These are the "reduced-fat shredded cheddar and mozzarella cheeses" I refer to in all recipes.

Parmesan cheese

Parmesan cheese is high in fat; however, the amounts called for do not add unreasonable amounts of fat. I therefore suggest using regular Parmesan cheese and have calculated the recipes accordingly. If you would like to use fat-free instead, please do. (I have also had great results mixing regular and fat-free 50–50.)

Canola oil, olive oil, sesame oil

There are many different types of vegetable oils on the market. For the best ratio of mono-unsaturated fat (the good fat), to saturated fat (the bad fat), the winners are canola and olive oil. I tend to use canola in baked goods and olive in tomato-based dishes. If you prefer to stock just one oil, make it light olive oil or canola. Either provides the most versatility and can be substituted for the others.

Sesame oil lends incredible flavor to oriental-style dishes; e.g., stir-fry. You'll only need a small bottle of this and, I promise, it's worth getting. Be sure to store it out of the light, or refrigerated, as it will go rancid after a time.

You may be surprised to see that I call for one tablespoon of oil quite often in sautéing. One tablespoon of oil is perfectly acceptable for serving four people if the total fat for the rest of the meal is minimal. A handy way to make sure you don't use too much is to use a pump-spray bottle containing your favorite canola, olive, or sesame oil and spritz it on instead of pouring it on.

Margarine

Margarine goes through a process called hydrogenation that makes it thick and spreadable. This process creates "trans-fatty acids," which are now believed to be as artery-clogging as the saturated fat in butter. So, instead of butter or margarine, opt for small amounts of oil. Yes, oil. In almost every recipe, I've managed to use a moderate amount of oil instead of margarine. Do buy a small tub of light "zero grams of trans fat per serving" margarine to store in the back of your refrigerator and use sparingly. Why sparingly if it's "zero grams of trans fat"? Because the FDA allows up to .4 grams of trans fat per serving and still say "zero grams of trans fat." So if you eat more than one serving a day, you may very well be consuming trans fat when you think you aren't! For more information about breaking the margarine habit, and whether or not butter is better, see my tip on page 282.

Miracle Whip Light

While I'm aware that fat-free Miracle Whip and mayonnaise are available, I've found that for taste, many people prefer the light versions instead of completely fat-free. I have called for and calculated the nutrition information using Miracle Whip Light for all recipes throughout the book. You are welcome to substitute fat-free if you prefer and you'll save a few more fat grams if you do.

Spaghetti sauce

The goal is to find a sauce that contains 350 mg or less of sodium per 1/2 cup. Or, my personal favorite, which is "no salt added" and organic (which I've used in all the recipes). I encourage you to shop around for the sauce you like best. Refer to pages 176 and 336 for eye-opening tips about spaghetti sauce.

Whole-wheat pastry flour

This flour is a very nutritious whole-grain flour, yet it is light and cakey in texture, similar to that of white flour. It can be used in equal amounts to replace white flour in any non-yeast recipe. (For more information about this flour, see my tip on page 288.)

Because it is considered a specialty flour, it may be found among special brands like Arrowhead Mills, Bob's Red Mill, or Hodgson Mill. If not, request it from your grocer. I buy it in bulk quantities at natural food stores, co-ops, or from one of these companies Web sites. Until you find it, you can substitute as follows:

> For each cup of whole-wheat pastry flour: 1/2 cup all-purpose and 1/2 cup whole-wheat flour (which you can find easily in the store) OR (as a last resort) use 1 cup all-purpose flour.

Oat bran

Uncooked oat bran is located in the cooked cereal section, often in a box. You can also buy it in the specialty baking section, or by the pound in the bulk food section. Brand names include Arrowhead Mills, Bob's Red Mill, or Hodgson Mill. It's a great way to add cholesterol-lowering soluble fiber to baked goods, etc.

Handy Conversions, Abbreviations, and International Conversions

Handy Conversions

3 tsp	= 1 T
2 T	= 1/8 cup
4 T	= 1/4 cup
$5^1/_3$ T	= 1/3 cup
8 T	= 1/2 cup
16 T	= 1 cup
1 cup	= 8 liquid oz
1 pint	= 2 cups
1 qt	= 4 cups or 2 pints
1 gallon	= 4 qt
1 cup shredded cheese	= 4 oz (weight)
1 skinless, boneless chicken breast half	= 4 oz (weight)

Abbreviations

C	=	cup
T	=	tablespoon
tsp	=	teaspoon
oz	=	ounce
lb	=	pound
g	=	gram
mg	=	milligram
ml	=	milliliter
pkt	=	packet
pkg	=	package
dz	=	dozen
qt	=	quart
pt	=	pint
min	=	minutes
sm	=	small
med	=	medium
lg	=	large
opt	=	optional
0-1	=	some weeks you will buy 0, some weeks you will buy 1 (or 2 or 3, as stated)
1+	=	buy 1 or more, for your family's needs

Hello, Canada & England!

1 oz	=	28 g
1 lb (16 oz)	=	453 g
1 T	=	15 ml or g
1 cup	=	237 ml or g
1 qt	=	.946 liter (946 ml)

Breakfast

"Breakfast is your most important meal of the day."

I know you've heard this a million times before. (I even bet I know from whom!) I also balked at my mother's advice for the first 22 years of my life. But then in a college classroom, Mom's advice took on new appeal. A study found different rates of weight loss between two groups of people, although their calorie intakes were identical. The group that ate their calories across breakfast, lunch, and dinner lost more weight than the group eating their calories across lunch and dinner only. This shows how our gastrointestinal tract burns calories simply by digesting food. Starting that process early in the morning (when your metabolism is high) means a higher total calorie burn for the day.

I don't know how this sounds to you, but to me it sounds like breakfast is the most important meal of the day.

So try these great recipes to make your most important meal of the day the most delicious meal of the day!

Lickety-Split Diabetic Meals

Lickety-Split Tip

Coffee: Morning Hydration Alert

Did you know that chances are you wake up in the morning dehydrated? You haven't consumed any liquids for 8 hours or longer. Charging off to work on 2 cups of coffee may not be the ideal hydrator your body needs. For many people, a cup of caffeinated coffee works like a diuretic. For every cup you drink, you excrete 1 1/2 cups. No wonder so many people get headaches by mid-afternoon, which is a classic sign of dehydration. Coupled with fatigue, this means you're definitely not operating at your optimal level.

Solution:

Make it a goal to drink a glass of water or diluted juice **FIRST THING** in the morning before having any coffee or tea. In fact, you may find it convenient to just open up in the shower! (Think about it. There isn't anything weird about using your showerhead as a drinking fountain. Try it!)

Breakfast Casserole

Hands-on – 10 min. Oven – 40 or 45 min.   **Serves 4 or 8**

Here's a special breakfast recipe that's not labor-intensive like pancakes or omelettes, yet is every bit as delicious. It's ideal to put in the oven before you head out to do your morning exercise. Be sure to keep this in mind for when you have overnight company—they'll love it!

Preheat oven to 375°
Coat baking dishes with cooking spray.
(Be sure to coat the sides of the dish, too.)

Great as a morning
- *Oven*
- *Exercise*
- *Eat!*

Menu

Breakfast Casserole

English Muffins

Strawberries, Melon, or Grapes

For 4	For 8	
3 cups	6 cups	**Ore Ida Potatoes O'Brien** (hash browns with onions & peppers)
1/2 cup	1 cup	**reduced-fat shredded cheddar cheese†**
2 oz	4 oz	**lean ham or Canadian bacon or low-fat smoked sausage**

Use an 8" × 8" baking dish for 4 servings and a 9" × 13" dish for 8 servings.

Place the frozen potatoes in the bottom of the baking dish. Break up large chunks. Cut the meat into small chunks. Sprinkle the meat and cheese over the potatoes.

For 4	For 8	
2	4	**whole eggs**
4	8	**egg whites**
2 T	1/4 cup	**skim milk**
2 T	1/4 cup	**Dijon mustard**
1/4 tsp	1/2 tsp	**thyme**

In a small bowl, whip lightly with a fork. Pour evenly over the potato mixture.

For 4	For 8	
20 grinds	40 grinds	**fresh ground pepper**

Top casserole with pepper. Place in oven uncovered and set timer for 40 minutes (4 servings) or 45 minutes (8 servings). No, don't read the paper; how about using one of those aerobic videos you have?

Serve with toasted English muffins and fresh fruit.

Nutrition information for 1 cup casserole
Exchanges/Choices: 1 Starch, 2 Lean Meat

†See reduced-fat cheese tip on page viii (Introduction).

Calories	183	Fat	5 g	Fiber	2 g	Sodium	457 mg	Total Carbohydrate	19 g
Calories from Fat	23%	Saturated Fat	2 g	Cholesterol	117 mg	Protein	15 g	Sugars	<1 g

Lickety-Split Tip

The Vegetarian Omelette: Friend or Foe?

Did you know that a "restaurant" vegetarian omelette, made with 3 eggs and cheese, served with buttered toast, hashbrowns, and an 8-oz glass of juice racks up 50 grams of fat, 90 grams of carbohydrates, and enough calories to fuel a pro football player? Talk about starting the day off with artery-clogging fats and a surging blood sugar!

Thank goodness, knowledge is power and you have choices! Next time you're at a restaurant for breakfast, try ordering my recommendation:

■ A vegetarian omelette made with egg substitute or 1 egg and 2 whites (yes, they will do this for you), hold the cheese and double the veggies (don't forget the spinach).

■ Dry whole-wheat toast and hold the hashbrowns.

■ For the juice, share with someone or only drink half (4 oz is the max), or better yet, order fresh fruit instead.

■ If you have a hankering for hashbrowns (30 grams of carbohydrates and 11 grams of fat), skip the toast. Or eat half the hashbrowns and one slice of toast.

■ Better yet, stay home and make Scrambled Omelette!

Either way, you will have slashed 50 grams of fat down to 8, halved the carbohydrates for half the blood sugar, and knocked out 360 calories. And you'll feel lighter and more alert all day!

Super Time-Saving Tip

Skip microwaving the potatoes and chopping the pepper and onion by using 2 cups of Ore Ida Potatoes O'Brien (a frozen hashbrown product called for in previous recipe). It has no fat, just chopped potatoes, onions, and peppers, and saves you loads of time!

Scrambled Omelette

Hands-on — 20 min.   **Serves 4**

Not patient enough to make an omelette, but crave the taste? Here's the compromise—and it's healthy too!

Menu

Scrambled Omelette

Whole-Wheat Toast or
English Muffins

Sliced Cantaloupe

2 small	(4 oz each) potatoes* (opt)	Scrub thoroughly and pierce each potato with a fork. Microwave on high for 7 minutes. (If you prefer your omelette without potatoes, then skip this step.)
1/2 1 small	green bell pepper, seeded and chopped* onion, chopped*	Chop (or save time and use pre-prepped frozen!)
2	Homemade Turkey Sausage patties** or 4 slices Canadian bacon, chopped (opt)	Spray a large nonstick skillet with cooking spray. Sauté onion and pepper with sausage over medium-high heat. Break sausage patties into chunks. When potatoes finish, chop and add to sauté.
2	English muffins or 4 slices whole-wheat bread	Put in toaster.
4 lg 6 lg 1/4 cup	whole eggs egg whites (yes, throw those yolks away!) skim milk	In a medium bowl, whip together with a fork. Add to sauté and stir constantly.
1 1/2 cup 15 grinds	tomato, chopped reduced-fat shredded cheddar cheese† fresh ground pepper	Fold in when eggs are almost completely done. Turn off heat, cover, and let set 1 minute. Top with ground pepper. Serve with English muffins or toast and cantaloupe. Note: If not using meat, you may wish to sprinkle on 1/4 tsp. salt.

Nutrition information for 1 cup omelette made with Turkey Sausage** and 1/2 English muffin

* See my Lickety-Split Tip above.

** See recipe on page 13.

†See reduced-fat cheese tip on page viii (Introduction).

Exchanges/Choices: 2 Starch, 3 Lean Meat

Calories	309	Fat	8 g	Fiber	3 g	Sodium	497 mg	Total Carbohydrate	29 g
Calories from Fat	24%	Saturated Fat	2.8 g	Cholesterol	229 mg	Protein	27 g	Sugars	6 g

Lickety-Split Diabetic Meals

Lickety-Split Tip

Cinnamon to Your Blood Sugar Rescue!

Here's a little-known tip to help lower blood sugar: Sprinkle cinnamon (make that "spoon" cinnamon) on oatmeal, yogurt, applesauce, and even meat. Not only does adding cinnamon help provide a convenient illusion of sweetness to foods like cereal so you require less (if any) sweetener, cinnamon also contains polyphenols. Early studies have shown that these polyphenols improve insulin function, thereby, improving blood sugar control. As if this exciting news isn't enough, these compounds are known for their antioxidant, anticancer, and anti-inflammatory functions as well. Now this is all a **HUGE** fringe benefit beyond the sweet and yummy taste! I encourage you to buy the big bottle of cinnamon and add it liberally (1/2 to 1 teaspoon a day) to your foods. Surprisingly, "spooning" 1/2 teaspoon of cinnamon in a single serving of oatmeal or cup of yogurt or applesauce tastes perfectly delicious. Give it a try!

Scrumptious Swiss Oats 'n Fruit

Hands-on – 5 min. (p.m.) – 15 min. (a.m.)

Serves 4 or 8

Think you don't like oatmeal 'cause it's gloppy? Have you tried uncooked oats, the Swiss way? You won't believe how absolutely delicious this dish is! Thanks to Elizabeth Wagner (culinary wizard, caterer, and new-found friend) for this dish you'll be proud to serve your family. It saves time on the morning rush and is perfect for overnight guests. This also makes a great "dish to pass" for a morning meeting. Bye-bye doughnuts!

Menu

Swiss Oats 'n Fruit
English Muffins (opt)

For 4	For 8	
1½ cups	3 cups	oats (quick-cooking or old-fashioned)
1½ cups	2½ cups	skim, 1/2%, or soy milk
2 T	1/4 cup	honey
1/2 tsp	1 tsp	ground cinnamon

Night before:

Stir together in a large bowl and allow to soak in refrigerator, covered, overnight.

For 4	For 8	
3 cups	6 cups	any variety of fresh or dried fruit you fancy: • sliced banana • sliced kiwi • strawberries, hulled and cut in half • blueberries • raspberries • bite-size chunks of cored apple • raisins • dried cranberries • dried cherries • dried chopped apricots
1/4 cup	1/2 cup	chopped walnuts, pecans, or almonds

In the morning:

Add and gently mix together.

Serve in large attractive bowl with matching small bowls. Include toasted English muffins on the side if you wish.

Needs to soak for at least 4 hours.

Nutrition information for 1½ cup serving with blueberries, banana, and apple

Exchanges/Choices: 1 1/2 Starch, 1 1/2 Fruit, 1 1/2 Fat

Calories	282	Fat	8 g	Fiber	7 g	Sodium	44 mg	Total Carbohydrate	49 g
Calories from Fat	25%	Saturated Fat	1 g	Cholesterol	1 mg	Protein	9 g	Sugars	23 g

Lickety-Split Diabetic Meals

Lickety-Split Tip

Don't Have Time For Breakfast?

Trust me, breakfast doesn't have to be time-consuming. Here are 5 fast breakfasts you can count on:

The Eat While You Drive:
1 banana or juice box and 1 small or 1/2 large whole-grain bagel with peanut butter, or 2 Breakfast in a Cookie cookies with a glass of milk or soy milk

The Eat at Your Desk While the Boss Isn't Looking:
8 oz low-fat yogurt with 1/4 cup Grape-Nuts, wheat germ, flax seed, or granola mixed in and 1 Breakfast in a Cookie cookie

The 3-Minute Favorite:
Cereal and skim or soy milk and a piece of fresh fruit

The Stick to Your Ribs When You Know You Won't Be Getting Lunch Until Late:
Whole-grain bagel with a thin spread of natural peanut butter, glass of skim or soy milk or juice

The Quickie:
8 oz glass of skim or soy milk and a 4-oz glass of orange juice. (Although this liquid breakfast may not seem ideal, it gives you 30% of your calcium needs, good carbohydrates and protein, and 100% of your vitamin C needs.)
Throw in 2 Breakfast in a Cookie cookies and you really do have a meal!

Breakfast in a Cookie

Hands-on – 50 min. Oven – 30 min. **60 cookies**

This is a brilliant way to get your bowl of oatmeal, milk, and fruit all in a convenient, not to mention delicious cookie! This recipe makes a lot so you can freeze plenty for weeks of quick breakfasts, desserts, and snacks.

Menu
2 Breakfast Cookies
Glass of Skim or Soy Milk

Position oven racks to accommodate 2 sheets at a time in the center of oven. Preheat oven to 375°.
Coat nonstick cookie sheets with cooking spray.

1 cup	oat bran (dry, uncooked)	Mix together in a small bowl and set aside to soak for 10 minutes.
3/4 cup	orange juice	

1 cup + 1 T	applesauce, unsweetened	Meanwhile, combine in a large bowl, using an electric mixer, until smooth.
2 T	canola oil	
1 cup	honey	
1/3 cup	firmly packed brown sugar	
3 lg	eggs	
1½ T	vanilla extract	
1 T	grated orange rind or 2 tsp orange extract	

3 cups	whole-wheat pastry flour*	Measure into a sifter and sift over applesauce mixture.
1 T	baking powder	
1½ tsp	baking soda	

1 cup	nonfat dry milk	Add the soaked oat bran and remaining ingredients to the large bowl and mix thoroughly with a strong wooden spoon. Drop by slightly heaping tablespoons 1" apart. (To save time, load cookie sheets up with as many cookies as possible, baking 2 trays at a time. Stagger trays 1 to the left and 1 to the right, to allow air circulation around each outer edge.) Bake until lightly browned or 12 to 14 minutes.
2½ cups	oats (quick-cooking or old-fashioned)	
1 cup	nuts	
1 cup	raisins	
1 cup	ground flax seed (opt)	

*If you don't have whole-wheat pastry flour, you can substitute with 1 1/2 cups whole-wheat and 1 1/2 cups all-purpose flour. To learn about whole-wheat pastry flour, see page ix.

Nutrition information for 2 cookies
Exchanges/Choices: 2 1/2 Carbohydrate, 1 Fat

Calories	220	Fat	7 g	Fiber	5 g	Sodium	127 mg	Total Carbohydrate	37 g
Calories from Fat	29%	Saturated Fat	<1 g	Cholesterol	22 mg	Protein	6 g	Sugars	17 g

Lickety-Split Diabetic Meals

Lickety-Split Tip

If I eat breakfast, I'm hungry again mid-morning, again at lunch, and I seem to eat all day long...

It amazes me that people think this is bad. This is good! This is eating to match your metabolism. I promise that after a day of this, you'll find it much easier to eat a light dinner with only a little evening snack, and before you know it, your morning blood sugars will be greatly improved.

Freezing Bananas

Do your bananas sometime over ripen before you can eat them all? Try this—peel them and slip them into a resealable baggie to freeze. Later, add the still frozen bananas to the Smoothie recipe for a frosty-fruity sensation.

You can also thaw and mash the bananas to use in 'Nana Bread or Banana Nut Cake or Muffins (pages 305 and 313).

P.S. A Smoothie is an ideal energy booster after a workout!

Hands-on — 5 min.   **Serves 4**

These nutrition-packed drinks are very dessert-like. Kids and adults alike love them for breakfast or a snack. Smoothies are especially good for an after-exercise pick-me-up. Use blueberries instead of strawberries for your kids and call them "Blue's Clues" Smoothies. The smoothies can be made with yogurt, skim milk, or soy milk, based on your personal nutrition goals.

Menu

Smoothie

1/2 Bagel or one Breakfast in a Cookie (page 9)

1 cup	skim milk, soy milk, or nonfat plain yogurt
1 T	sugar
2 cups	frozen strawberries, unsweetened (roughly 1/2 of a 20-oz bag)
1	(6 oz) banana (a ripe frozen one is especially good)
3 T	wheat germ and/or ground flax seed (opt)
3	ice cubes (if your strawberries aren't frozen)

Buzz together in a food processor or blender. This produces a thick, frozen consistency, perfect for eating with a spoon.

1/2–1 cup	orange juice

Add fruit juice to attain the desired consistency, perfect for sipping through a straw.

Serve with a bagel or a Breakfast in a Cookie for a complete meal or snack.

Nutrition information for 1 1/4 cup serving made with optional wheat germ and 1/2 cup orange juice

Exchanges/Choices: 2 Carbohydrate

Calories	128	Fat	<1 g	Fiber	3 g	Sodium	30 mg	Total Carbohydrate	28 g
Calories from Fat	5%	Saturated Fat	0 g	Cholesterol	1 mg	Protein	5 g	Sugars	18 g

Lickety-Split Diabetic Meals

Lickety-Split Tip

Why go to the effort to make Homemade Turkey Sausage?

Regular Pork Sausage................... 20–24 grams of fat/serving.........75–84% of calories from fat

Commercial Turkey Sausage........ 8–11 grams of fat/serving ....60–70% of calories from fat

Homemade Turkey Sausage .... 1 gram of fat/serving..................7% of calories from fat

And it's more than just for breakfast . . .

This Homemade Turkey Sausage is called for in the following recipes: Scrambled Omelette (page 5), Herbed Italian Sausage over Pasta (page 175), and Hot & Spicy Pizza with Sausage (page 189). So, make some up for the freezer today!

Money-Saving Tip!

Watch for turkey breast to go on sale. Skin, bone, and grind it yourself for delicious turkey sausage—the guilt-free way!

Homemade Turkey Sausage

Hands-on — 30 min. **Makes 16 or 48 (2-oz) Patties**

Since truly low-fat sausage is so hard to find, here's one you can make yourself. This sausage is rock-bottom low in fat and delicious. It's easy to make and you can enjoy it for months to come. The larger recipe makes enough to serve sausage every Sunday morning for a family of 4 for 3 months!

Menu
Homemade Turkey Sausage
Scrambled Eggs
Toast

For 16	For 48	Cut 16 or 48 10" squares of freezer wrap or wax paper.
2 pkgs	6 pkgs	(20 oz each) extra lean ground turkey breast*
1 tsp	1 T	black pepper**
1½ tsp	1½ T	dried sage
1½ tsp	1½ T	dried thyme
1½ tsp	1½ T	dried rosemary
1/4 tsp	3/4 tsp	red pepper flakes**
1/4 tsp	3/4 tsp	cayenne**
10 grinds	30 grinds	fresh ground pepper**
3/4 tsp	2 tsp	salt
1 T	3 T	oil (canola or olive)
3/4 cup	2¼ cups	applesauce, unsweetened

Mix ingredients together very thoroughly.
Use your hands if necessary. (Wash them first!)

Divide the sausage mixture into 4 equal portions in the bowl.

From each portion, make 4 (small batch) or 12 (large batch) 2" balls.
Place each ball in the center of a paper square.

Fold the square up from the bottom, the sides, and then the top.
This will flatten the ball into a patty.

Put 4 to 8 patties each in a resealable freezer bag and freeze.

To cook:

Coat a large nonstick skillet with cooking spray. Place over medium-high heat.

Unwrap frozen patties (no need to thaw) and place in skillet.

Cook patties 6 minutes on each side (less if not frozen) until no longer pink inside. (Do not overcook or they will be dry.)

Serve with scrambled eggs and toast.

*If grinding turkey yourself, use cutter for either fine or coarse sausage, depending on which you like best.

**Four types of pepper are used to enhance flavor.

Nutrition information for 1 turkey sausage patty
Exchanges/Choices: 2 Lean Meat

Calories	90	Fat	1.8 g	Fiber	<1 g	Sodium	160 mg	Total Carbohydrate	<1 g
Calories from Fat	18%	Saturated Fat	<1 g	Cholesterol	28 mg	Protein	16 g	Sugars	1 g

Lickety-Split Diabetic Meals

Lickety-Split Tip

But I'm never hungry in the morning!
The mere thought of food makes me nauseous...

As soon as I hear this from a client, I quickly ask about their nighttime nibbling. If you overeat at night, very little digestion occurs during sleep. You wake up with a full stomach, so of course you are not going to feel hungry. When you start matching your eating to your metabolism and eat less at night, you will be hungry in the morning (and not surprisingly, your blood sugars are in target range in the morning). So stop eating two or three hours before bed (except for a pre-portioned snack according to your eating plan) and be ready to start the next day with a nutritious breakfast!

Whole-Grain Pancakes

Hands-on – 20 min.   **Serves 6**

While you may think you love the white flour pancakes you grew up with, wait 'til you change over to whole grain. These offer texture without being too grainy. And talk about nutrition packed! A great way to start your day!

Menu

Whole-Grain Pancakes

Applesauce or Light Syrup

Fresh Fruit

Canadian Bacon

2 cups	whole-wheat pastry flour*
1/2 cup	wheat germ (or just use more flour)
1/4 cup	ground flax seed (opt)
2 tsp	baking powder
1 T	sugar
3 dashes	cinnamon (opt)

In a medium-size bowl, stir together until baking powder is well distributed.

1	egg
2	egg whites
1/2 tsp	vanilla (opt)
2½ cups	skim milk or soy milk

Add all at once to dry mixture and mix just until combined.

Heat griddle over medium-high heat. Spray with nonstick cooking spray. (It should be hot enough so that when you sprinkle drops of water on the surface, they dance.)

Use a 1/4 cup measuring cup to measure and pour the cakes. Turn when bubbles come to the surface and pop, and the edges are slightly dry.

Serve with applesauce or light syrup and fresh fruit.

Makes approximately 18 pancakes. Leftover pancakes can be re-warmed in the microwave the next day, or frozen for another day.

* If you don't have whole-wheat pastry flour, you can substitute 1 cup whole-wheat and 1 cup all-purpose flour. To learn about whole-wheat pastry flour, see page 342.

Nutrition information for 3 pancakes

Exchanges/Choices: 2 1/2 Starch, 2 1/2 Fat-Free Milk, 1/2 Fat

Calories	278	Fat	5 g	Fiber	8.5 g	Sodium	209 mg	Total Carbohydrate	45 g
Calories from Fat	16%	Saturated Fat	<1 g	Cholesterol	37 mg	Protein	14 g	Sugars	8 g

Lickety-Split Diabetic Meals

Lickety-Split Tip

Tame Your Sweet Tooth

It is possible for you to change your taste for sweetness. For instance, if you like to pour 1/2 cup of syrup on your pancakes, you can gradually reduce this amount. Soon, you are topping pancakes with only fruit.

Likewise, if you like 3 teaspoons of sugar on cereal or oatmeal, you can slowly cut back to 1. Sprinkling cinnamon, raisins, and other fruits on your cereal sweetens it while adding nutritional value.

These strategies are important for everyone in the famiy, those with diabetes and without.

Banana-Oat Pancakes

Hands-on – 25 min.

Serves 4

Since we are big fans of pancakes, I thought you'd like both of our favorite recipes.
If we have bananas, we make these. If not, we make the previous Whole-Grain Pancakes. Enjoy!

Menu

Banana-Oat Pancakes

Homemade Turkey Sausage
(page 13)

3/4 cup	dry oats (quick-cooking or old fashioned) or oat bran (dry, uncooked)	Mix these together in a medium-size bowl, and let them sit for 5 minutes to give them some extra "soaking" time.
2 cups	skim milk or soy milk	
1 cup	whole-wheat pastry flour*	In a small bowl, mix together with a fork. Be sure the baking powder is evenly distributed. Add to the soaking oats and stir.
1 T	baking powder	Gently mix in.
3 dashes	cinnamon (opt)	
1	egg (or 2 egg whites)	Slice bananas very thin. Fold bananas and nuts into batter.
1/2 tsp	vanilla (opt)	Heat griddle over medium heat, spray with cooking spray. (It should be hot enough so that when you sprinkle drops of water on the surface, they dance.)
2	(6 oz each) bananas, peeled	Use 1/4 cup of batter for each pancake, cooking over medium heat. After spooning the batter onto the pan, give the pan a quick shake to spread the batter out slightly. Cook for about 2 minutes or until bubbles appear on the surface. Flip the pancakes and cook for another minute or so.
1/4 cup	chopped walnuts (opt)	

Serve with reduced-calorie syrup, fruit spread, or applesauce on top, and Homemade Turkey Sausage on the side. Makes approximately 12 pancakes.

* If you don't have whole-wheat pastry flour, you can substitute 1/2 cup whole-wheat and 1/2 cup all-purpose flour. To learn about whole-wheat pastry flour, see page 342.

Nutrition information for 3 pancakes

Exchanges/Choices: 3 Starch, 1/2 Fruit, 1/2 Fat-Free Milk, 1 Fat

Calories	350	Fat	8 g	Fiber	8 g	Sodium	370 mg	Total Carbohydrate	60 g
Calories from Fat	22%	Saturated Fat	1 g	Cholesterol	55 mg	Protein	14 g	Sugars	17 g

Lickety-Split Diabetic Meals

Lickety-Split Tip

Favorite Exercise Videos

Speaking of buns, one of my favorite exercise videos is "8-Minute Buns." These are very effective exercises for firming up. Also available are "8-Minute Abs," "8-Minute Arms," and "8-Minute Legs," all of which are excellent and worthwhile.
Visit *www.collagevideo.com* or call Collage Video at 800-433-6769 to order.

Glazed Cinnamon Nut Buns

Hands-on – 30 min. Oven – 15–17 min.

Serves 9

What a delicious holiday treat! You'll especially enjoy serving these to your overnight guests. Waking them up with this mouth-watering aroma will make you a favorite host or hostess!

Menu		

Menu

Glazed Cinnamon Nut Buns
Scrambled Eggs
Sliced Fresh Fruit

1	frozen honey-wheat bread dough (1 lb) (unbaked loaf)	**Night before (about 10:00 p.m.)**

Night before (about 10:00 p.m.)

Remove dough from freezer and plastic bag. Place in a medium-size bowl. Cover with plastic wrap. Set out to thaw and rise overnight.

In the morning (about 7:30 a.m.)

Prepare a clean work surface and dust lightly with flour. (I use the countertop or a cutting board.) Punch down dough and roll out to a 10" x 12" rectangle.

Set frozen dough out the night before to rise.

3 T	light corn syrup

Evenly spread across dough.

Coat an 8" × 8" baking dish with cooking spray.

3 T	sugar
1½ tsp	cinnamon
1/4 cup	chopped almonds, pecans or walnuts (opt)

Mix together in a 1 cup measuring cup and sprinkle across dough.

Begin to roll up, starting on the long side, to form a long cylinder. Pinch the seams together to seal. Cut roll into 9 equal slices and place in baking dish with spirals facing up and sides touching.

Preheat oven to 350°.

Cover rolls with a kitchen towel and allow to sit on top of the stove for 45 minutes to 1 hour while the oven preheats to 350°. The warmth of the oven will help facilitate the 2nd rise. (I use this time to grab a shower!)

About 8:45 or 9:00 a.m.

Place in oven to bake 15 to 17 minutes. Meanwhile, scramble eggs and slice fresh fruit.
Cool the rolls 5 minutes before removing from pan.

1/2 cup	powdered sugar
2½ tsp	skim milk
1/4 tsp	vanilla extract

Mix together in a small cup. Transfer rolls to serving platter. Drizzle with glaze.

About 9:15 a.m.

Serve with scrambled eggs and fresh fruit, and watch your guests' eyes pop!

Nutrition information for 1 bun

Exchanges/Choices: 3 Carbohydrate

Calories	213	Fat	3 g	Fiber	1 g	Sodium	250 mg	Total Carbohydrate	42 g
Calories from Fat	13%	Saturated Fat	0 g	Cholesterol	0 mg	Protein	4 g	Sugars	18 g

Lickety-Split Diabetic Meals

Lickety-Split Tip

Add a Pinch of Protein in the Morning

In my co-authored weight-loss novel, *Water with Lemon*, Fowler serves a slice of low-fat cheese with his whole-grain French toast to increase the protein content of the meal. This added protein helps keep blood sugar more stable throughout the morning—a valuable addition since breakfast meals like French toast or pancakes are often low in protein.

I always use peanut butter on French toast and pancakes instead of butter. Peanut butter provides valuable protein, fiber, and various nutrients that butter or margarine does not, and is lower in saturated and trans fats. Oddly enough, it goes great with the blueberries. Don't knock it until you've tried it!

Whole-Grain French Toast

Hands-on —15 min.   **Serves 4**

In my co-authored weight-loss novel, Water with Lemon, Fowler makes this delicious and nutritious French Toast for Karen while revealing another of his winning weight-loss habits.

Menu
Whole-Grain French Toast
Blueberry Topping
Fresh Fruit
Cheese Slice

Preheat a griddle to medium-high.

1	egg	In a wide-bottom bowl, toss lightly with a fork until scrambled.
2	egg whites	
1/2 tsp	vanilla	
1 T	skim or 1/2% milk	
3 dashes	cinnamon	

3 cups	frozen unsweetened blueberries	Place in a microwave-safe bowl and cook on high for 4 minutes. (These will eventually cook down to about 1½ cups.)

8 slices	whole multi-grain bread	Once the griddle is hot, coat with non-stick cooking spray. Dip bread in egg mixture, one by one, just until each side is completely coated and place on hot griddle. Cook until brown (about 1–2 minutes) then flip and cook 1 minute on second side. If your griddle only accommodates 4 slices at a time, repeat process with the remaining 4.

1 tsp	corn starch	Meanwhile, stir into the warm blueberry liquid. Cook 2 minutes more, until thick and bubbly.

Serve each person two slices of French Toast with approximately 1/3 cup blueberry topping. Add sliced fresh fruit of your choice like melons, oranges, peaches, or pears. For added protein and staying power, add a 1/2 oz slice of reduced-fat cheese.

Nutrition information for 2 slices of French Toast with 1/3 cup of blueberry topping.

Exchanges/Choices: 2 Starch, 1/2 Fruit, 1 Fat

Calories	235	Fat	4.5 g	Fiber	7 g	Sodium	365 mg	Total Carbohydrate	40 g
Calories from Fat	17%	Saturated Fat	1 g	Cholesterol	53 mg	Protein	11 g	Sugars	12 g

Lickety-Split Diabetic Meals

Lickety-Split Tip

This sleepyhead's goof-proof method for getting up early to exercise:

1. The night before, I lay out exercise clothes in the bathroom (not beside the bed as that has **NEVER** worked!) appropriate for both indoor and outdoor temperatures. (You know how plans may change, depending upon what the morning brings.)

2. I set my bedside alarm for 5:55 a.m. and a second alarm in the bathroom for 6:00 a.m. (The first alarm warns me before I actually have to get up.) The screaming bathroom alarm is my insurance to be up by 6:00 a.m. And there, lo and behold, are my exercise clothes, waiting for me!

3. While brushing my teeth, I focus on how good it feels to get my workout in before work and how disappointed I would be if I didn't. (This is key—associating more pleasure with my new habit and pain to my old one.)

4. Once downstairs, I drink diluted juice to rehydrate and provide carbohydrates to get me going.

5. Music is my next saving grace. It does wonders for waking me up and energizing me. Out the door I go, or onto my exercise equipment.

While you may still feel groggy the first couple of days, your body will adjust. Be persistent! Before you know it, you'll be a die-hard morning exerciser too!

Ambrosia Rice

Hands-on — 10 min.

Serves 8

The next time you find yourself with 2 cups of leftover plain rice, turn it into this! Not only does it make a delicious breakfast, but it's also a delight for the lunch box, picnic basket, or dessert table.

Great way to use leftover cooked rice

Menu

Ambrosia Rice

2 cans	(8 oz each) pineapple tidbits, in its own juice
1 can	(15 oz) Mandarin oranges

Open cans and drain. Reserve pineapple juice for another use. Place in large bowl.

2 cups	cooked brown rice, chilled
1/2 cup	chopped walnuts, pecans, or almonds
1/4 cup	oat bran (dry, uncooked)
2 cups	seedless red grapes, washed well, patted dry
1/2 cup	raisins or chopped dried apricots
1 container	(8 oz) strawberry nonfat yogurt*
dash	cinnamon and nutmeg (opt)

Add and mix gently.

Serve now or later. Will keep in refrigerator, covered, for 2 days.

*If all you have is plain nonfat yogurt, simply stir in 2 tablespoons strawberry jam or preserves to 1 cup plain yogurt. Other flavors, like raspberry and peach, work great as well.

Nutrition information for 1 cup

Exchanges/Choices: 1 1/2 Starch, 1 1/2 Fruit

Calories	220	Fat	5 g	Fiber	3 g	Sodium	32 mg	Total Carbohydrate	41 g
Calories from Fat	20%	Saturated Fat	<1 g	Cholesterol	0 mg	Protein	6 g	Sugars	24 g

Lickety-Split Diabetic Meals

Lickety-Split Tip

"The day I turned 65, something told me I would feel a lot younger if I lost weight. So, with guidance from Zonya, I embarked step by step upon my new way of life. I did not follow a diet, just ate nutritious food and didn't deprive myself of anything. By the time I ate all the recommended fruits and vegetables, I was too full to eat junk foods. I felt then, as I do now, that I can eat so many tasty things, all without counting calories. I also began walking for 30 minutes over my lunch hour—raincoat, umbrella, and all. Now that I'm retired, my husband and I walk 3 miles 4 days a week. I absolutely love my new way of life!"

—Betty S., maintaining a 60-pound weight loss for 18 months and counting.

"Appeteasers"

You're invited over to friends on Friday night. Great! You've been asked to bring an appetizer. Hmmm! What should you bring? The pressure to bring something everyone will like, and that you'll be proud of, can be quite nerve-racking. You want it to be attractive, delicious, unsuspectingly healthy, and above all, FAST. Wonder no more; it's all right here!

This is a collection of my favorite appetizers that I bring to parties time and time again. No more shuffling through mounds of recipes to find something tasty and easy, just thumb through these. That's a time saver in itself! And if you've used the Lickety-Split grocery list, you have all the ingredients you need.

Keep in mind these other recipes, which also make great "appeteasers."

- Guiltless Nachos Supreme (page 89)
- Shrimp Pizza (page 197) or any of the pizzas

The following "appeteasers" can be made as delicious entrées.

- Benito Bean Dip (for burritos)
- 7-Layer Bean Dip
- Marinated Sesame Chicken Kabobs
- Simple Tofu Bites (to stuff pitas or top salads)
- Oklahoma Bean Dip (to stuff pitas or top salads)
- Herbed Salmon Spread (to make sandwiches)

Enjoy these "appeteasers"; they are fast, fun, and tasty!

Lickety-Split Diabetic Meals

Lickety-Split Tip

Get Your Vitamin D! (Part 1)

Yes, Vitamin D has been known for its job to boost calcium absorption for fighting osteoporosis. But research also shows that Vitamin D aids in the prevention and/or treatment of muscle weakness, gum disease, arthritis, multiple sclerosis, hypertension, several cancers, and diabetes and insulin resistance. Yes, Vitamin D helps the pancreas release insulin. People with low blood levels of Vitamin D produce less insulin and their bodies' cells are less sensitive to the hormone, causing double trouble.

Even though our bodies can synthesize Vitamin D from sunshine, many people are deficient. This may be a result of a lifestyle of staying inside or our use of sunscreen (which blocks the production of Vitamin D in the skin). If you live north of the latitude running generally through Los Angeles and Atlanta, you are typically sun-deprived and consequently, low in Vitamin D, especially during the fall and winter months. Curious about your own Vitamin D status? Ask your doctor for a blood test of 25-hydroxy vitamins D.

Benito Bean Dip

My husband makes more of this almost as soon as we run out. Also perfect for making Benito Bean Burritos (page 67) and Chicken & Bean Enchiladas (page 151).

A favorite at parties!

3	green onions (opt)	**5 minutes before serving:** Chop in food processor.
1 jar 1 cup 1/2 tsp 1/4 cup	(48 oz) pinto beans, rinsed and drained salsa Zippy Zonya Mexi Mix‡ fresh cilantro leaves (opt)	Add to processor and blend until smooth. Serve at room temperature or slightly chilled.
1 lg bag	baked tortilla chips	Serve with baked tortilla chips or Bagel Chips (page 37).

‡See recipe on page 40.

Nutrition information for 2 T dip with 5 baked tortilla chips

Exchanges/Choices: 1 Starch

| Calories | 73 | Fat | <1 g | Fiber | 2.5 g | Sodium | 191 mg | Total Carbohydrate | 15 g |
| Calories from Fat | 7% | Saturated Fat | <1 g | Cholesterol | 0 mg | Protein | 2.5 g | Sugars | 0 g |

Lickety-Split Diabetic Meals

Lickety-Split Tip

Get Your Vitamin D! (Part 2)

Your best bet is to include several servings daily of Vitamin D–rich or fortified foods (e.g., salmon, mackerel, sardines, shrimp, fortified milk, cereals, or orange juice) as well as take a supplement. Taking a One-A-Day vitamin containing 400 IU of Vitamin D is not too much. We may see the current 400 IU daily value being raised to 2,000 or more. Time and more studies will tell.

7-Layer Bean Dip

Hands-on – 20 min.

Serves 32 or 4

32 as an appetizer

4 as a meal

Thanks to our neighbors, Dan & Karen Hettel, you can make this popular party appetizer that has been a hit at many of our get-togethers. It's both attractive and delicious!

2 cups	Benito Bean Dip (page 27)	**20 minutes before serving:** Spread this mixture all across a large decorative serving platter.

3	green onions, chopped	Layer over Bean Dip in the order listed.
2 cups	shredded lettuce	
1	green pepper, seeded and chopped	
2	tomatoes, chopped	
1/2 cup	reduced-fat shredded cheddar cheese†	
15 slices	black olives (opt)	

Also makes a delicious, yet healthy, Friday night meal!

1 lg bag	baked tortilla chips	Open chips, it's party time!

†See reduced-fat cheese tip on page viii (Introduction).

Nutrition information for approximately 2 T dip with 5 baked tortilla chips

Exchanges/Choices: 1 Starch

Calories	72	Fat	1 g	Fiber	2 g	Sodium	176 mg	Total Carbohydrate	13 g
Calories from Fat	12%	Saturated Fat	0 g	Cholesterol	1 mg	Protein	3 g	Sugars	0 g

Lickety-Split Diabetic Meals

Lickety-Split Tip

Party Survival Tip #1: Halve it and you can have it!

The next time you're faced with an assortment of yummy dips, gooey sweets, or irresistible fried treats, think, "Halve it and I can have it." This strategy works anytime, anywhere, and will keep you from feeling deprived while halving the calories, carbs, and fats you would normally eat. Not only does adopting this mindset help you at parties, but can really be adopted for everyday living when those office doughnuts appear, followed by the church potluck, and on and on! Yes, not only does halving it mean a better blood sugar for you today and a better A1C (blood test reflecting blood sugar averages over the past 2–3 months) at your next doctor visit, 250-calorie savings performed daily for a year means you can quite possibly shed 26 pounds in a year. Not bad for not ever depriving yourself.

Party Survival Tip #2: Plan ahead

Eat a low-fat breakfast and lunch to save up a few extra fat grams to spend at the party. However, do NOT arrive at the party overly hungry, either. In fact, eating a small snack before you go is a good idea.

Party Survival Tip #3: Include exercise before you go

Let's face it, parties generally mean a few more calories than you usually eat. Overindulge on a day you don't exercise and your fat cells will grow all night long! To prevent this from happening, be sure to exercise before you go.

Oklahoma Bean Dip

Hands-on – 12 min.   **Serves 48**

My thanks to Gloria Edwards for this tasty recipe that has become a regular at our family get-togethers. Great with
Baked Tostitos, rolled up in a flour tortilla, or stuffed into a pita pocket for a quick sandwich.
For a real change, try this served on top of tossed salad. You won't need dressing, since it's already in!

1 can	(14 oz) black-eyed peas	**2 or more hours before serving:**
2 cans	(15½ oz each) garbanzo beans	Drain and rinse. Place in medium bowl.

2 med	tomatoes	Chop and add to beans.
4	green onions	
1 tsp	chopped garlic (2 cloves)	
2	jalapeno peppers (opt)	
1/2 cup	fresh parsley	

Also makes a quick meal!

1 bottle	(8 oz) fat-free or lite Italian dressing	Add to mixture and mix well.
1 tsp	oregano	Refrigerate for 2 hours or more before serving. This will keep for 5 days in your refrigerator.

1 lg bag	baked tortilla chips	**Just before serving:**
		Toss beans gently and serve with chips.

Nutrition information for approximately 2 T dip with 5 baked tortilla chips

Exchanges/Choices: 1 Starch

Calories	68	Fat	<1 g	Fiber	2 g	Sodium	194 mg	Total Carbohydrate	13 g
Calories from Fat	7%	Saturated Fat	0 g	Cholesterol	0 mg	Protein	2 g	Sugars	<1 g

Lickety-Split Diabetic Meals

Lickety-Split Tip

Party Survival Tip #4: Mingle AWAY from the food

Standing beside a big bowl of cashews or Spanish peanuts can really throw a monkey wrench into your weight-loss efforts. Think I'm kidding? Just try to stand or sit near an enticing bowl of nuts and **NOT** unconsciously eat a little handful here, another handful there. Although you swear it wasn't much, it was an unconscious downing of 10 grams of fat and 110 calories per handful!

Suggestion:
Take out 5 whole cashews (equivalent to 5 grams of fat) and line them up on your napkin or plate. Enjoy them one by one, with lots of time in between. Take a break and enjoy other foods like raw vegetables and fruit. Repeat with 5 more if you really want them. Decide that you're finished and move away from them!

Herbed Salmon Spread

Hands-on – 12 min.   **Makes 24 Appetizers**

This makes an excellent party appetizer. Serve inside a hollowed-out round loaf of pumpernickel bread and eat with the bread cubes. This is also wonderful served with bagel or pita chips, or crackers. Try it as a lunchtime sandwich spread!

2 cups	plain nonfat yogurt	**16 hours before serving:**
		Line a strainer with a paper coffee filter or cheesecloth. Place over a bowl. Spoon yogurt onto coffee filter, cover and refrigerate for 10 to 14 hours.
		Yogurt will now be thick. Discard the collected liquid beneath or use it in soups or breads. Remove yogurt from the filter and place in a medium bowl.

1 can	(15 oz) red or pink salmon packed in water, drained and picked over for skin and bones	**2 to 4 hours before serving:**
1 T	Miracle Whip Light	Gently mix into yogurt. Refrigerate 2 or more hours before serving.
1 T	fresh parsley, chopped	Note: If "water puddles" appear after the dip has sat awhile, simply stir.
1 T	green onion, tops and bottoms, chopped	
1/4 tsp	dill weed	
1/4 tsp	thyme	

6	whole-wheat pita breads (6-inch rounds)	Lightly toast each in a toaster and cut into triangles to serve. Also excellent served with Bagel Chips (page 37).

Nutrition information for approximately 2 T spread on 2 pita triangles

Exchanges/Choices: 1/2 Starch, 1 Lean Meat

Calories	70	Fat	2 g	Fiber	1 g	Sodium	172 mg	Total Carbohydrate	8 g
Calories from Fat	25%	Saturated Fat	0 g	Cholesterol	5 mg	Protein	6 g	Sugars	2 g

Lickety-Split Diabetic Meals

Lickety-Split Tip

Party Survival Tip #5: Use a plate

One thing that puts on weight and soars blood sugars is eating more than you're aware of. Anytime you nibble on things directly from the bowl, you can end up eating more than if you put all the food on a plate. Therefore, create a healthful boundary for yourself: Everything goes on a plate. Make it a small plate for even better results!

P.S. There's freedom within boundaries.

Holiday Crab Dip

So simple and delicious yet very low in fat and calories.

1 tub	**(8 oz) fat-free cream cheese, softened**	Mash and spread across bottom of a decorative serving platter.
1/2 cup	**seafood cocktail sauce**	Spread over cream cheese.
1 can	**(6 oz) crab meat, well drained**	Sprinkle chunks over sauce. Circle the platter with low-fat whole-wheat crackers or Bagel Chips (page 37).

Nutrition information for approximately 2 T dip and 2 Bagel Chips

Exchanges/Choices: 1 Carbohydrate

Calories	74	Fat	1 g	Fiber	1.7 g	Sodium	241 mg	Total Carbohydrate	11 g
Calories from Fat	12%	Saturated Fat	0 g	Cholesterol	11 mg	Protein	6 g	Sugars	2 g

Lickety-Split Diabetic Meals

Lickety-Split Tip

Party Survival Tip #6:

Put foods to the "pinch, slip, and shine test"

One way to scout out calories-climbing fat is to perform what I call the "pinch, slip, and shine test." The test is simple. If upon pinching the item, you see a lot of "slip and shine" on your fingers, that tells you there is a lot of fat. The following are appetizers that will undoubtedly give you a positive slip and shine reading, therefore alerting you to limit them.

Egg rolls • Buttery crackers • Potato chips • Pigs-in-a-blanket • Chicken wings Meatballs • Anything wrapped in bacon

These bagel chips pass the test with no sign of "slip and shine." By contrast, a bag of commercial bagel chips has enough "slip" to shine several pairs of shoes!

Remember, while fat is enemy number one, number two is too many carbohydrates. Be mindful even of the number of baked chips you are eating. Smart selections **AND** portion control are what you need for successful management of both weight and blood sugars.

Bagel Chips

Looking for a snack that's a hit? These are absolutely terrific served with any dip, but especially Herbed Salmon Spread (page 33), Holiday Crab Dip (page 35), or Benito Bean Dip (page 27). Also makes a delicious "road trip" munchie all by itself.

Position oven racks to accommodate 2 baking sheets at a time in center of oven. Preheat oven to 350°.

4	**(3 oz each) whole-wheat bagels, onion, plain, or garlic (preferably unsliced)**	Using a sharp serrated knife, slice each bagel vertically (from top to bottom) into 8 very thin slices. Arrange in single layer on 2 ungreased nonstick baking sheets.
	Nonstick cooking spray or I Can't Believe It's Not Butter spray	Lightly spray bagel slices.
1 tsp	**oregano**	Sprinkle on bagel slices.
dash	**garlic powder**	Bake until crisp, about 12 minutes.
		Let cool and enjoy! Store in an airtight container for up to 1 week.

Nutrition information for approximately 4 Bagel Chips

Exchanges/Choices: 1 Starch

Calories	85	Fat	1 g	Fiber	3 g	Sodium	100 mg	Total Carbohydrate	18 g
Calories from Fat	11%	Saturated Fat	0 g	Cholesterol	0 mg	Protein	4 g	Sugars	3 g

Lickety-Split Diabetic Meals

Lickety-Split Tip

Party Survival Tip #7: Avoid drinking all your calories

"But I hardly ate a thing all holiday season! How did I gain weight?"

Think before you drink:

Egg Nog (4 oz): 355 calories

Wine (3 oz): 85 calories

Beer, regular (12 oz): 150 calories

Beer, light (12 oz): 100 calories

Cider (12 oz): 180 calories

Fruit punch (12 oz): 180 calories

Piña colada (6 oz): 325 calories

Opt for: Club soda or sparkling water to dilute punch or fruit juice; mineral water, low-calorie soda, or diet tonic water. Or better yet, add a slice of lemon or lime to a refreshing glass of pure water!

Spinach Dip in Pumpernickel

Hands-on – 30 min.   **Serves 32**

Makes 4 cups (2 T per serving)

Here's a delicious dip that is always a hit at parties, minus the hit on your hips!
Don't tell anyone it's low-fat; they'll never guess on their own.

Also good with rye bread.

1½ cups	plain nonfat yogurt or fat-free sour cream	**3 hours before serving:** Mix together in medium bowl so the dried soup can begin rehydrating.
1 cup	Miracle Whip Light	
1 pkg	dried vegetable soup mix	
3 pkg	(10 oz each) frozen chopped spinach	Thaw spinach in microwave. Squeeze out all excess water. Stir into yogurt mixture.
1 can	(8 oz) sliced water chestnuts, drained	Chop into small pieces. Stir into mixture. For best results, refrigerate 3 hours before filling pumpernickel loaf and serving.
1 lg	round loaf pumpernickel bread*	**Just before serving:** Using a knife, hollow out a large hole. Fill hole with dip. Cube the bread you've removed to serve on the side for dipping. When the cubes are gone, invite guests to tear bread from the "bowl."

* If you can't find a large round unsliced loaf of pumpernickel bread, simply buy sliced pumpernickel, cube it and serve with the dip.

Nutrition information for 2 T dip with 3 cubes bread (or 1/2 slice)

Exchanges/Choices: 1 Carbohydrate

Calories	80	Fat	2 g	Fiber	2.3 g	Sodium	290 mg	Total Carbohydrate	13 g
Calories from Fat	23%	Saturated Fat	0 g	Cholesterol	0 mg	Protein	3 g	Sugars	2 g

Lickety-Split Tip

Party Survival Tip #8: Bring a healthy dish to pass

I've lost count of the number of times that I've gone to a potluck to find NO vegetables and NO fruits and NO whole grains anywhere—only starchy, high-fat, high-sodium, high-calorie dishes to choose from. What dish should you take to pass? How about choosing a recipe from this chapter and you can rest assured that at least one thing on your plate won't pack on the pounds. As for the other items, use a small plate and choose just a little of two or three options.

My South of the Border Roll-ups make a great party dish to pass. By following my reduced-fat cheese tip and flavoring this with my Zippy Zonya Mexi Mix, you will lower the fat AND sodium while making a great-tasting, HEALTHY party favorite!

Zippy Zonya Mexi Mix

Instead of using prepared packets of taco or fajita mixes, I realized how easy it is to make my own and save a full teaspoon of salt plus monosodium glutamate each time. All you have to do is mix up this recipe, place it in an empty spice bottle, label, and date it. You no longer need to buy commercial, high-sodium taco and fajita seasoning packets.

Simply use 3 tablespoons of Zippy Zonya Mexi Mix to replace one packet of the commercial mixes.

5 T ground cumin
1 T cumin seeds (opt)
6 T chili powder
1 tsp garlic powder (make sure it's powder, not salt)
1 tsp onion flakes
1/4 tsp black pepper
1/4–1/2 tsp cayenne pepper (opt)

South of the Border Roll-ups

Hands-on – 30 min. **Serves 16**

Thanks to my neighbor Suzy Crossley for the recipe for this popular appetizer.
It has been a hit at many neighborhood parties.

1 tub	(8 oz) fat-free cream cheese	**4 hours before serving:**
1 cup	fat-free sour cream	Mix together in medium bowl.
1 T	Zippy Zonya Mexi Mix‡	
1/2 – 1 cup	salsa of your choice (to taste)	
1 can	(4 oz) chopped green chilies	
4	green onions (tops & bottoms chopped)	Gently stir in.
1 cup	reduced-fat shredded cheddar cheese†	
10	6" flour tortillas	Lay out 5 tortillas at a time. Using 1/2 the cheese mixture, divide and spread evenly across the 5 tortillas. Roll up creating spirals inside. Repeat with remaining 5 tortillas.

Lightly dampen 10 sheets of paper towel. Wrap each roll in one.
Refrigerate 3 to 4 hours.

Just before serving:

Unwrap each roll and slice 1" apart.

Arrange on decorative platter.

†See reduced-fat cheese tip on page viii (Introduction).
‡See recipe on page 40.

Nutrition information for 4 bites (using 1/2 cup salsa total)
Exchanges/Choices: 1 Carbohydrate, 1 Lean Meat

Calories	115	Fat	2 g	Fiber	1 g	Sodium	293 mg	Total Carbohydrate	15 g
Calories from Fat	16%	Saturated Fat	1 g	Cholesterol	4 mg	Protein	7 g	Sugars	1 g

Lickety-Split Diabetic Meals

Lickety-Split Tip

Party Survival Tip #9: Keep your focus away from the food

While good food is certainly an important part of an enjoyable party, be sure you keep it in perspective. Appreciate the other great things: Socializing, the beautiful decorations, music, games, and activities.

Why tofu?

See page 80 to find out!

Simple Tofu Bites

Hands-on – 5 min. Oven – 30 min.   **Serves 4**

Serve these at your next party. When your guests ask what these delicious little cheese chunks are,
watch their jaws drop when you tell them it's tofu!

16 oz	firm tofu

3 or more hours before serving:

Slice the tofu into small bite-sized chunks, or into 1/8" "lunchmeat" slices for sandwiches. Place in a glass baking dish.

2 T	soy sauce, reduced-sodium or tamari sauce
1/2 tsp	low-sodium Spike or Mrs. Dash seasoning mix

In a small bowl, mix the soy or tamari sauce with the seasoning. Pour over tofu, making sure to coat evenly. Marinate the tofu in the refrigerator, covered, for 2 or more hours.

Coat a nonstick baking sheet with cooking spray.

6	red-tipped lettuce leaves, or purple kale (opt)

45 minutes before serving:

When marinating time is almost up, heat oven to 425°. Place the tofu on the baking sheet. Bake 30 minutes. Tofu should become slightly browned.

Line platter with red tipped lettuce leaves and layer on the chunks. Stab chunks with toothpicks and serve hot or cold.

Note: This simple marinade works great with chicken, too.

Use as meat slices for sandwiches or sprinkle the chunks on a tossed salad.

Nutrition information for approximately 8 chunks
Exchanges/Choices: 2 Lean Meat, 1/2 Fat

Calories	120	Fat	6 g	Fiber	0 g	Sodium	288 mg	Total Carbohydrate	3 g
Calories from Fat	45	Saturated Fat	<1 g	Cholesterol	0 mg	Protein	12 g	Sugars	0 g

Lickety-Split Diabetic Meals

Lickety-Split Tip

Party Survival Tip #10: Stop eating early

Even if you stay late, decide when you will quit eating and do just that: Quit eating. This strategy can do wonders to prevent that continuous "just because it's there" munching, saving you hundreds of calories and, most likely, a high blood sugar reading the next morning.

Tzatziki & Vegetables

Hands-on – 8 min.   **Serves 16**

My thanks to Carol Brickenden and Stacy Rafalko for this simple and delicious dip for vegetables. It is also the traditional Greek sauce used in pita sandwiches. Try using this instead of butter or mayonnaise in a sandwich.

2 cups	plain nonfat yogurt

12 to 24 hours before serving:

Line a strainer with a paper coffee filter or cheesecloth. Place over a bowl. Spoon yogurt into coffee filter, cover, and refrigerate for 12 to 24 hours.

Yogurt will now be thick. Discard the collected liquid beneath or use it in soups or breads. Remove yogurt from the filter and place in a small bowl.

1/2	cucumber, peeled, seeded, and shredded
2 large	cloves of garlic, minced
1/2 tsp	dill weed*
1/4 tsp	salt
2 tsp	lemon juice
1 tsp	olive oil

1 hour before serving:

Mix into yogurt.

6 cups	any combination of fresh vegetables (see right)

Serve with a variety of fresh vegetables like: fresh green beans (lightly steamed), green, red, or yellow peppers, carrots, celery, zucchini, yellow squash, tomatoes, cucumbers, radishes, broccoli, and cauliflower. Also delicious with pita triangles and Bagel Chips (page 37).

*Can use 1 tsp chopped fresh dill instead.

Nutrition information for approximately 2 T dip

Exchanges/Choices: Free Food

Calories	20	Fat	0 g	Fiber	0 g	Sodium	57 mg	Total Carbohydrate	3 g
Calories from Fat	0%	Saturated Fat	0 g	Cholesterol	0 mg	Protein	1.5 g	Sugars	2 g

Lickety-Split Diabetic Meals

Lickety-Split Tip

Party Survival Tip #11: No matter what, stay positive

Even if you did overdo it at the party, keep things in perspective. You do not need to be "perfect" all the time, and one event does not make you an overweight person or give you high cholesterol, or make your blood sugar uncontrollable. Say, "It's no big deal," and start your next day back on your healthy fitness regime.

Marinated Sesame Chicken Kabobs

Here's a great way to add a lean protein source to your finger-food party menu. Festive, delicious, and easy to eat, your guests will love them!

12 as an appetizer
(Two 6-inch skewers per person)

6 as a meal
(Two 12-inch skewers per person)

1/4 cup	tamari or soy sauce (reduced-sodium)
1 tsp	sesame oil
1 T	firmly packed brown sugar
1/2 tsp	ginger (fresh grated is best)
8 grinds	fresh ground pepper
1/4 tsp	minced garlic
2 T	sesame seeds

5 hours before serving or night before:

Mix together in a large bowl for marinating.

Kids' Favorite!

6	(4 oz each) skinless, boneless chicken breasts

Slice chicken into 2"× 1/2" strips. Thoroughly coat with marinade, cover, and refrigerate for 5 hours or overnight.

Preheat BBQ grill or oven broiler.
Position oven rack 6 inches from broiler.

Optional additions

Whole mushrooms, green and red pepper chunks, onion wedges, cherry tomatoes, pineapple chunks

10 minutes before serving:

If using these, mix with chicken and marinate a few minutes before assembling. (Overexposure to the salty marinade causes vegetables to wilt.)

Using 6" bamboo skewers for appetizers* and 12" for dinner entrées, begin assembling kabobs. Pierce 1 end of the chicken strip, then hook it around and pierce the other end. Or pierce the whole strip lengthwise (use a weaving motion if desired). Alternate with the colorful vegetables if using. Broil or grill 6 to 8 minutes or until chicken is fully cooked.

6	red-tipped lettuce leaves

Serve warm or cold on a lined tray of red-tipped lettuce leaves.

*Simply cut 12" skewers in half.

Nutrition information for two 6-inch skewers (without optionals)
Exchanges/Choices: 2 Lean Meat

Calories	84	Fat	2 g	Fiber	<1 g	Sodium	240 mg	Total Carbohydrate	2 g
Calories from Fat	21%	Saturated Fat	<1 g	Cholesterol	33 mg	Protein	14 g	Sugars	1 g

Lickety-Split Diabetic Meals

Lickety-Split Tip

How do you eat right when your job has you on the road ALL the time?

"Restaurants used to be my downfall, but not anymore. My secret is I no longer look at the menu. That took care of the fried mozzarella sticks and chicken wings staring me in the face. Now, instead of ordering from the menu, I ask the server, 'Can you make me a broiled chicken breast, with lots of steamed vegetables, no butter, some marinara sauce, and a baked potato?' No more surprises and it's NEVER too many calories."

—*Sue Kloc, Management Analyst*

Celebrating the loss of 20 pounds and normalization of her high blood pressure without drugs.

1-Minute Mini-Meals

We've all been there. It's 6:50 p.m. and you're walking in the door. You have a 7:00 meeting to go to and it takes 5 minutes to get there. You have 5 minutes, so frantically you scrounge through the fridge and cupboards for anything to eat. The only thing you're thinking is, **"FOOD NOW!"**

There's no time for cooking anything, you'll just have to "grab." Is there something you can throw together in 1 minute that suffices as a meal and happens to be healthy and tastes good? In the past, half a bag of chips would have done the trick, but not anymore! Assuming you've shopped using the Lickety-Split grocery list, you're in business to make ANY of these tasty and good-for-you 1-Minute Mini-Meals!

Lickety-Split Diabetic Meals

Lickety-Split Tip

True or False?

Popcorn should be reserved as a snack and a snack only. It would be unhealthy to serve popcorn as the grain in your meal.

Answer: FALSE!

Popcorn is corn and corn is a healthy contribution to a meal, right? Corn is actually a grain (sorry, not a vegetable), and grains or starches should be an important part of every meal. Who says potatoes, rice, pasta, and bread are the only starches and grains allowed at mealtime? As long as your popcorn is healthfully prepared (including the truly low-fat versions of microwave popcorn), it's fine to include popcorn in a meal. My personal favorite combinations are beans and popcorn, and soup and popcorn!

1-Minute Mini-Meals

Quick Nachos

- Spread 20 Baked Tostitos on a microwave-safe plate.
- Sprinkle with 1/4 cup reduced-fat shredded cheddar cheese.
- Microwave on high 45 to 60 seconds.
- Eat with fat-free refried beans and salsa along with baby carrots and fruit juice.

Serves 1

Exchanges: 2 Starch, 1 Fruit, 1 Vegetable, 1 Lean Meat, 1 Fat

Nutritional Information

Calories 310
  Calories from Fat 55
Total Fat 6.0 g
  Saturated Fat 3.0 g
  Trans Fat 0.0 g
Cholesterol 15 mg
Sodium 860 mg
Total Carbohydrate 55 g
  Dietary Fiber 7 g
  Sugars 18 g
  Protein 13 g

Cheese Pita Pizza

- Spread 2 T spaghetti sauce on a pita.
- Sprinkle with 2 T reduced-fat shredded mozzarella cheese and 2 tsp Parmesan cheese. (Add any vegetables you have lying around, too!)
- Microwave on high until cheese is melted.

Serves 1

Exchanges: 2 Starch, 1 Vegetable, 1 Lean Meat, 1/2 Fat

Nutritional Information

Calories 260
  Calories from Fat 45
Total Fat 5.0 g
  Saturated Fat 2.2 g
  Trans Fat 0.0 g
Cholesterol 10 mg
Sodium 60 mg
Total Carbohydrate 41 g
  Dietary Fiber 3 g
  Sugars 6 g
  Protein 13 g

Quick Quesadilla

- Place a flour tortilla on a plate.
- Sprinkle with 2 T reduced-fat shredded cheddar cheese.
- Microwave 20 seconds on high.
- Meanwhile, chop a tomato for topping. (Salsa may also be used.)
- Roll and eat.

Serves 1

Exchanges: 1 1/2 Starch, 1 Vegetable, 1 Fat

Nutritional Information

Calories 200
  Calories from Fat 55
Total Fat 6 g
  Saturated Fat 2.2 g
  Trans Fat 0.0 g
Cholesterol 5 mg
Sodium 385 mg
Total Carbohydrate 30 g
  Dietary Fiber 3 g
  Sugars 5 g
  Protein 8 g

Zonya's Stress-Relieving Beans & Popcorn

- Place a bag of Orville Redenbacher Smart Pop in the microwave on high.
- Open a can of Eden seasoned beans.
- Eat 1/2 cup of the beans while waiting for the popcorn.
- Chase beans with popcorn.
- Have 1/2 cup unsweetened applesauce sprinkled with cinnamon for dessert

Serves 3

Exchanges: 2 1/2 Starch, 1 Fruit

Nutritional Information

Calories 265
  Calories from Fat 20
Total Fat 2.5 g
  Saturated Fat 0.6 g
  Trans Fat 0.0 g
Cholesterol 0 mg
Sodium 380 mg
Total Carbohydrate 57 g
  Dietary Fiber 12 g
  Sugars 13 g
  Protein 10 g

1-Minute Mini-Meals

Beans & Crackers

- Eat 1/2 cup of baked beans with 5 reduced-fat Triscuits.
- Any baked beans are OK, however, Eden baked beans can't be beat for being the most nutritionally smart.
- Chase with a handful of baby carrots.

Serves 1

Exchanges: 2 1/2 Starch, 1 Vegetable, 1/2 Fat

Nutritional Information

Calories 240
  Calories from Fat 20
Total Fat 2.5 g
  Saturated Fat 0.8 g
  Trans Fat 0.0 g
Cholesterol 0 mg
Sodium 260 mg
Total Carbohydrate 45 g
  Dietary Fiber 10 g
  Sugars 7 g
Protein 10 g

Snappy Sandwich Roll

- Spread mustard on a 6" flour tortilla or lavash flat bread.
- Add 1½ oz (3 deli-thin slices) 97% fat-free lunch meat or low-fat cheese.
- Place a couple of carrots and celery sticks lined up end to end.
- Roll and eat.

Serves 1

Exchanges: 1 Starch, 1 Vegetable, 1 Lean Meat,

Nutritional Information

Calories 155
  Calories from Fat 25
Total Fat 3.0 g
  Saturated Fat 0.7 g
  Trans Fat 0.0 g
Cholesterol 20 mg
Sodium 625 mg
Total Carbohydrate 18 g
  Dietary Fiber 2 g
  Sugars 2 g
Protein 13 g

Fiesta Bean Burrito

- Spread 1/2 cup fat-free refried beans and 1 T salsa in a 6" flour tortilla.
- Roll and eat.

Serves 1

Exchanges: 2 Starch, 1 Lean Meat

Nutritional Information

Calories 200
  Calories from Fat 20
Total Fat 2.5 g
  Saturated Fat 0.6 g
  Trans Fat 0.0 g
Cholesterol 0 mg
Sodium 770 mg
Total Carbohydrate 34 g
  Dietary Fiber 7 g
  Sugars 2 g
Protein 9 g

Yogurt & Grape-Nuts

- Pour 1/4 cup Grape-Nuts (or 2 T ground flax seed) into 6 oz nonfat yogurt.
- Stir and eat.

Tip: If all you have is plain yogurt, simply stir in 1 T fruit jam or preserves.

Serves 1

Exchanges: 1 1/2 Starch, 1 Fat-free Milk

Nutritional Information

Calories 180
  Calories from Fat 10
Total Fat 1.0 g
  Saturated Fat 0.3 g
  Trans Fat 0.0 g
Cholesterol 10 mg
Sodium 255 mg
Total Carbohydrate 36 g
  Dietary Fiber 4 g
  Sugars 13 g
Protein 11 g

1 Minute Mini-Meals

English Muffin Melt

- Toast an English muffin.
- Lay 1/2 slice low-fat cheese on each half.
- Microwave on HIGH 15 seconds.
- Add a tomato slice, if you like. Eat with a small apple.

Serves 1

Exchanges: 2 Starch, 1 Fruit, 1 Lean Meat

Nutritional Information

Calories 225
  Calories from Fat   15
Total Fat 1.5 g
  Saturated Fat 0.3 g
  Trans Fat 0.0 g
Cholesterol 5 mg
Sodium 550 mg
Total Carbohydrate 44 g
  Dietary Fiber 5 g
  Sugars 15 g
Protein 10 g

Applesauce & Cottage Cheese

- Place 1/2 cup each of unsweetened applesauce and nonfat cottage cheese side by side.
- Sprinkle with ground cinnamon if desired.
- Slightly mix together as you eat.

Serves 1

Exchanges: 1 Fruit, 2 Lean Meat

Nutritional Information

Calories 130
  Calories from Fat 0
Total Fat 0.0 g
  Saturated Fat 0.0 g
  Trans Fat 0.0 g
Cholesterol 5 mg
Sodium 410 mg
Total Carbohydrate 19 g
  Dietary Fiber 1 g
  Sugars 14 g
Protein 14 g

Cottage Cheese & Fruit

- Place 1/2 cup of drained fruit (pineapple, peaches, or apricots, packed in their own juice) over 1/2 cup of nonfat cottage cheese.
- Eat with 5 low-fat whole-wheat crackers.

Serves 1

Exchanges: 1 Starch, 1 Fruit, 2 Lean Meat

Nutritional Information

Calories 215
  Calories from Fat 20
Total Fat 2.0 g
  Saturated Fat 0.7 g
  Trans Fat 0.0 g
Cholesterol 5 mg
Sodium 525 mg
Total Carbohydrate 34 g
  Dietary Fiber 4 g
  Sugars 16 g
Protein 17 g

Easy Cheesy Tomatoes

- Open a 14½-oz can diced tomatoes, no salt added.
- Pour into a microwave-safe bowl and sprinkle with 2 oz reduced-fat shredded mozzarella cheese, 1 tsp Parmesan cheese, and a dash each dried oregano and pepper.
- Microwave on HIGH until cheese is melted.
- Eat with 5 low-fat whole-wheat crackers (per person).

Serves 2

Exchanges: 1 Starch, 1 Vegetable, 1 Lean Meat

Nutritional Information

Calories 170
  Calories from Fat 20
Total Fat 2.5 g
  Saturated Fat 0.8 g
  Trans Fat 0.0 g
Cholesterol 5 mg
Sodium 540 mg
Total Carbohydrate 27 g
  Dietary Fiber 6 g
  Sugars 7 g
Protein 12 g

Lickety-Split Tip

Pop Quiz

If you change from drinking 2 cups of 2% milk each day to drinking 2 cups of 1/2% milk each day, you'll lose:

A.   6 pounds in a year

B.   10 pounds in a year

C.   12.5 pounds in a year

Answer: C. 12.5 pounds in a year!

That's the Power of One Good Habit!

1-Minute Mini-Meals

Pepper Strips & Cottage Cheese

- Slice and seed 1 red or green bell pepper.
- Pour a puddle of light Thousand Island dressing on a lunch plate.
- Plop 1/2 cup nonfat cottage cheese on the side for 2-step dipping.
- Eat with a small nectarine, pear, or orange.

Serves 1

Exchanges: 1 Fruit, 1/2 Carbohydrate, 1 Vegetable, 2 Lean Meat

Nutritional Information
Calories 210
  Calories from Fat 20
Total Fat 2.0 g
  Saturated Fat 0.1 g
  Trans Fat 0.0 g
Cholesterol 5 mg
Sodium 585 mg
Total Carbohydrate 33 g
  Dietary Fiber 5 g
  Sugars 23 g
Protein 17 g

Bagelwich

- Slice a 3-oz whole-grain bagel and throw on 1½ oz (3 deli-thin slices) 97% fat-free turkey lunch meat with some mustard.
- Eat with a handful of baby carrots and radishes.

Serves 1

Exchanges: 3 Starch, 1 Lean Meat

Nutritional Information
Calories 290
  Calories from Fat 20
Total Fat 2.0 g
  Saturated Fat 0.3 g
  Trans Fat 0.0 g
Cholesterol 20 mg
Sodium 855 mg
Total Carbohydrate 49 g
  Dietary Fiber 7 g
  Sugars 9 g
Protein 21 g

Pita Wedges & Veggies Dipped in Hummus

- Rinse some fresh broccoli florets and baby carrots.
- Slice a pita into 8 triangles.
- Dip pita triangles and veggies into hummus and eat.

Note: You can buy ready-made hummus in a case near the deli section of your grocery store.

An 8-oz tub of hummus serves 2 to 4

Exchanges: 1 1/2 Starch, 1 Vegetable, 1 Fat

Nutritional Information
Calories 200
  Calories from Fat 55
Total Fat 6.0 g
  Saturated Fat 0.9 g
  Trans Fat 0.0 g
Cholesterol 0 mg
Sodium 405 mg
Total Carbohydrate 29 g
  Dietary Fiber 6 g
  Sugars 6 g
Protein 9 g

Sardines & Crackers

- Pop open a 3¾ oz can of sardines in mustard sauce.
- Eat with 5 reduced-fat Triscuits or Wheat Thins and a handful of baby carrots, celery, and pepper strips.

Serves 1

Exchanges: 1 Starch, 1 Vegetable, 3 Lean Meat

Nutritional Information
Calories 255
  Calories from Fat 90
Total Fat 10.0 g
  Saturated Fat 4.7 g
  Trans Fat 0.0 g
Cholesterol 60 mg
Sodium 645 mg
Total Carbohydrate 22 g
  Dietary Fiber 5 g
  Sugars 4 g
Protein 20 g

Lickety-Split Tip

Pop Quiz!

Your fruit bin and baskets are typically:

A.   Stocked with the season's best selection, replenished at least once if not twice each week.

B.   Full after shopping, but empty for days between trips, since it's hard to get to the store.

C.   Home to a few apples or oranges, or other fruits with a long shelf life.

D.   What bin or basket?

Correct Answer: A.

With all the anti-aging compounds in fresh fruit, it's hard to name a habit more beneficial to your health than eating 3 to 4 pieces of fruit each day. And in order to eat fruit, you have to **BUY** fruit. Establish the habit of making a midweek stop at a produce market so you'll always have enough!

P.S. Fruit is fast food!
P.P.S. Fruit is nature's candy!

1-Minute Mini-Meals

Garden Lentil Salad & Crackers

- Eat 1 cup of salad directly from container.
- Eat with 5 low-fat whole-wheat crackers.

Note: You can buy this delicious ready-made salad from the deli section of your grocery store.

Serves 1

Exchanges: 1 Starch, 1 Fruit, 1 Vegetable, 1 1/2 Fat

Nutritional Information

Calories 240

  Calories from Fat 80

Total Fat 9.0 g

  Saturated Fat 2.3 g

  Trans Fat 0.0 g

Cholesterol 5 mg

Sodium 300 mg

Total Carbohydrate 37 g

  Dietary Fiber 7 g

  Sugars 14g

Protein 8 g

Turkey Rolls with Potato Chips

- Spread hot mustard on 2 slices 97% fat-free turkey lunch meat.
- Place a couple of carrots lined up end to end.
- Roll and eat.
- Chase with 15 Baked Lay's potato chips and a juice box.

Serves 1

Exchanges: 2 Starch, 1 Fruit, 1 Lean Meat

Nutritional Information

Calories 250

  Calories from Fat 20

Total Fat 2.5 g

  Saturated Fat 0.1 g

  Trans Fat 0.0 g

Cholesterol 15 mg

Sodium 505 mg

Total Carbohydrate 48 g

  Dietary Fiber 4 g

  Sugars 17 g

Protein 10 g

Mediterranean Lavash Roll-up

- Spread 1/4 cup hummus and 1/2 cup tabouli on a lavash flat bread or flour tortilla.
- Roll and eat with 10 cherry tomatoes.

Note: You can buy ready-made hummus and tabouli in a case near the deli section of your grocery store.

Serves 1

Exchanges: 2 1/2 Starch, 1 Vegetable, 1 Meat

Nutritional Information

Calories 315

  Calories from Fat 80

Total Fat 9.0 g

  Saturated Fat 1.3 g

  Trans Fat 0.0 g

Cholesterol 0 mg

Sodium 535 mg

Total Carbohydrate 50 g

  Dietary Fiber 9 g

  Sugars 10 g

Protein 12 g

Quick Chicken Sandwich

- Open a 10-oz can cooked white chicken, rinse, and drain.
- Mix with 2 T Miracle Whip Light and 1 T Dijon mustard.
- Spread chicken mixture on 3 slices of whole-grain bread and eat with a small apple, pear, or nectarine.

Serves 3

Exchanges: 1 Starch, 1 Fruit, 1 Lean Meat

Nutritional Information

Calories 245

  Calories from Fat 35

Total Fat 4.0 g

  Saturated Fat 0.4 g

  Trans Fat 0.0 g

Cholesterol 55 mg

Sodium 730 mg

Total Carbohydrate 29 g

  Dietary Fiber 5 g

  Sugars 14 g

Protein 25 g

Lickety-Split Tip

Pop Quiz!

Which best describes your vegetable consumption yesterday?

A.   Cup of vegetable soup, large stir-fry including peppers, broccoli, and carrots

B.   Small iceberg salad with tomato fragment, half cup overcooked green beans

C.   Ketchup, pickles, and French fries

If you answered anything besides A, you're in big trouble!

Vegetables are loaded with high fiber for controlling blood sugar, not to mention other cancer-fighting and heart-disease-fighting compounds your body needs. Say yes to a double serving of vegetables at dinner, and munch on raw vegetables at lunch. Your body will thank you with improved weight and blood sugar control, plus a reduced risk of cataracts, clogged arteries, and cancer!

P.S. Raw veggies are fast food!

Baked Tortilla Chips & Spicy Pintos

- Eat 1/2 cup Eden Spicy Pintos with 15 baked tortilla chips.
- Chase with 1/2 cup unsweetened applesauce sprinkled with cinnamon.

Serves 1

Exchanges: 2 1/2 Starch, 1 Fruit

Nutritional Information

Calories 255
  Calories from Fat 20
Total Fat 2.0 g
  Saturated Fat 0.4 g
  Trans Fat 0.0 g
Cholesterol 0 mg
Sodium 350 mg
Total Carbohydrate 56 g
  Dietary Fiber 10 g
  Sugars 13 g
Protein 9 g

String-Cheese Standby

- Eat a piece of string-cheese with 5 crackers and a small apple, orange, or pear.

Serves 1

Exchanges: 1 Starch, 1 Fruit, 1/2 Fat-Free Milk, 1 Lean Meat

Nutritional Information

Calories 230
  Calories from Fat 45
Total Fat 5.0 g
  Saturated Fat 2.3 g
  Trans Fat 0.0 g
Cholesterol 15 mg
Sodium 345 mg
Total Carbohydrate 36 g
  Dietary Fiber 5 g
  Sugars 17 g
Protein 12 g

Simple Salad Supper

- Pour pre-cleaned salad greens into a bowl.
- Top with 1/2 can of drained, rinsed Eden garbanzo beans.
- Add a plop of nonfat cottage cheese, a bunch of canned beets and other fresh veggies.
- Top with 2 T light Thousand Island dressing and croutons.

Serves 1

Exchanges: 2 Starch, 1/2 Carbohydrate, 2 Vegetable, 1 Lean Meat

Nutritional Information

Calories 305
  Calories from Fat 45
Total Fat 5.0 g
  Saturated Fat 0.3 g
  Trans Fat 0.0 g
Cholesterol 5 mg
Sodium 780 mg
Total Carbohydrate 50 g
  Dietary Fiber 10 g
  Sugars 21 g
Protein 17 g

Salmon Pita Sandwich

- Open a 7-oz can of salmon, rinse, and drain.
- Mix with 2 T Miracle Whip Light. (Smash bones with a fork.)
- Stuff into a pita.
- Add lettuce and tomato and eat.

Serves 3

Exchanges: 1 Starch, 1 Vegetable, 1 Lean Meat, 1 Fat

Nutritional Information

Calories 200
  Calories from Fat 55
Total Fat 6.0 g
  Saturated Fat 1.2 g
  Trans Fat 0.0 g
Cholesterol 25 mg
Sodium 560 mg
Total Carbohydrate 22 g
  Dietary Fiber 2 g
  Sugars 4 g
Protein 15 g

Lickety-Split Tip

Pop Quiz!

Which best describes the high-calcium foods you consumed yesterday?

A.   Milk on cereal, 6 oz yogurt, and 1 oz low-fat cheese on broccoli

B.   Cheese on pizza, ice cream

C.   No dairy; you avoid it because of allergy or intolerance.

Correct Answer: A.

Calcium is a **VERY** important anti-aging food. It helps prevent osteoporosis (weak and porous bones) helps to improve insulin production and, therefore, blood sugar control. If you answered A, great. If you answered B, that amount of calcium is not only insufficient, but your intake also contains excessive saturated fat and calories. C means you just plain need to start taking a calcium supplement with Vitamin D. Don't delay. Start doing it now!

1-Minute Mini-Meals

Tuna Cracker Sandwiches

- Pop open a 3-oz single serving can of water-packed tuna, rinse, and drain.
- Make cracker sandwiches and chase with a can of low-sodium V-8.

Serves 1

Exchanges: 1 Starch, 2 Vegetable, 2 Lean Meat

Nutritional Information

Calories 205
  Calories from Fat 25
Total Fat 3.0 g
  Saturated Fat 0.9 g
  Trans Fat 0.0 g
Cholesterol 25 mg
Sodium 465 mg
Total Carbohydrate 24 g
  Dietary Fiber 4 g
  Sugars 6 g
Protein 21 g

Hard-Boiled Egg with Crackers

- Crack and peel 1 egg you've previously hard-boiled.
- Eat with 5 reduced-fat Triscuits and a small apple.

Serves 1

Exchanges: 1 Starch, 1 Fruit, 1 Medium-Fat Meat

Nutritional Information

Calories 210
  Calories from Fat 65
Total Fat 7.0 g
  Saturated Fat 2.3 g
  Trans Fat 0.0 g
Cholesterol 210 mg
Sodium 180 mg
Total Carbohydrate 30 g
  Dietary Fiber 5 g
  Sugars 11 g
Protein 8 g

Tuna, Rice & Veggie Salad

- Rinse and drain a 6-oz can of tuna or chicken.
- Add to bowl along with 1 cup leftover brown rice and chopped peppers and carrots.
- Toss with 4 T light salad dressing of your choice.

Serves 2

Exchanges: 1 1/2 Starch, 1/2 Carbohydrate, 1 Vegetable, 2 Lean Meat

Nutritional Information

Calories 260
  Calories from Fat 25
Total Fat 3.0 g
  Saturated Fat 0.4 g
  Trans Fat 0.0 g
Cholesterol 25 mg
Sodium 540 mg
Total Carbohydrate 35 g
  Dietary Fiber 3 g
  Sugars 8 g
Protein 23 g

Tuna in a Pita

- Spread 1 T Miracle Whip Light inside a pita.
- Pop open a 3 oz single-serving can of water-packed tuna, rinse, and drain. Stuff into pita.
- Add any vegetables that you have.

Serves 1

Exchanges: 2 Starch, 1 Vegetable, 2 Lean Meat

Nutritional Information

Calories 290
  Calories from Fat 25
Total Fat 3.0 g
  Saturated Fat 0.6 g
  Trans Fat 0.0 g
Cholesterol 25 mg
Sodium 725 mg
Total Carbohydrate 39 g
  Dietary Fiber 3 g
  Sugars 5 g
Protein 26 g

Lickety-Split Tip

Dashboard Dining Tips

My family secrets to dashboard dining include:

1. Keeping a baggie filled with napkins, plastic forks, knives and spoons, wet-wipes, and yes, even a can opener in the glove compartment. You are now in a better position to grab something healthy from a grocery store salad bar or deli, or even healthy leftovers grabbed out of your own refrigerator.

2. Keeping the cabinet beside the door leading to the garage stocked with the following easy grab-and-go items:
   • single-serving cans of low-sodium V-8 juice
   • bottles of water
   • snack-size baggies of trail mix
   • soy nuts
   • envelopes of tuna (new seasoned types are great)
   • cans of baked beans and other seasoned beans (visit *www.EdenFoods.com* for my favorites)
   • low-fat whole-grain crackers (Kashi makes trans-fat free)
   • raisins and dried apricots
   • whole-grain bagels and cookies

3. Keeping the fridge always stocked with baby carrots, a tub of hummus, whole-wheat pita bread, mozzarella cheese sticks, and fruit.

4. Lavash flatbread too, as turkey and lettuce drizzled with low-fat dressing makes a super quick roll-up dinner to go. Wrap in plastic wrap and "peel and eat" as you drive.

5. Grabbing 2 or 3 Breakfast in a Cookie cookies (page 9) from the freezer plus 8-oz box of EdenSoy.

While I don't recommend "dashboard dining" as a rule, I know from personal experience that it's unavoidable sometimes. The point is to plan enough ahead that it doesn't **HAVE** to turn into a drive-thru window nightmare on the nutrition scoreboard.

And always remember to not let your fast-paced lifestyle make you eat so fast that you don't realize how much you've eaten, and you eat more than you need in order to be satisfied.

1-Minute Mini-Meals

Peanut Butter Rice Cake

- Spread 1 T peanut butter thinly on a couple of rice cakes.
- Eat with a small banana.

Serves 1

Exchanges: 1 Starch, 1 Fruit,
1/2 Fat-Free Milk, 1 Meat

Nutritional Information

Calories 265
  Calories from Fat 80
Total Fat 9.0 g
  Saturated Fat 1.9 g
  Trans Fat 0.0 g
Cholesterol 5 mg
Sodium 195 mg
Total Carbohydrate 38 g
  Dietary Fiber 3 g
  Sugars 16 g
Protein 10 g

Quick 2-Bean Salad

- Rinse and drain a 15-oz can of kidney beans and a 14½-oz can of green beans.
- Transfer to a medium bowl and toss with 1/4 cup lite or fat-free Italian dressing.
- Eat with low-fat whole-wheat crackers (5 per person).

Serves 2

Exchanges: 3 Starch, 1 Vegetable,
1 Lean Meat

Nutritional Information

Calories 300
  Calories from Fat 25
Total Fat 3.0 g
  Saturated Fat 0.7 g
  Trans Fat 0.0 g
Cholesterol 0 mg
Sodium 970 mg
Total Carbohydrate 56 g
  Dietary Fiber 14 g
  Sugars 8 g
Protein 16 g

Corny Chicken Salad

- Rinse and drain a 10-oz can cooked chicken and a 15-oz can of corn, no salt added.
- Flake chicken and toss together in a bowl with 3 T lite or fat-free Italian dressing.
- Eat with widely cut strips of red pepper.

Serves 2

Exchanges: 1 1/2 Starch, 4 Lean Meat

Nutritional Information

Calories 275
  Calories from Fat 40
Total Fat 4.5 g
  Saturated Fat 0.3 g
  Trans Fat 0.0 g
Cholesterol 75 mg
Sodium 830 mg
Total Carbohydrate 24 g
  Dietary Fiber 6 g
  Sugars 16 g
Protein 35 g

Black Bean & Corn Salad

- Rinse and drain a 15-oz can each of black beans and corn, no salt added.
- Transfer to a medium bowl and toss with 2 cups of salsa.
- Eat as a dip with 15 Baked Tostitos per person.

(Also great rolled up in a whole-wheat tortilla or as a tossed salad topper.)

Serves 4

Exchanges: 2 1/2 Starch, 2 Vegetable

Nutritional Information

Calories 255
  Calories from Fat 20
Total Fat 2.0 g
  Saturated Fat 0.4 g
  Trans Fat 0.0 g
Cholesterol 0 mg
Sodium 940 mg
Total Carbohydrate 52 g
  Dietary Fiber 10 g
  Sugars 11 g
Protein 11 g

Lickety-Split Tip

Can you think of any foods that may have contributed to your long and healthy life?

"For 30 years, we raised sweet potatoes, and boy did we eat a lot of them. I've always cooked up a pot of beans weekly. (Yes, with a ham bone!) But probably the biggest thing has been my years of home-cooked meals, not processed restaurant foods."

—My grandmother Minnie Burgess, type 2 diabetic at age 90 when she was still climbing the stairs of her home effortlessly, countless times a day.

5-Minute Meals

It just astounds me how many people go out to eat. "I don't have time to cook," they say. But eating out takes **SO MUCH** time! Even going through a drive-through takes time. My husband and I firmly believe that the fastest way to get a meal is to make it yourself. The secret is keeping the right ingredients on hand and, of course, using this book!

When we want a meal in 5 minutes, we mentally pick from among these 3 things:

• Roll-ups (bean burrito or a lavash roll-up)

• Quick Pita Sandwich or Pita Pizza

• Canned beans (mix with canned corn or tuna)

Once you decide, you'll be eating 5 minutes later!

Lickety-Split Diabetic Meals

Lickety-Split Tip

What is fiber and where do you find it?

Fiber is the portion of plant foods that you cannot digest, also known as "roughage."

It is not found in any animal foods.

Yes	**No**
Plant foods	Animal foods
Fruits	Chicken
Vegetables	Beef
Grains	Pork
Whole-grain flours	Veal
Whole-grain baked goods	Fish
Dried beans and peas	Milk
Nuts and seeds	Eggs

Benito Bean Burritos

Hands-on – 5 min.

Serves 8

Burritos without the refried beans. Soon to be a household favorite!

3	**green onions (opt)**	Chop in the food processor.
1 jar	**(48 oz) pinto beans, rinsed and drained**	Add to processor and blend until smooth.*
1 cup	**salsa of your choice**	Transfer mixture to microwave safe container and heat on HIGH for 2 or more minutes.
1/2 tsp	**Zippy Zonya Mexi Mix‡**	
1 med	**tomato (opt)**	Rinse and chop for extra toppings, if desired.
1 cup	**chopped lettuce (opt)**	
8	**6" flour tortillas**	Microwave on HIGH about 5 seconds per tortilla.
1/2 cup	**salsa of your choice (1 T per burrito)**	Use as desired for topping your burrito.
1/2 cup	**reduced-fat shredded cheddar cheese†** **(1 T per burrito)**	Assemble by spreading approximately 1/4 cup Benito Spread on each tortilla and layer on any additional ingredients you choose. Fold in the ends and roll up.
1/2 cup	**fat-free sour cream or nonfat yogurt** **(1 T per burrito)**	Slice 2 apples into wedges and place on table with baby carrots.

If you must eat on the run, just roll your burrito up in a paper towel, and take it with you. Don't forget your apples and carrots.

*This step can be replaced by simply opening a can of fat-free refried beans. My husband and
 I still prefer the flavor of this old-fashioned method.

†See reduced-fat cheese tip on page viii (Introduction).

‡See recipe on page 40.

Nutrition information for 1 burrito
Exchanges/Choices: 3 Starch, 1 Lean Meat

Calories	295	Fat	4.5 g	Fiber	9 g	Sodium	685 mg
Calories from Fat	14%	Saturated Fat	1.3 g	Cholesterol	3 mg	Protein	14 g

Total Carbohydrate	49 g
Sugars	3 g

Lickety-Split Diabetic Meals

Lickety-Split Tip

Why is fiber so important?

• Yields no calories! Helps control your weight by filling you up on fewer calories.

• Plays an important role in intestinal health. (Your intestinal tract is 24 feet long and needs to be kept clean!) Helps keep you "regular."

• Greatly reduces your risk of cancer, especially colon cancer.

• Helps lower blood cholesterol.

• Helps control blood sugar levels for people with diabetes.

Great Northern Tuna Salad Stuffer

Quickly mix this up for a delicious pita pocket stuffer, flour tortilla roll-up, or to add on top of a tomato or bed of salad greens. Friends will rave!

Keeps in the refrigerator for 4 days. Use for lunches all week.

1 lg can	(12 oz) water packed tuna, drained	Toss together in medium bowl.
2 cans	(15 oz each) **Great Northern beans, rinsed and drained**	

1/2 tsp	dill weed	Add and mix gently.
1/3 cup	light Thousand Island dressing	

Optional:		Add if you have time.
1	green onion, chopped	Serve 3/4 cup stuffed into 2 pita halves, rolled in a flour tortilla, placed on top of a tomato or salad greens, or simply eat with low-fat, whole-wheat crackers.
1/2	red bell pepper, chopped	
1/4 cup	fresh parsley, chopped	

Nutrition information for 3/4 cup including the optional veggies

Exchanges/Choices: 1 1/2 Starch, 2 Lean Meat

Calories	202	Fat	3 g	Fiber	7 g	Sodium	503 mg	Total Carbohydrate	25 g
Calories from Fat	12%	Saturated Fat	0 g	Cholesterol	14 mg	Protein	19 g	Sugars	3 g

Lickety-Split Diabetic Meals

Great Northern Tuna Salad Stuffer

Lickety-Split Tip

How much fiber do you need?

The recommended intake is 20–30 (or more) grams per day.

On the average, people eat only 11 grams of fiber per day, with some people eating even less than that. (YIKES!)

Almond Chicken Salad

Hands-on — 5 min.   **Serves 4**

This makes a very special luncheon dish served in 1/2 of a cantaloupe. It's also great for sprucing up brown bag lunch.

| 1 can | (8 oz) pineapple tidbits, in its own juice | Open cans and drain. Reserve pineapple juice for another use. |
| 1 can | (15 oz) Mandarin oranges* | |

| 2 cups | diced cooked chicken or turkey or 1 can (10 oz) white chicken, rinsed and drained | Place in a medium bowl with the fruit. |

| 1/4 cup | Miracle Whip Light | Mix together in a 2 cup measuring cup. Fold into fruit and chicken. |
| 1/4 cup | nonfat plain yogurt | |

| 1/4 cup | slivered almonds | Gently mix in. |

Use to make a sandwich, stuff a pita, top lettuce greens, or fill half a cantaloupe.

*Try substituting 1 cup of grape halves for variety.

Nutrition information for approximately 1 cup
Exchanges/Choices: 1 Fruit, 2 Lean Meat, 1 Fat

| Calories | 182 | Fat | 8 g | Fiber | 2 g | Sodium | 303 mg | Total Carbohydrate | 19 g |
| Calories from Fat | 39% | Saturated Fat | <1 g | Cholesterol | 19 mg | Protein | 10 g | Sugars | 16 g |

Lickety-Split Diabetic Meals

Almond Chicken Salad

Lickety-Split Tip

How can you get 20–30 grams of fiber each day?

Think "10 + 10 + 10".................................. To achieve this each day, EAT:

10 grams from fruit.. 3 or more pieces of fruit

10 grams from vegetables .... 3 or more 1/2-cup servings of vegetables

10 grams from whole grains.......................... 4 or more servings of whole-grain bread,
cereals, brown rice, oatmeal, etc.

Also include beans on a weekly basis:
Pinto, kidney, garbanzo, navy, lima beans, and lots of peas and corn.

This Black Bean & Corn Salad at 16 grams of fiber per serving helps get you to your daily
goal of 20–30 grams in a hurry!

Black Bean & Corn Salad

Hands-on – 5 min.

Serves 4

This is so simple, it's almost obscene! Thanks to Karen Pender for this incredibly simple and delicious dish! She brought it to a 4th of July potluck picnic where many of us fell in love with it.

1 can	(16 oz) corn, no-salt-added	Place in a strainer to drain. If using frozen corn, run warm water over it to thaw. Transfer to medium bowl.
2 cans	(16 oz) black beans or black soybeans (Eden)	Drain and rinse in strainer, then add to bowl.
1 cup	fresh tomato salsa*	Add to bowl and mix contents gently.
1 tsp	Zippy Zonya Mexi Mix‡ (opt)	
3 dashes	cayenne pepper (opt)	

Eat as a salad, or rolled up in a tortilla as a quick sandwich or dip with baked tortilla chips. Also makes a wonderful accompaniment for outdoor-grilled chicken or fish.

*If you only have canned salsa, try adding some chopped fresh tomatoes and minced cilantro or parsley for fresh color and flavor.

‡See recipe on page 40.

Also makes a great appetizer.

Nutrition information for approximately 1 cup salad without tortilla chips

Exchanges/Choices: 3 Starch, 1 Lean Meat

Calories	290	Fat	2 g	Fiber	16 g	Sodium	627 mg	Total Carbohydrate	50 g
Calories from Fat	6%	Saturated Fat	0 g	Cholesterol	0 mg	Protein	15 g	Sugars	6 g

Lickety-Split Diabetic Meals

Lickety-Split Tip

Why buy lavash?

1. It's very nutritious since you can buy 100% whole-wheat lavash bread that has no added fat.

2. It allows you to make a sandwich out of a leftover stir-fry or just about anything!

3. It's a nice change from eating sandwiches all the time.

4. It easily allows you to include all kinds of vegetables.

5. It's perfect for eating on the run!

Turkey & Hot Mustard Roll-ups

I don't know what we would do without these lavash breads. Be sure to try this. A great way to get a meal on the run!

Also an excellent party appetizer.

1	10" lavash flat bread* or flour tortilla	Lay out on flat surface.
2 T	fat-free cream cheese	Spread across entire lavash or tortilla.
2 tsp	Honeycup mustard (or to taste) (any spicy mustard will do)	Spread on top of the cream cheese.
2 oz	sliced home-cooked turkey breast	Place ingredients in a row side by side.
2	baby carrots, cut into fourths lengthwise	Get ready to roll! Starting from the edge of a long side, roll it up. Cut in half. If eating later, wrap in plastic wrap.
1/4	cucumber, cut lengthwise	To eat as a sandwich, peel back a few inches of plastic wrap, eat, peel some more, eat… you get the idea!
1/2	tomato, cut into wedges	
1/4 cup	alfalfa sprouts	To eat as an appetizer, let them "set" in the refrigerator for 2 or 3 hours. Then, remove the plastic wrap. Cut the rolls into 1" slices, using a sawing motion.
10	red-tipped lettuce leaves or purple kale (opt)	Serve cut side up on a platter garnished with red-tipped lettuce or purple kale.

P.S. Make more!

Note: If you use processed turkey instead of homemade, the sodium for this sandwich soars!

*Find lavash (sometimes spelled lawash) in the deli or bakery sections of your grocery store. It's a large flat bread like a tortilla.

Nutrition information for a half roll-up

Exchanges/Choices: 1 Starch, 1 Vegetable, 1 Lean Meat

Calories	152	Fat	3 g	Fiber	2 g	Sodium	564 mg	Total Carbohydrate	17 g
Calories from Fat	18%	Saturated Fat	0 g	Cholesterol	1 mg	Protein	14 g	Sugars	2 g

Lickety-Split Diabetic Meals

Lickety-Split Tip

Go Mediterranean!

The Mediterranean diet has become increasingly popular, spotlighting the health benefits of legumes, vegetables, olive oil, and garlic. Purchasing ready-made hummus and tabouli are two great ways to conveniently reap these benefits.

Hummus: Ground chickpeas, sesame seed paste (called tahini), lemon juice, and garlic. Excellent for dipping vegetables, pita bread triangles, or crackers.

Tabouli: Bulgur (wheat kernels that have been steamed, dried, and crushed), parsley, lemon juice, olive oil, and garlic. Excellent as a side salad or stuffed into a pita or rolled in a lavash.

The combination of hummus and tabouli together in these sandwiches is awesome! You must try it!

Mediterranean Roll-ups

Hands-on – 5 min. **Serves 2**

You'll never say "Where's the meat?" when eating this delicious super-fast vegetarian sandwich. Just stop by the specialty section of your grocery store deli for prepared tabouli and hummus, and a package of lavash.

Also an excellent party appetizer.

1	10" lavash flat bread* or flour tortilla	Lay out on a flat surface.
1/4 cup 1/4 cup	ready-made hummus ready-made tabouli	Pile each in a long row, side by side on lavash or tortilla.
10	romaine lettuce leaves, whole or chopped	Add generously.

1 cup	alfalfa or bean sprouts (opt)	Add as desired.
2 lg	tomatoes, chopped	Get ready to roll! Starting from the edge of a long side, roll it up. Cut in half. If eating later, wrap in plastic wrap.

To eat as a sandwich, peel back a few inches of plastic wrap, eat, peel some more, eat… you get the idea!

To eat as an appetizer, let "set" in the refrigerator for 2 or 3 hours. Then remove the plastic wrap. Cut the rolls into 1" slices, using a sawing motion.

10	red-tipped lettuce leaves or purple kale (opt)	Serve cut side up on a platter garnished with red-tipped lettuce or purple kale. P.S. Make more!

*Find lavash (sometimes spelled lawash) in the deli or bakery sections of your grocery store. It's a large flat bread like a tortilla.

Nutrition information for a half roll-up
Exchanges/Choices: 1 1/2 Starch, 1 Vegetable, 1 Fat

Calories	187	Fat	6 g	Fiber	5 g	Sodium	364 mg	Total Carbohydrate	29 g
Calories from Fat	28%	Saturated Fat	0 g	Cholesterol	0 mg	Protein	7 g	Sugars	1 g

Lickety-Split Diabetic Meals

Lickety-Split Tip

How many fat grams can I have each day?

It is recommended to consume no more than 30 to 60 grams of fat per day depending on your health needs.*

If you are less active and/or want to lose weight, make it closer to 30 grams.

If you are more active and/or want to maintain weight, choose closer to 60 grams.

*Studies by Dean Ornish, MD, author of *Reversing Heart Disease Without Drugs or Surgery*, suggest that a vegetarian diet as low as 15 grams of fat per day in combination with exercise and meditation can reverse heart disease in diseased patients.

Did you know?

Every 5 grams of fat listed on a label = 1 teaspoon of lard or shortening!

Some Americans eat over 100 grams of fat per day!

That's almost a 1/2 cup of lard or shortening **EACH DAY**!

Vegetable & Spinach Dip Roll-ups

Hands-on – 5 min.

Serves 2

Have leftover spinach dip? Here's the perfect way to use it.

Also excellent as a party appetizer.

1	10" lavash flat bread* or flour tortilla	Lay out on a flat surface.
1/4 cup	Spinach Dip (see page 39)	Spread across entire lavash or tortilla.
2	baby carrots, cut into fourths lengthwise	Line up the vegetables each in a row, side by side.
1/4	cucumber, peeled, seeded, and cut lengthwise	Get ready to roll! Starting from the edge of a long row, roll it up. Cut in half. If eating later, wrap in plastic wrap.
1/2	tomato, cut into wedges	To eat as a sandwich, peel back a few inches of plastic wrap, eat, peel some more, eat… you get the idea!
		To eat as an appetizer, let them "set" in the refrigerator for 2 or 3 hours. Then remove the plastic wrap. Cut the rolls into 1" slices, using a sawing motion.
10	red-tipped lettuce leaves or purple kale (opt)	Serve cut side up on a platter garnished with red-tipped lettuce or purple kale. P.S. Make more!

*Find lavash (sometimes spelled lawash) in the deli or bakery sections of your grocery store. It's a large flat bread like a tortilla.

Nutrition information for a half roll-up
Exchanges/Choices: 1 Starch, 1 Vegetable, 1/2 Fat

Calories	122	Fat	2.7 g	Fiber	3 g	Sodium	405 mg	Total Carbohydrate	20 g
Calories from Fat	19%	Saturated Fat	0 g	Cholesterol	0 mg	Protein	5.5 g	Sugars	5 g

Lickety-Split Diabetic Meals

Lickety-Split Tip

What IS tofu?

Tofu is made from soy milk by adding a coagulant and pressing the curds into blocks like cheese. It's high in protein and happens to be the staple meat alternative in Asian countries.

Why should we eat tofu?

Soybeans contain a powerhouse of antioxidants and other disease-fighting agents. Thirty-four studies have shown that soy protein lowers cholesterol by 15% or more. In study after study, consumption of soy foods is associated with lower risk of heart disease, breast and prostate cancers, and osteoporosis.

Eating soy is like taking a sip from the fountain of youth!

More ways to incorporate beneficial soy:

Soy milk on your cereal. (I personally like the EdenSoy Extra, both vanilla and original.) Try cooking your oatmeal in it. Makes great-tasting pudding, too!

Black soy beans (you can buy these canned and ready to eat from Eden). Add to chili or any dish that would use beans. They are very much like black beans, but black soy beans are incredibly high in healthful soy compounds.

Tofu (see more recipes listed in the Index).

Commercial soy burgers (a majority of these products have had most of the beneficial soy compounds removed; however, they are still healthier than eating meat).

Eggless Salad Stuffer

You can make this great summertime salad with chicken and tofu, or only tofu. Never tried tofu?
Combined with the chicken, it's a tasty way to become a tofu believer!

12 oz	firm tofu	Drain water from tofu. Crumble the tofu with a fork in a medium bowl.
	or	If using chicken, add to bowl and flake apart.
6 oz	firm tofu	
	and	
1 can	(10 oz) chicken breast meat, rinsed and drained	

2	celery stalks	Chop vegetables. Add to bowl and mix.
1/2 small	onion	
1/2	red pepper	

2 T	Dijon mustard	Add to the bowl and mix well.
1/4 cup	Miracle Whip Light	Serve in a pita pocket or on whole-wheat bread with lettuce and tomatoes. This is also delicious as a dip for crackers or celery sticks.

Nutrition information for approximately 1/2 cup salad (no chicken, without bread)

Exchanges/Choices: 1/2 Carbohydrate, 1 Medium-Fat Meat

Calories	95	Fat	5 g	Fiber	1 g	Sodium	213 mg	Total Carbohydrate	5 g
Calories from Fat	47%	Saturated Fat	<1 g	Cholesterol	2 mg	Protein	6 g	Sugars	2 g

Lickety-Split Diabetic Meals

Lickety-Split Tip

What do you think is the secret to your youthfulness?

"Since I feel my best on the days I get out and about, I sure think that's important. Each day I always eat 3–4 pieces of fruit and always have. I drink a lot of water, 2 glasses of 1/2% milk, and hot water instead of coffee."

—*Charlotte Brownell, at age 82, still volunteering at the thrift store, 15 years and counting.*

15-Minute Meals

It's 5:45 p.m. and the family is starved. Is it humanly possible to get a hot and satisfying dinner on the table in 15 minutes?

Welcome to 15-Minute Meals! You'll discover how to make Crispy Chicken Dijon or Creamy Chicken Dijon over Noodles all within 15 minutes! Or how about stuffed baked potatoes, sloppy joes, or nachos? They're all here, and you'll learn how to get the complete meal on the table in 15 minutes or less. Guaranteed!

Remember: If it takes a bit longer than 15 minutes, refer back to the Introduction about how to "speedisize" your kitchen. To really achieve this kind of efficiency, it's imperative to have every drawer, cupboard, and utensil in full cooperation.

Lickety-Split Diabetic Meals

Lickety-Split Tip

What is the glycemic index?

The glycemic index is a measure of a food's effect on a person's blood sugar level. The quicker the rise in blood sugar, the higher the glycemic index. In general, "simple"carbohydrates—those with more processing—have a higher glycemic index than "complex" carbohydrates—those with minimal processing. Complex carbohydrates are rich in dietary fiber, which slows down a rise in blood sugar.

Are low glycemic foods the only foods people with diabetes should eat?

Because many factors are typically involved in a rise in blood sugar, glycemic index is more of a prediction. Factors typically include a person's age, physical activity level, and rate of digestion, as well as how a food is cooked and what else is eaten with the food. Foods that contain carbohydrates affect blood sugar the most, but by eating a mixture of fuels at a meal or snack—including carbohydrate, protein, and fat—blood sugar rises more slowly.

Glycemic index is calculated based on blood sugar release after consuming a serving of food that contains 50 grams of carbohydrate. Often, we do not eat a single food alone, and very often, we do not eat a portion that contains 50 grams of carbohydrate. In an effort to make the glycemic index more useful, experts are trying to convert the information to something more helpful like the "glycemic load," which takes into account portions commonly consumed.

The bottom line: Knowing the glycemic index (or load) of a food is another piece of the question, "Which foods are the most beneficial to my health and blood sugar?" On the other hand, this is a complicated and long list of numbers to try and memorize, and the numbers all change when portions are altered and foods are mixed together. It is good advice to eat nutrient-dense, lower glycemic index foods like vegetables, whole grains, beans (as this cookbook advises), and fruits for dessert rather than simple carbs like sugar, syrups, white flour, and milled grains. So, choose brown rice over white, a piece of fruit over fruit juice, and old-fashioned oats over quick-cooking oatmeal....you get the idea! **AND**, add servings of protein, such as fish, tofu, lean meat or poultry, or low-fat dairy products and some fat like olive oil to get a mixture of fuels at your meals.

Veggie & Cheese Stuffed Baked Potato

Here's what we serve most often in our house. It's a real "no-brainer."

1 small	(4 oz) baking potato	Scrub thoroughly and pierce 3 or 4 times with a fork. Wrap with damp paper towel. Place in microwave on HIGH 4 to 5 minutes. Make sure it's done by piercing with a fork. Cook more if necessary. Set aside.
1 cup	frozen California blend (broccoli, cauliflower, and carrots)	Place vegetables in a microwave-safe dish. Cover and cook 6 to 8 minutes on HIGH. Split potato open and top with vegetables (overflowing the spud!)
1/4 cup	reduced-fat shredded cheddar cheese†	Sprinkle on top and microwave the entire potato on HIGH 1 more minute until cheese melts.
4 grinds 2 dashes	fresh ground pepper dill weed	Top potato with pepper and dill, and a dollop of nonfat plain yogurt or fat-free sour cream. Serve with a side of nonfat cottage cheese and canned light peaches.

†See reduced-fat cheese tip on page viii (Introduction).

Nutrition information for entire recipe

Exchanges/Choices: 1 Starch, 1 Vegetable, 1 Medium-Fat Meat

Calories	180	Fat	3 g	Fiber	5 g	Sodium	388 mg	Total Carbohydrate	23 g
Calories from Fat	15%	Saturated Fat	2 g	Cholesterol	12 mg	Protein	13 g	Sugars	4 g

Lickety-Split Diabetic Meals

Lickety-Split Tip

I heard people with diabetes should never eat potatoes because they turn to pure sugar in the bloodstream. Is this really true? (I think I'll die if I can never eat a potato again!)

The humble spud does have a higher glycemic index, similar to white bread and sugar. But, does that mean you can never eat a potato again? Absolutely not! You must have some carbohydrates at each meal—eat a small or medium potato—(and limit bread, corn, and dessert consumed at the same meal), and enjoy it with a "mixture of fuels," for instance a little butter, low-fat cheese, or cottage cheese, or meat, chicken, or fish along with a generous portion of low-carbohydrate vegetables. Also know that a white potato has more potassium than a banana and offers dietary fiber too. Aren't you relieved?

Chicken Dijon Stuffed Baked Potatoes

Hands-on – 15 min.

Serves 3

Here's another great way to make a quick meal out of a baked potato.
The sour cream replaces the mayonnaise for a perfect complement atop a potato.

Menu

Chicken Dijon Stuffed Baked Potatoes

Unsweetened Applesauce

3 small	(4 oz each) baking potatoes	Scrub thoroughly and pierce each potato 3 or 4 times with a fork. Wrap with damp paper towel. Microwave on HIGH 8 minutes. Test doneness by piercing with a fork. Cook longer if necessary. Meanwhile, place a steamer with water over high heat.
1 bunch	asparagus (about 18 spears) or broccoli	Rinse vegetables. Snap off asparagus bottoms. Seed and slice pepper into long strips. Place all in the steamer, which should be boiling by now. Steam 8 to 10 minutes, until crisp tender.
1	red bell pepper	
1 can	(10 oz) cooked white chicken, rinsed and drained	Place in a medium microwave-safe bowl. Flake meat with a fork.
1/4 cup	fat-free sour cream or nonfat plain yogurt	Add to chicken. Mix well. When potatoes are done, microwave the chicken mixture 1½ to 2 minutes on HIGH. To serve, cut potatoes in half, spoon the chicken salad evenly over each potato half, and top evenly with steamed vegetables. Serve with applesauce.
1 T	Dijon mustard	
1	green onion, chopped, or 1 tsp dried onion flakes	

Nutrition information for 1 stuffed baked potato (2 halves)

Exchanges/Choices: 1 1/2 Starch, 1 Vegetable, 2 Lean Meat

Calories	220	Fat	2 g	Fiber	7 g	Sodium	280 mg
Calories from Fat	8%	Saturated Fat	<1 g	Cholesterol	28 mg	Protein	20 g

Total Carbohydrate 32 g
Sugars 9 g

Lickety-Split Diabetic Meals

Lickety-Split Tip

True or False?

Nachos are a fattening appetizer, and could never pass as a "healthy dinner."

TRUE for most restaurant nachos.
FALSE for your own homemade!

Sitting down to a mounded plate of nachos covered with beans, cheese, and sour cream sounds like a major binge, right? Not at all, thanks to all the new low-fat foods available and proper portion control. Baked tortilla chips can count as a healthful serving of grain. Add vegetables, beans, reduced-fat cheese, salsa, and nonfat sour cream or nonfat plain yogurt (all on a small plate), and you have a most delicious, satisfying, and completely guilt-free meal!

Compare this to a restaurant serving of Nachos Supreme, at 800 calories and 55 grams of fat!

Note: To achieve the recommended vegetable quota at dinner,
munch on raw vegetables while you're making this recipe.

Guiltless Nachos Supreme

Hands-on – 15 min.   **Serves 4**

Here's my favorite Friday night "veg-out" dinner. We munch on raw carrots, broccoli, and cauliflower as we put it together.

Menu

Guiltless Nachos Supreme

Raw Veggies

Grapes

Turn broiler on and keep oven door ajar.
Adjust oven rack to 6" from heating element.

1/2 lb	extra-lean ground turkey breast	Coat a large nonstick skillet with cooking spray and place over medium-high heat. Sauté until meat is no longer pink and vegetables are soft.
1 small	onion, chopped (opt)	
1	green bell pepper, seeded and chopped (opt)	
1 tsp	Zippy Zonya Mexi Mix‡	

Kids' Favorite!

1 can	(15 oz) no-salt-added pinto or black beans, drained and rinsed	Add and sauté 1 minute.
60	bite-sized baked tortilla chips (about 8 oz)	Spread out over an ungreased nonstick baking sheet. Layer bean mixture over chips.
1 cup	reduced-fat shredded cheddar cheese†	Sprinkle on top of bean mixture. Broil 4 to 6 minutes, or until cheese melts and browns slightly.
1/4 cup	salsa of your choice	Serve on the side for dipping. Fresh grapes make the ideal dessert.
1/4 cup	fat-free sour cream or nonfat plain yogurt	

†See reduced-fat cheese tip on page viii (Introduction).

‡See recipe on page 40.

Nutrition information for 1/4 the recipe

Exchanges/Choices: 3 Starch, 3 Lean Meat

Calories	363	Fat	6 g	Fiber	7 g	Sodium	587 mg	Total Carbohydrate	46 g
Calories from Fat	15%	Saturated Fat	2 g	Cholesterol	35 mg	Protein	30 g	Sugars	1 g

Lickety-Split Diabetic Meals

Lickety-Split Tip

Tips to help "obesity-proof" your kids....

"The Clean-Plate Syndrome"

Try to refrain from asking your children to clean their plates. Insisting they finish their food when their stomachs are full, is teaching them to ignore their innate "obesity fighting" signal. Instead, say to them, "When your stomach tells you you've had enough, you can be excused." Then cover unused portions and refrigerate for the next meal or snack time.

"The Big Eater"

Do you remember being praised for eating more food than anyone else?

When your child does eat a big meal, avoid the temptation to say, "good boy" or "good girl." Instead, keep your comments low-key and focused on their "gut" feelings, like, "Wow, you were hungry tonight, weren't you?" Responses like these go a long way in preventing the overeating habit.

Crafty ways to sneak positive foods into your child

Make vegetables FUN by allowing your kids to eat broccoli like dinosaurs! Stick the broccoli spears in their pile of mashed potatoes and then have them growl "GRRRRRR," as they grab the stalks with their mouths, eating like dinosaurs. Once they actually begin eating the veggies, you can put a fork in their hands and have them advance to eating like humans again!

Turkey Joes

Hands-on – 15 min.   **Serves 6**

These Joes are fast and healthy. You can make your own Sloppy Joe sauce to save on the sodium, but when you need it fast, the can will do.

Kids' Favorite!

Menu

Turkey Joes

Sunshine Carrot-Raisin Salad (page 259)

Unsweetened Applesauce

20 oz	extra-lean ground turkey breast	Brown in a large nonstick skillet over medium-high heat.
1 med	onion, chopped	
1 can	(16 oz) Sloppy Joe sauce	Add to the skillet. Cover and simmer 3 more minutes.
6	whole-wheat hamburger buns	Ladle 1/6 of batch on top of each hamburger bun.

Serve with Sunshine Carrot-Raisin Salad and applesauce on the side.

Nutrition information for 1 Turkey Joe with bun

Exchanges/Choices: 2 Starch, 3 Lean Meat

Calories	270	Fat	3 g	Fiber	3 g	Sodium	670 mg	Total Carbohydrate	31 g
Calories from Fat	10%	Saturated Fat	<1 g	Cholesterol	38 mg	Protein	27 g	Sugars	10 g

Lickety-Split Diabetic Meals

Lickety-Split Tip

Buying chicken:
Save yourself time, money, and headaches

I've found buying bags of individually frozen, skinless, boneless chicken breasts saves a lot of time, money, and effort. This product is so convenient because you can reach into the resealable bag and grab however many you need. The chicken breasts are a uniform size and thickness. No need to plan ahead; they defrost in minutes in your microwave. For recipes that use liquid, add them to the pan while still frozen. They will thaw and cook in no time. How terrific!

Look for this type of chicken in the freezer section of your grocery store.

Sodium Alert

Check the label and avoid brands containing over 200 mg of sodium per serving. (Sometimes they go overboard injecting with a salt-water solution to promote juiciness.)

Crispy Chicken Dijon

Hands-on – 15 min.   **Serves 4**

Add this to your "must try" list. It's absolutely terrific!
My thanks to Diana Dyer, MS, RD, for her discovery of the tasty tofu option*.

Menu

Crispy Chicken Dijon
Baked Sweet Potatoes
Green Beans & Carrots

2	(8 oz each) sweet potatoes or 4 baking potatoes (4 oz each)	Scrub thoroughly and pierce 3 or 4 times with a fork. Wrap in a damp paper towel. Place in microwave 12 minutes on HIGH. Test doneness by piercing with a fork. Cook longer if necessary.
1 pkg	(10 oz) frozen green beans, broccoli, or pea pods	Place steamer basket in a pan and add 1" water. Place over medium-high heat. Add vegetables and cover. When you notice it's boiling, set timer for 8 minutes.
1 pkg	(10 oz) frozen sliced carrots	
1/2 cup	dry bread crumbs, unseasoned	Take out 2 cereal bowls and place bread crumbs in one, mustard in the other.
1/4 cup	Dijon mustard	
1 T	olive oil	Heat over medium heat in a medium nonstick skillet.
4	(4 oz each) boneless, skinless chicken breast*	Dip chicken in mustard, then roll in the crumbs. Brown each side in the skillet 4 to 5 minutes, until cooked all the way through.

*Crispy Tofu Dijon:

Substitute 16 oz. of extra-firm tofu for the chicken, cut into 8½" slices. (Serve 2 slices per person.)

If vegetable timer goes off before you're ready, remove from heat and partially remove lid (to allow steam to escape but to keep vegetables warm).

Serve with vegetables and half a sweet potato (or whole 4-oz white potato).

Nutrition information for 1 chicken breast, 1/2 sweet potato, 1 cup vegetables

Exchanges/Choices: 2 Starch, 1 Vegetable, 4 Lean Meat

Calories	360	Fat	5.5 g	Fiber	7 g	Sodium	580 mg	Total Carbohydrate	38 g
Calories from Fat	15%	Saturated Fat	1 g	Cholesterol	66 mg	Protein	32 g	Sugars	9 g

Lickety-Split Diabetic Meals

Crispy Chicken Dijon

Lickety-Split Tip

Simple Cutting Tip

Cutting chicken into strips is easy when the chicken is still mostly frozen. Set individually frozen chicken breasts on your cutting board to thaw for about 5 minutes. Then cut quickly and easily with a chef's knife (the kind with a big wide blade). Be careful, they can be a little slippery!

Creamy Chicken Dijon over Noodles

Hands-on — 15 min.
Serves 4 or 6

Unexpected guests? Proudly serve this delicious 15-minute "company food" meal. Guests will rave and family will feel like guests!

Delegate someone to: Prep asparagus, tomatoes, cucumbers, and fruit.

Menu
Creamy Chicken Dijon
Egg Noodles
Asparagus
Sliced Tomatoes & Cucumbers
Fresh Fruit Cup

Place a large kettle of water on to boil.

For 4	For 6		
1 T	1½ T	olive oil	Sauté 7 or 8 minutes over medium-high heat until chicken is no longer pink.
1 tsp	1½ tsp	minced garlic (2 or 3 cloves)	
1 lb	1½ lb	skinless, boneless chicken breast strips	
4 oz	6 oz	dry egg noodles, preferably whole wheat	Meanwhile, add to boiling water. Set timer for 6 minutes.
1 small	1 lg	bunch fresh asparagus	Meanwhile, wash asparagus. Snap off bottoms, cut diagonally into 1½" slices, and set aside.
1 can	2 cans	(7 oz each) mushrooms, drained	Add to chicken and cook 1 minute.
1/4 cup	1/3 cup	Dijon mustard	Meanwhile, mix together in a 2-cup measuring cup. Add to bubbling chicken and mushrooms and heat only until hot throughout.
1/2 cup	3/4 cup	fat-free sour cream or nonfat plain yogurt	When timer goes off, toss asparagus in with the bubbling noodles.

Set timer for 2 minutes. At the sound of the timer, quickly drain.

Serve the chicken over the noodles with asparagus. Place sliced tomatoes and cucumbers and a fresh fruit cup on the side.

Nutrition information for 3 oz chicken breast, 1 cup noodles & asparagus, 1/4 cup sauce

Exchanges/Choices: 2 Starch, 1 Vegetable, 4 Lean Meat

| Calories | 325 | Fat | 6 g | Fiber | 1.6 g | Sodium | 573 mg | Total Carbohydrate | 28 g |
| Calories from Fat | 16% | Saturated Fat | 1 g | Cholesterol | 92 mg | Protein | 33 g | Sugars | 4 g |

Lickety-Split Diabetic Meals

Lickety-Split Tip

Pop Quiz!

Which of the following best describes your consumption of cooked dried beans?

A. Each week: A cup of bean soup, garbanzo beans on a salad, a bean burrito, and a serving of mixed vegetables (including lima beans).

B. Two bean entrees per week including another serving from the leftovers for lunch on the following day (4 servings per week).

C. Refried beans in Mexican food, once a week.

D. Chili twice a year, baked beans twice a year.

E. Beans? Are you crazy? I tasted them when I was 7 years old and hated them!

Correct answer: A and B

Dried beans are among the best foods on the planet! They are jam-packed with disease-fighting phytochemicals, vitamins, minerals, and cholesterol-lowering fiber. They are rich in protein and are, therefore, a wonderful meat alternative. When beans replace meat at a meal, the benefit is magnified even more.

Q: For a person with diabetes, aren't beans high in carbs?

A: They do contain carbs, but one of the "best" carbs you'll have all day. Thanks to their high soluble fiber content, beans tout a low glycemic index or low glycemic load, meaning they turn into blood sugar at a slower rate than other carbohydrates. Just remember that every half cup of beans trades out for a bread/starch serving. (Think of beans as your "new and improved croutons."

Do yourself a favor: Think "cholesterol sponges and blood sugar buffers," I mean beans, **FOUR** times a week!

White Beans with Tomato, Basil & Parmesan

Serve this hot or cold, as a main or side dish. Great with Cornbread or whole-grain bread and raw veggies.

Menu

White Beans with Tomato, Basil & Parmesan

Cornbread (page 283) or 9-grain bread

Raw Vegetables & Dip

Lemon Sorbet

Note: If you're planning to have Cornbread (page 283), mix that up first. Start this recipe once you have the cornbread in the oven.

1 T	olive oil	In a 12" nonstick skillet, sauté over medium heat for 3 minutes.
1 tsp	minced garlic (2 cloves)	
2 cans	(15 oz each) navy, Great Northern, or white kidney beans, rinsed and drained	Stir in and cook about 7 minutes longer.
1 lg	ripe tomato, chopped (or 1 cup canned diced tomatoes, drained)	Meanwhile, slice bread and prep raw veggies.
1/4 cup	minced fresh parsley (opt)	
1 tsp	dried basil	
1/2 cup	grated Parmesan cheese	Mix in just before serving.
1 T	lemon juice	Serve with Cornbread or 9-grain bread and raw vegetables and dip. Try lemon sorbet for dessert.

*Serves 4 as the main course or 8 as a side dish.

Nutrition information for 1 cup (main course serving)

Exchanges/Choices: 2 Starch, 1 Lean Meat, 1 Fat

Calories	250	Fat	7 g	Fiber	11 g	Sodium	501 mg	Total Carbohydrate	32 g
Calories from Fat	25%	Saturated Fat	2 g	Cholesterol	9 mg	Protein	14 g	Sugars	0 g

Lickety-Split Diabetic Meals

Lickety-Split Tip

Monitoring your blood sugar control

Hopefully you know the value of monitoring your blood sugar each day at home. While you may be tempted to skip it, **DON'T**! Whether your diabetes educator has you monitoring just in the morning or several times during the day, this handy invention tells you immediately how you are doing and if you've overdone it at a previous meal. Bringing these records to your diabetes appointments also lets them know how they can adjust diet and medications to keep you healthy and in tight control.

But what about that blood test your doctor can do that tells you how your blood sugar has averaged over the past 3 months? This test is often referred to as an A1C (officially known as glycated hemoglobin or HbA1C). This simple blood test is a great way to know how well your diabetes treatment plan has been working over time.

So, in addition to knowing your day-to-day numbers, be sure to learn about the A1C as well. It's another great tool to help you!

Cheesy Potato Skillet with Mixed Vegetables

Talk about a "no-brainer," this is fast and satisfying after a super hectic day.

Menu

Cheesy Potato Skillet with Mixed Vegetables

Nonfat Cottage Cheese

Sliced Apples, Oranges, or Kiwis

1 T	oil (olive or canola)	Place in a large nonstick skillet over medium-high heat 4 minutes. Stir frequently.
1 bag	(16 oz) frozen mixed vegetables (peas, corn, carrots, green beans, lima beans)	

4 cups	frozen Ore Ida Potatoes O'Brien (hash browns with onions and peppers)	Add and cook 6 minutes longer, stirring frequently. (Look for fruit to serve like oranges, apples, and kiwi.)

1/2 cup	reduced-fat shredded mozzarella cheese†	Sprinkle over vegetables, turn off heat, cover, and let stand 1 minute.
10 grinds	fresh ground pepper	Serve with orange sections, apple wedges, or kiwi slices and nonfat cottage cheese, if desired.
2 T	grated Parmesan cheese	

†See reduced-fat cheese tip on page viii (Introduction).

Nutrition information for 1½ cups

Exchanges/Choices: 2 Starch, 1 Vegetable, 1 Lean Meat

Calories	234	Fat	6 g	Fiber	5 g	Sodium	274 mg	Total Carbohydrate	36 g
Calories from Fat	23%	Saturated Fat	1 g	Cholesterol	6 mg	Protein	11 g	Sugars	5 g

Lickety-Split Diabetic Meals

Lickety-Split Tip

Beans, Beans, the Magical Fruit...

I suppose it's time to talk about GAS. If you find yourself avoiding beans because of this problem, try these tips:

1. Many people's digestive tracts gradually adjust in their ability to produce the necessary enzymes to digest beans. Therefore, add beans to your diet in small servings several times per week. Not eating beans on a consistent basis and then digging into a big batch of chili and beans is what shocks your system, causing excessive gas.

2. Start with easier-to-digest beans like lentils and split peas.

3. Consider a supplement like Beano. It provides the enzyme that your body is not sufficiently producing. Available at your pharmacy.

4. If all else fails, take frequent walks.

Whatever it takes, get your body used to eating a small portion of beans, **FOUR** times per week!

Caribbean Black Beans with Squash

I'm always on the lookout for recipes using the nutrition dynamo winter squash.
This recipe features a special variety of seasoned black beans from Eden and is worth the effort
to find them by visiting www.edenfoods.com.

Menu
Caribbean Black Beans
with Squash
Brown Rice
Tossed Salad

| 3/4 cup | Uncle Ben's whole-grain instant brown rice, dry | Place rice and water in a 2-quart microwave-safe dish. Cover and cook 12 minutes on HIGH. |
| 1 1/3 cups | water | |

2 cans	(15 oz) Eden Organic Caribbean Black Beans	Meanwhile, mix together in a large saucepan and place over medium-high heat. Do not drain or rinse beans.
1/2 cup	water	
1/2 tsp	salt or 1 tsp lite salt	

| 1 small | butternut squash | Meanwhile, peel, seed, and cut into chunks. Place in a food processor and pulse a few times to create pieces slightly larger than the beans. |
| | | Add squash to beans and simmer 8 minutes or until squash is tender. |

| 3 T | white wine | Stir into bean mixture and serve over rice. Serve fruit on the side. |
| 1/2 cup | sliced green onions (tops & bottoms) | |

Delegate someone to: Make a tossed salad and set table.

Nutrition information for 1 cup of beans and squash and 1/2 cup rice

Exchanges/Choices: 3 1/2 Starch

| Calories | 258 | Fat | 1 g | Fiber | 12 g | Sodium | 348 mg | Total Carbohydrate | 58 g |
| Calories from Fat | 3% | Saturated Fat | 0 g | Cholesterol | 0 mg | Protein | 11 g | Sugars | 5 g |

Lickety-Split Diabetic Meals

Lickety-Split Tip

What does tofu taste like?

No one can say tofu tastes bad. It simply has no taste at all! The good news is that tofu takes on the flavors of whatever spices or flavorings you use with it. In fact, a good rule of thumb is to increase spices and seasonings by one-half whenever using tofu.

See page 80 for information about what tofu is and its benefits.

Super Time-Saving Tip:

Skip microwaving the potatoes and chopping the pepper and onion by using 2 cups of Ore Ida Potatoes O'Brien. It has no fat, just chopped potatoes, onions, and peppers, and saves you loads of time!

Cheesy Scrambled Tofu

Hands-on – 15 min.   **Serves 4**

This is the very first recipe I learned to make using tofu. Makes a great dinner or breakfast.
You can save a lot of fat grams by using your favorite fat-free cheese.

Menu

Cheesy Scrambled Tofu

Whole-Wheat Toast or English Muffins

Grapes and Strawberries

2 small	(4 oz each) potatoes*	Scrub potatoes clean. Pierce each 3 or 4 times with a fork. Wrap in damp paper towels. Microwave on HIGH 6 to 8 minutes.
1/2	green bell pepper, seeded*	Meanwhile, chop vegetables. Coat a large nonstick skillet with cooking spray. Begin to sauté.
1/2	onion*	
Optional extras:		Add any optional extras.
1 cup	frozen corn	
1	chopped tomato	
1 cup	sliced mushrooms	
1 cup	fresh or frozen snow peas	
12 oz	firm tofu, crumbled	Add to the sauté. It is important for the tofu to absorb the flavors from the vegetables and spice. When potatoes are done, peel, chop, and add to sauté and cook 5 minutes.
1 tsp	ground cumin, dill weed, or dried oregano (pick your favorite)	
4 slices	whole-wheat bread, or 2 English muffins	Make toast.
1/4 cup	reduced-fat shredded cheddar cheese†	Sprinkle both kinds of cheese on top. Cover and cook 2 minutes more.
1/4 cup	reduced-fat shredded mozzarella cheese†	Meanwhile, set table and set out fresh fruit and toast.

*See my Super Time-Saving Tip above. †See reduced-fat cheese tip on page viii (Introduction).

Nutrition information for 1½ cups, including optional extras and 1 slice bread
Exchanges/Choices: 2 1/2 Starch, 1 Vegetable, 1 Medium-Fat Meat, 1/2 Fat

Calories	320	Fat	9 g	Fiber	6 g	Sodium	444 mg	Total Carbohydrate	46 g
Calories from Fat	25%	Saturated Fat	2 g	Cholesterol	5 mg	Protein	19 g	Sugars	9 g

Lickety-Split Diabetic Meals

Cheesy Scrambled Tofu

"I'm so proud of you, Mommy, because you teach all the other mommies and kids about 'grow' food."

—My son, Ridge, at age 5, after sitting with me to review my TV show, "Zonya's Health Bites."

30-Minute Meals

While researching the needs of families, I heard several shared wishes:

• "Easy meals for more quality dinner time at home."

• "To eliminate unnecessary steps."

• "To create less mess."

• "To put the entire meal on the table in 30 minutes."

Welcome back to Kansas, Dorothy. There's no place like home. It's back to the family, gathered around the table for a home-cooked meal. All in only 30 minutes!

Lickety-Split Tip

Whole grains help fight type 2 diabetes

Did you know that study after study finds that people who get their carbs from whole grains have lower blood insulin levels and a lower risk for developing diabetes? In the Iowa Women's Health Study, researchers found that, as whole-grain intake went up, diabetes risks went down. Women who consumed the most whole grains had a 22% lower risk for diabetes compared with women eating refined products. And researchers at Tufts University found that people who eat three or more servings of whole grains a day, especially from high-fiber cereals, are less likely to develop insulin resistance and metabolic syndrome—common precursors of both type 2 diabetes and cardiovascular disease.

Why? Whole grains are a good source of both magnesium and chromium. Magnesium helps in the production, release, and activity of insulin, while chromium also helps insulin do its job. Combined with the fact that whole grains are rich in fiber, they fill us up without filling us out, so they help trim our waistlines. I like to say that whole-grain breads, pasta, and rice have "built-in-portion-control regulators." The fiber helps you feel full much sooner than you do eating the refined versions, and decreasing your portion size is the best blood sugar control of all!

Money-saving tip for brown rice

While instant whole-grain brown rice combines nutrition with convenience, it can also be a bit pricey. **Try this tip:** On any day that you are going to be around the house for an hour, cook 3 cups brown rice in 6 cups of water for 45 minutes to 1 hour. The rice will then keep in the refrigerator for 4 days or in the freezer for up to 3 months. Either way, reheating the rice in the microwave is as fast as using instant rice, without the cost!

Curried Chickpeas & Gingered Black Beans

Hands-on – 30 min.
Serves 4

Ready for a new twist for the old tastebuds? You know, I never thought I liked curry and avoided every recipe with it. What a mistake! The ginger and curry are awesome together and the presentation is beautiful. Try it!

Menu

Curried Chickpeas and Gingered Black Beans

Brown Rice

Broccoli & Carrots

Lemon Sorbet

1/2 cup	Uncle Ben's whole-grain instant brown rice, dry	Place in microwave-safe dish.
1 cup	water	
1 head	broccoli (cleaned and cut into florets)	Add to rice. Cover, place in microwave, and cook on HIGH until tender, about 10 minutes.
12	baby carrots	
1 small	onion	Cut onion into small wedges. Heat oil over medium-high heat in large nonstick skillet. Add onion and spices. Cook 2 minutes.
1 T	olive oil	
2 tsp	ginger (fresh grated is best)	
2 tsp	curry powder	
1 can	(14½ oz) diced tomatoes, no salt added	Add to skillet and simmer 5 minutes.
1 can	(15 oz) chickpeas, rinsed and drained	
1 can	(15 oz) black beans, rinsed and drained	
1/3 cup	chopped fresh parsley (opt)	
1 T	lemon juice (opt)	Stir in just before serving. Serve bean mixture over the rice and vegetables. Try a small scoop of lemon sorbet for dessert.

Nutrition information for approximately 1 cup bean mixture over 1/2 cup rice with 1 cup vegetables

Exchanges/Choices: 3 Starch, 2 Vegetable, 1 Lean Meat, 1 Fat

| Calories | 386 | Fat | 7 g | Fiber | 18 g | Sodium | 573 mg | Total Carbohydrate | 66 g |
| Calories from Fat | 15% | Saturated Fat | 0.5 g | Cholesterol | 0 mg | Protein | 18 g | Sugars | 8 g |

Lickety-Split Diabetic Meals

Curried Chickpeas & Gingered Black Beans

Lickety-Split Tip

Married with children?

Finding it hard to get a sitter for that once-a-week date your marriage desperately deserves? Follow the advice of my friends, Jay and Art Johnson. Pick one night a week for date night. Make the kids their favorite dinner while the two of you munch on raw veggies and dip. Get the kids to bed promptly at 8:00. Light candles. Make a simple, yet light and elegant dinner. Rent a movie. Presto! You have date night, without hiring a sitter!

Romantic dinner for two suggestions:

• Skillet Chicken & Vegetables in Wine (page 109)

• Crispy Chicken Dijon (page 93)

• Chicken or Salmon Marsala with Brown Rice and Peas (page 111)

• White Beans with Tomato, Basil & Parmesan (page 97)

• Our favorite, Guiltless Nachos Supreme (page 89)

Skillet Chicken & Vegetables in Wine

Serve this scrumptious meal with a tossed salad and whole-grain bread.

2 med	(12 oz each) sweet potatoes	Scrub thoroughly and pierce each 3 or 4 times with a fork. Wrap with a damp paper towel. Microwave on HIGH 8 minutes. Test doneness by piercing with a fork. Cook longer if necessary.
1 T	olive oil (garlic flavored if you have it)	Heat oil in medium nonstick skillet over medium-high heat. Add chicken and cook until browned. Turn and brown other side.
4	(4 oz each) skinless, boneless chicken breasts	
1	onion	Meanwhile, seed and cut peppers into strips and cut onion into wedges. Add to chicken along with peas and sauté 2 minutes.
1	red or yellow bell pepper	
1½ cups	frozen peas	
1/3 cup	white wine	Add to skillet and cover. The wine will begin evaporating quickly. When "brown bits" begin collecting in the skillet, the dish is done.
1/2 tsp	dried thyme	
1/4 tsp	dried rosemary	Serve with potatoes, salad, and whole-grain bread.
1/2 tsp	poultry seasoning	
5 grinds	fresh ground pepper	If you still have room for dessert, consider a small scoop of vanilla frozen yogurt.
1/2 tsp	salt	

Nutrition information for 1 chicken breast, 1/2 sweet potato, 3/4 cup vegetables

Exchanges/Choices: 2 1/2 Starch, 1 Vegetable, 3 Lean Meat

Calories	370	Fat	5 g	Fiber	9 g	Sodium	450 mg	Total Carbohydrate	44 g
Calories from Fat	13%	Saturated Fat	1 g	Cholesterol	66 mg	Protein	32 g	Sugars	15 g

Lickety-Split Diabetic Meals

Lickety-Split Tip

Germ-Free Cooking

The Center for Science in the Public Interest recommends that we assume all raw meat, poultry, and fish are contaminated with bacteria, and therefore handle them properly. To prevent even a mild case of food poisoning "flu" in your home, do not allow any uncooked meat to come in contact with cutting boards, plates or utensils that will touch foods that will not be further cooked.

Follow these important safe-handling tips:

• Own 2 cutting boards. Reserve one for meats, the other for vegetables. This helps reduce the chances of cross contamination.

• Thoroughly wash your cutting boards and knives immediately after prepping your meat. (Delaying this chore is an invitation for cross contamination to occur.)

• Use a **CLEAN** plate for serving meat off the grill (not the plate you used to bring the meat to the grill). Use a clean utensil as well.

• Discard meat marinade after use. (However, if you boil it, you can serve it as a dipping sauce.)

Chicken or Salmon Marsala

Hands-on — 30 min.   **Serves 4**

This is worth the extra effort to buy Marsala wine. You'll think you're eating restaurant food!
You'll be glad to know this really only takes 20 minutes, and it's fabulous with the salmon!

Menu

Chicken or Salmon Marsala

Brown Rice

Peas

Where's the Lettuce? Salad
(page 255)

Sliced Pears & Kiwi

1/2 cup	Uncle Ben's whole-grain instant brown rice, dry	Combine in a medium microwave-safe dish. Cover and cook on HIGH 9 to 10 minutes.
1 cup	water	
2 cups	frozen peas	

2 T	olive oil	Meanwhile, prep the onion. Heat oil in a nonstick skillet over medium-high heat. Add onion, garlic, and mushrooms to the skillet and begin sautéing.
1	onion, cut into wedges	
1 tsp	chopped garlic (2 cloves)	
1 can	(8 oz) mushrooms, drained or 10 fresh baby portabella mushrooms, sliced	

| 4 | (4 oz each) skinless, boneless chicken breast or salmon fillets | Add to skillet. Brown on each side 5 minutes. (Less time for the fish.) |

| 1/2 cup | Marsala wine | Add to skillet. It will begin evaporating quickly. |

1½ cups	chicken broth, 1/3 less sodium	Mix together in a measuring cup. Add to skillet. Reduce heat to low. Simmer about 5 minutes until chicken is done.
1/4 tsp	salt (opt)	
2 T	cornstarch	Serve chicken and sauce over rice and peas with Where's the Lettuce? Salad and sliced fruit for dessert.
4 grinds	fresh ground pepper	

Nutrition information for 1 chicken breast, 1/2 cup rice, and 1/2 cup peas with sauce (without salt)

Exchanges/Choices: 2 1/2 Starch, 4 Lean Meat, 1/2 Fat

| Calories | 416 | Fat | 9 g | Fiber | 5.5 g | Sodium | 675 mg | Total Carbohydrate | 41 g |
| Calories from Fat | 19% | Saturated Fat | 1 g | Cholesterol | 66 mg | Protein | 34 g | Sugars | 11 g |

Lickety-Split Diabetic Meals

Lickety-Split Tip

How to combat the after-work snack attacks

A good way to prevent coming home ravenous and out of control is to take a banana (or similar snack) to work with you. Save it to eat later in the afternoon or on your drive home. Eating a snack at this time allows the nourishment to "hit your stomach," so you will feel energized, instead of famished, upon arriving home. Chasing it with a bottle of water is also very filling and supplies needed hydration, which many people are lacking at this time of day.

Hungarian Chicken Paprikash

This is a nutri-sized version of Katherine Buss's original Hungarian recipe, and you won't believe how delicious it is. Katherine's granddaughter Stacy Rafalko and I were able to cut 21 grams of fat per serving off the original recipe. Grandma, can you tell?

Menu
Hungarian Chicken Paprikash
Egg Noodles
Green Beans
Tossed Salad

3 med	onions, chopped	Sauté in oil in a large nonstick skillet over medium-high heat 8 to 10 minutes.
1½ T	olive or canola oil	

Place a large kettle of water on to boil.

6	(4 oz each) skinless, boneless chicken breast	Add to onions and mix to coat chicken. Cover and cook 15 minutes, turning chicken occasionally.
3 T	paprika	
10 grinds	fresh ground pepper	
2 T	low-sodium chicken bouillon granules	
1½ tsp	salt	
3/4 cup	water	

8 oz	whole-grain noodles or pasta, dry (any shape)	Meanwhile, add to boiling water. Set timer for 10 minutes.

2 pkg	(10 oz each) frozen whole green beans	Place in a microwave-safe dish, cover, and microwave on HIGH 8 minutes. Use this time to prepare a tossed salad and set the table.

1½ cups	fat-free sour cream	Remove chicken from heat and stir in sour cream.
		Drain noodles. Pour chicken mixture over noodles and toss. Serve with green beans and salad.

Nutrition information for 1 chicken breast, scant 1 cup noodles and 1/2 cup green beans

Exchanges/Choices: 2 1/2 Starch, 2 Vegetable, 4 Lean Meat

Calories	415	Fat	6 g	Fiber	8 g	Sodium	731 mg	Total Carbohydrate	53 g
Calories from Fat	13%	Saturated Fat	<1 g	Cholesterol	65 mg	Protein	37 g	Sugars	13 g

Lickety-Split Diabetic Meals

Lickety-Split Tip

Attention: Macaroni and Cheese Fans!

Rescue a high-fat, high-calorie, low-fiber meal with the following 3 simple changes:

1. Use skim milk.

2. Reduce the margarine to 1 T (eventually none!) and make up the reduced liquid in extra milk. (Numerous clients agree that even finicky children do not notice this change.)

3. Reduce the portion of macaroni and cheese and serve ample vegetables and sliced fruit with the meal. (This helps increase the fiber while reducing your sodium intake.) You may choose to add vegetables right to the macaroni and cheese to get twice the benefit from the cheesy sauce.

Easy Succotash Dinner

Hands-on – 25 min.

Serves 4

You may think I'm crazy to call this dish a meal, but think about it! It's protein, grain, and vegetables all in one dish. It's as fast as macaroni and cheese, and much more delicious and nutritious.

Menu

Easy Succotash Dinner

Tossed Salad or Carrot Sticks

Frozen Yogurt and Gingersnaps

1 cup	water
1 bag	(16 oz) frozen corn
1 bag	(16 oz) frozen lima beans

Place together in a medium saucepan. Bring to a boil over medium-high heat. Cover, reduce heat to medium-low, and simmer for 13 minutes. Be sure to set your timer, this is the exact time before all the water boils away.

Search your refrigerator for some lettuce, vegetables, or fruit to make a salad. Raw carrots will do if that's all you can find.

1 cup	reduced-fat shredded cheddar cheese†
10 grinds	fresh ground pepper

At the sound of the timer, remove from heat and stir in. The cheese will melt in seconds.

Serve with salad or carrot sticks, or fruit.

Since this is a low-calorie meal, feel free to enjoy a small scoop of low-fat ice cream or frozen yogurt with 3 gingersnap cookies.

†See reduced-fat cheese tip on page viii (Introduction).

Nutrition information for 1¼ cup serving
Exchanges/Choices: 3 Starch, 2 Lean Meat

Calories	318	Fat	5 g	Fiber	8 g	Sodium	331 mg	Total Carbohydrate	53 g
Calories from Fat	14%	Saturated Fat	2 g	Cholesterol	12 mg	Protein	20 g	Sugars	6 g

Lickety-Split Diabetic Meals

Lickety-Split Tip

Fish Facts

It all started with studies showing that fish-loving Eskimos hardly ever get heart disease. Now we know the oil in fish reduces heart attack risk by warding off blood clots, lowering blood pressure, and bringing down high triglycerides (blood fats). By bringing down inflammation in the body, this reduces many disease processes including the number one leading killer for diabetics—heart disease—as well as being helpful in fighting arthritis.

Broiled Orange Roughy

Hands-on – 25 min.   **Serves 4**

Let's face it, who wants to cook on Friday night? (And it's time you had a break from pizza!)
This meal comes together so fast—you won't even know you cooked!

x

Menu
Broiled Orange Roughy
Vegetable Medley
Baked Sweet Potatoes
5 Gingersnaps

Turn broiler on. Position oven rack 6" from heating element. Don't forget to leave oven door ajar.

2	(12 oz each) sweet potatoes or baking potatoes	Scrub thoroughly and pierce each potato 3 or 4 times with a fork. Wrap in a damp paper towel. Microwave on HIGH 8 minutes. Test doneness by piercing with a fork. Cook longer if necessary.
1/2 head 1/2 head 8	cauliflower broccoli baby carrots	Clean and cut into pieces or save time and use 4 cups of frozen. Place in a steamer on top of the stove to cook for 8 to 10 minutes.
4 1	(4 oz each) fresh or frozen fish fillets (thin fillets of orange roughy) lemon, quartered	Place fresh or frozen fillets on broiling pan. (No need to defrost.) Squeeze 1/4 of the lemon over each fillet.
dash dash	paprika dill weed or oregano	Sprinkle as much as you wish over each fillet. Broil until cooked through, 8 to 12 minutes. Cut sweet potatoes in half. Place potatoes and vegetables on table and serve fish.

Since this is a low-calorie meal, feel free to satisfy your sweet tooth with 5 gingersnap cookies.

Note: Fish will not need to be turned to cook all the way through if fillets are thin. Fish is done when it flakes easily with a fork.

Nutrition information for 1 fish fillet, 1/2 potato, 1 cup vegetables

Exchanges/Choices: 2 Starch, 2 Vegetable, 2 Lean Meat

Calories	282	Fat	1.5 g		10 g	Sodium	184 mg	Total Carbohydrate	45 g
Calories from Fat	4%	Saturated Fat	0 g		23 mg	Protein	25 g	Sugars	13 g

Lickety-Split Diabetic Meals

Lickety-Split Tip

Need to lower your cholesterol?

Cooking from this book means that you'll be eating meals that can help lower cholesterol, because the recipes are low in fat, high in fiber, and moderate in carbohydrates.

In addition to using these recipes to help lower your cholesterol, choose oily fish like salmon, trout, and sardines 2 times per week. These fish employ the help of omega 3 fatty-acids to help lower both cholesterol and triglycerides and improve the elasticity of arteries. Eating a 4-ounce serving twice a week also keeps you within the FDA recommended guidelines of eating 12 ounces of low-mercury fish 2 times a week, to limit exposure to any PCBs or mercury that may be found in fish. The four types of fish that have been found to carry the highest amounts of mercury and ones you should NOT eat are shark, swordfish, tilefish, and king mackerel.

A smart move:
Replace prime rib with salmon to boost your health. Also, for convenience at home, consider cracking open a can of salmon, just as you would tuna, for salmon salad sandwiches. Aim to eat fish 2 times per week!

Salmon Burgers

Hands-on – 25 min.

Serves 4

These are delicious! A simple and tasty way to eat salmon, which is so good for you!
Serve as burgers on hamburger buns with lettuce and tomato, or serve with a baked potato
and green vegetables for a salmon patty dinner.

Menu

Salmon Burgers on Whole-Grain Bun

Steamed Asparagus or Green Beans

Watermelon

1 can	(15 oz) red or pink salmon, packed in water, rinsed and drained (or 2 cups flaked)	In a medium bowl, remove skin from fish and flake with a fork, mashing bones (great calcium).

8	crackers (saltines type)	Crush the crackers and add to bowl. Add remaining ingredients. Mix well. Set aside.
1/4 cup	seeded and diced red bell pepper	
3 T	Miracle Whip Light	
1 tsp	lemon juice (bottled or fresh squeezed)	
4 drops	Tabasco sauce	

1 bunch	fresh asparagus or green beans	Snap off asparagus bottoms or ends of green beans and place in a microwave-safe dish. Cover and microwave on HIGH 7 minutes, until crisp tender.
		Shape the salmon mix into 4 patties. Coat a large nonstick skillet with cooking spray and place over medium heat. Cook salmon cakes, turning once, until lightly browned on each side. Assemble into burgers.

4	hamburger buns (preferably whole-grain)	Serve with asparagus and watermelon on the side.
4	lettuce leaves	
1	tomato, sliced	

4 cups	watermelon cubes

Nutrition information for 1 Salmon Burger on whole-grain bun, 6 asparagus spears, and 1 cup watermelon

Exchanges/Choices: 2 Starch, 1/2 Fruit, 1 Vegetable, 3 Lean Meat, 1 Fat

Calories	396	Fat	15 g	Fiber	5 g	Sodium	716 mg	Total Carbohydrate	42 g
Calories from Fat	32%	Saturated Fat	2.4 g	Cholesterol	42 mg	Protein	27 g	Sugars	17 g

Lickety-Split Diabetic Meals

Lickety-Split Tip

Pepper Power!

Among the vegetable superstars stand sweet peppers. Red, yellow, orange, and green; they pack a powerful punch of valuable nutrition. Even the natural "color" of the peppers is tremendously valuable to your body and its defenses against cancer and heart disease.

My advice to you: Buy, cook, and snack on them as often as possible!

Super time- and money-saving tip:

When you find peppers on sale (particularly the red, yellow, and orange ones, which can be quite pricey), buy as many as you can. Wash, seed, and chop them. Place them in resealable baggies and freeze. (Add chopped onions if you like.) Every 20 minutes over the next hour, reach in and shake the bags. This keeps them from freezing in one big chunk. Set the timer to remind yourself.

You will now have a fast and economical supply of chopped peppers ready in your freezer for directly adding to any stir-fry or vegetable sauté. They keep up to 3 months. However, use fresh peppers for raw dishes like salads.

Unstuffed Peppers

Hands-on – 30 min.

Serves 6

Who has time for fancy stuffed peppers? This recipe skips that step, yet delivers the characteristic flavor in a fast and simple stove-top dish.

Menu
Unstuffed Peppers
Tossed Salad
Sliced Fruit

1 lg	onion	Cut all the vegetables into small wedges.
1 each	green, red, and yellow bell pepper	
2 tsp	minced garlic (4 cloves)	
20	baby carrots	

1 T	olive oil (garlic or red pepper flavored is good)	Heat oil in a large nonstick kettle and sauté the vegetables and garlic.

20 oz	extra-lean ground turkey breast	Crumble the turkey and add to sauté.

2 tsp	Mrs. Dash or Spike seasoning	While waiting for the meat to brown, add seasonings to sauté. Open the cans. Once the meat is completely brown, add broth, tomatoes, and frozen spinach.
2 tsp	dried oregano	
1/4 tsp	salt (opt)	
2 cans	(14½ oz each) diced tomatoes, no salt added	
1 can	(14½ oz) chicken broth, 1/3 less sodium	
1 box	(10 oz) frozen chopped spinach	

Keeps warm in a crock pot for buffet-type entertaining.

2 cups	Uncle Ben's whole-grain instant brown rice, dry	Bring the mixture to a boil and add rice and cheese. Stir well. Cover and set timer for 5 minutes.
1/2 cup	grated Parmesan cheese	Meanwhile, search through the refrigerator for tossed salad "fixin's." Slice apples, kiwi, oranges, or any other fruit you have. When timer goes off, dinner is ready!

Nutrition information for 1½ cup serving (including optional salt)
Exchanges/Choices: 2 Starch, 4 Vegetable, 2 Lean Meat

Calories	360	Fat	5 g	Fiber	5 g	Sodium	430 mg	Total Carbohydrate	52 g
Calories from Fat	13%	Saturated Fat	1 g	Cholesterol	32 mg	Protein	26 g	Sugars	10 g

Lickety-Split Diabetic Meals

Unstuffed Peppers

Lickety-Split Tip

Cholesterol-lowering tip

By including soy products as much as possible, you could lower your cholesterol an additional 6 percent. Try out soy nuts, soy milk, and tofu (see Index for 10 of the best tofu recipes). Soy also contains powerful antioxidants that help slow the oxidation of cholesterol with your artery wall.

Tofu Fiesta

Hands-on — 30 min.

Serves 4

You can have this delicious, vegetarian meal on the table in no time at all!

Menu

Tofu Fiesta

Tossed Salad

Fruit Bowl

2 med	(6 oz each) baking potatoes	Scrub thoroughly and pierce each 3 or 4 times with a fork. Wrap in a damp paper towel. Microwave on HIGH 7 minutes. Test doneness by piercing with a fork. Cook longer if necessary.

1 med	onion	Coat a large nonstick skillet with cooking spray. Chop onion and seed and cut peppers into wedges or strips. Sauté all over medium-high heat 3 minutes.
1/2	green bell pepper	
1/2	red bell pepper	
1 tsp	minced garlic (2 cloves)	
1 cup	frozen corn	
1/2 cup	chopped fresh parsley or cilantro (reserve 1/4 cup for garnish)	

12 oz	firm tofu, crumbled	Add tofu and spices. Drain and rinse beans. Add to skillet. Sauté 5 minutes more.
1 can	(15 oz) pinto beans	
1 T	Zippy Zonya Mexi Mix‡	Meanwhile, peel and chop cooked potatoes into small pieces and add to sauté.

2 cups	salsa of your choice (fresh is best)	Add salsa. Cover and cook 3 minutes more.
1/4 cup	reserved chopped parsley or cilantro	To serve, sprinkle remaining parsley or cilantro on top. Accompany with a tossed salad and a bowl of fruit for dessert.

‡See recipe on page 40.

Nutrition information for approximately 1 cup

Exchanges/Choices: 2 1/2 Starch, 1 Vegetable, 1 Medium-Fat Meat

Calories	290	Fat	5 g	Fiber	9 g	Sodium	511 mg	Total Carbohydrate	48 g
Calories from Fat	16%	Saturated Fat	<1 g	Cholesterol	0 mg	Protein	17 g	Sugars	10 g

Lickety-Split Diabetic Meals

Lickety-Split Tip

Bring on the Beef!

You're standing in the beef aisle. Can you make a healthy choice? Absolutely! And here's a list of the leanest cuts of meat to make your selection. Each 3-ounce serving on this list has less than or the same amount of total fat and saturated fat as a 3-ounce serving of skinless, boneless chicken thigh. So go ahead! Be a smart beef shopper and enjoy!

Just remember to calculate 1/4 pound of raw meat per person, which cooks down to 3 ounces of cooked meat. If this seems small to you, try cutting into strips or chunks for stir-fries and stews to make the meat "seem" like more.

Eye Round Roast and Steak
Sirloin Tip Side Steak
Bottom Round Roast and Steak
Top Sirloin Steak
Brisket, Flat Half
95% Lean Ground Beef
Round Tip Roast and Steak
Round Steak
Shank Cross Cuts
Chuck Shoulder Pot Roast
Sirloin Tip Center Roast and Steak
Chuck Shoulder Steak
Shoulder Petite Tender and Medallions
Flank Steak
Shoulder Center (Ranch) Steak

Grilled Beef or Chicken Teriyaki

Hands-on – 10 min. (a.m.) 20 min. (p.m.)

Serves 4

When I was growing up, I remember mom let us pick what we wanted to have for our birthday dinner. I always chose Beef Teriyaki. It's now my husband's favorite recipe for venison. This marinade is so versatile you can use it for any of your favorite meats, fish, or even for tofu!

Menu

Grilled Teriyaki

Brown Rice

Broccoli & Carrots

Sliced Nectarines or Simple Summer Fresh Fruit Pie (page 287)

1/4 cup	soy sauce, reduced-sodium
1 T	firmly packed brown sugar
2 T	water
2 tsp	sesame oil
1/2 tsp	ginger (fresh grated is best)
5 grinds	fresh black pepper
1/4 tsp	minced garlic (1 clove)

Night before or early morning:

Mix together in a bowl big enough to hold the meat you will be marinating.

1 lb	lean trimmed top round, sirloin, flank steak, chicken breasts, venison, fish, or 24-oz tofu, cut into chunks or strips

Add and toss to coat. Allow to marinate, covered in refrigerator 8 hours or overnight. (Exception: for fish, do not exceed 2 hours in marinade.) Toss several times during marination.

Consider making Simple Summer Fresh Fruit Pie.

Preheat gas grill or broiler.
Position oven or grill rack 6" from heat source.

1 cup	Uncle Ben's whole-grain instant brown rice
1¾ cups	water
1 head	broccoli, cut into florets
12	baby carrots

30 minutes before dinner:

Place in microwave-safe dish. Cover and place in microwave.
Cook on HIGH 10 minutes, until tender.

Remove meat from marinade and grill or broil. Check meat frequently for doneness. Discard marinade. Serve with rice and vegetables, and fruit or fruit pie for dessert.

Nutrition information for 3 oz top round beef, 1 cup rice, 1 cup vegetables

Exchanges/Choices: 3 Starch, 2 Vegetable, 4 Lean Meat

Calories	472	Fat	9 g	Fiber	8 g	Sodium	712 mg	Total Carbohydrate	58 g
Calories from Fat	17%	Saturated Fat	2 g	Cholesterol	76 mg	Protein	42 g	Sugars	9 g

Lickety-Split Diabetic Meals

Lickety-Split Tip

"The most important aspect about exercise for me is that it builds a confidence level that carries me through all aspects of my life. I feel exercise is a celebration of life and a blessing on the whole day."

—Kay V. E., Retired second-grade teacher and consistent exerciser for over 24 years. Once 168 pounds, now 125.

Oven • Exercise • Eat

The Road to Dinner

You've just gotten home with an hour to go before dinner. Your early morning meeting kept you from exercising this morning. How are you going to fit in your workout before you're too pooped? Your personal experience tells you that inertia is five times stronger in the hours after dinner. If only you could fit exercise in BEFORE dinner.

Well, now you can, with Oven • Exercise • EAT! This is a collection of complete meal recipes that are quick to go in the oven, so you can exercise during the baking time and dinner will be ready when you are done. Just flip through and see what looks good tonight. Note the length of prep-time and oven/exercise-time that work best for you. And assuming you've shopped using the Lickety-Split grocery list, you will have all the ingredients you need!

Lickety-Split Diabetic Meals

Lickety-Split Tip

Keeping the "Exercise" in Oven • Exercise • Eat

If you're like most of us, you'll probably be tempted to use your bake time to do other seemingly important things, like laundry or housekeeping. But unless you've already exercised today, **DON'T GIVE IN!** A clean house has nothing over a clear mind and healthy body!

Have a great workout and enjoy a healthy and delicious meal, hot out of the oven, when you're done!

Oven-Baked Lentils & Rice

Hands-on – 10 min. Oven/Exercise – 90 min. **Serves 6**

Yes, this recipe makes a huge batch. You're going to enjoy it so much that you'll be glad you made the extra for lunch "planned overs." It keeps in the refrigerator for 5 days and freezes well, too. Serve with steamed vegetables, salad and fruit.

Menu
Oven-Baked Lentils & Rice
Steamed Vegetables
Tossed Salad
Mandarin Oranges

Preheat oven to 350°.

2 small	onions
2 cans	(14½ oz each) chicken broth, 1/3 less sodium
1¾ cups	water
1/2 cup	white wine
1½ cups	dry lentils, rinsed and picked over for stones
1 cup	dry brown rice (not quick-cooking)
1 small jar	(2 oz) chopped pimentos
1 tsp	dried basil
1 tsp	dried oregano
1/2 tsp	dried thyme
1/4 tsp	garlic powder
15 grinds	fresh ground pepper

Chop onions. Mix ingredients together in a large baking dish. Set timer for 90 minutes and bake uncovered.

Meanwhile… how about 9 holes of golf? Remember, you don't need a cart!

1½ cups	reduced-fat shredded mozzarella or Swiss cheese†

After 90 minutes of baking, sprinkle over top and bake 15 minutes longer to melt.

Use this time to steam vegetables, make a salad, and set table.

†See reduced-fat cheese tip on page viii (Introduction).

Nutrition information for 1¼ cup serving

Exchanges/Choices: 3 Starch, 1 Lean Meat

Calories	360	Fat	3.5 g	Fiber	8 g	Sodium	595 mg	Total Carbohydrate	53 g
Calories from Fat	9%	Saturated Fat	1.2 g	Cholesterol	8 mg	Protein	26 g	Sugars	3 g

Lickety-Split Diabetic Meals

Lickety-Split Tip

Exercising Consistently: Here's How to Make Your Good Intentions Come True!

If you are just getting into an exercise routine, it's important to establish positive feelings of accomplishment, so you will want to continue and be consistent.

WEEK 1
Try starting with only 5 minutes* of easy exercise, but do it 5 times that week. Try marching in place in front of the TV or spinning on your exercise bike. (Keep your intensity low.) You can always find 5 minutes! What's important is to do it 5 times per week. Do it at the same time each day, which will become your routine exercise time.

WEEKS 2, 3, 4, and 5
How does it feel to have exercised 5 times last week? Pretty good, huh? Now, over the next 4 weeks, increase your exercise time up to 7 minutes, then 10, 12, 15, 20, 25, 30. Keep your intensity fairly low. Be sure to keep up 5 times a week!

WEEK 6
Now, don't you feel GREAT having exercised 5 times a week for 5 weeks? Congratulations!

Now you're ready to add intensity. Increase your walking speed or turn up the resistance on the stationary bike.

*If you are particularly fit, you can start with 10 minutes, but not more. The point is NOT to do all you are physically capable of doing, but rather to establish the concrete habit for CONSISTENCY. Most people agree, consistency is the hardest part!

Reminder: ALWAYS CHECK WITH YOUR DOCTOR FIRST BEFORE STARTING ANY EXERCISE PROGRAM!

Pizzucchini with Redskins

Hands-on – 20 min. Oven/Exercise – 60 min.   **Serves 6**

Here's a delicious summer dish that uses up your extra zucchini and tomatoes. Pizzucchini gets its name from smelling like pizza while baking. We serve this with corn on the cob and cantaloupe.

Menu

Pizzucchini with Redskins

Corn on the Cob

Cantaloupe

Preheat oven to 375°.

Coat a 9" × 13" baking pan with cooking spray.

3 small	zucchini	Slice vegetables 1/8 inch thick. Separate onion slices into rings.
1 med	onion	
4 med	tomatoes	

6 T	grated Parmesan cheese	Mix together in a medium bowl.
1 cup	reduced-fat shredded mozzarella cheese†	Make 2 layers in the baking dish, using half the ingredients each time in the order listed: zucchini, onion, tomatoes, cheese mixture (repeat).
2 tsp	dried oregano	
1 tsp	garlic powder	

6 small	(4 oz each) red skin potatoes, cut in 1/2	Scrub potatoes and slip in around edges of casserole. Cover and bake 1 hour. (Remember to set timer.)

Popular summer feast!

How about swimming?

After 1 hour, remove cover and bake 15 minutes more. Use this time to cook some corn on the cob and slice some cantaloupe. Enjoy!

†See reduced-fat cheese tip on page viii (Introduction).

Nutrition information for 1 cup

Exchanges/Choices: 1 1/2 Starch, 1 Vegetable, 1 Lean Meat

Calories	190	Fat	3.5 g	Fiber	4.5 g	Sodium	280 mg	Total Carbohydrate	28 g
Calories from Fat	16%	Saturated Fat	1.6 g	Cholesterol	9 mg	Protein	12 g	Sugars	5 g

Lickety-Split Diabetic Meals

Lickety-Split Tip

Don't let the weather control your workout.

Always have a back-up plan for nasty weather. If the weather is nice, I walk, jog, rollerblade, or ride my bike. If not, I work out indoors doing aerobics or on an exercise machine. Develop a plan that works best for you.

Tuna Noodle Casserole

Hands-on – 10 min. Oven/Exercise – 50 min. **Serves 6**

Yes, it's your all-American favorite! This time it's made lower in fat and sodium, and without the time-wasting step of boiling the noodles first. Plan on a good workout tonight with 50 minutes of oven time!

Menu
Tuna Noodle Casserole
Tossed Salad
Whole-Wheat Rolls
Sliced Pears

Preheat oven to 375°.

1 can	(10¾ oz) cream of mushroom soup (Campbell's, Healthy Request)	Mix together in a large casserole dish.
1¼ cups	skim milk	

2 cans	(6 oz each) water-packed tuna, rinsed, drained, and flaked	Add to dish and mix well.
1 tsp	dried onion flakes	Put in oven, covered. Set timer for 50 minutes.
1/2 tsp	dill weed	How about heading outside for some "active" gardening or yard work?
1/4 cup	grated Parmesan cheese	
1½ cups	frozen peas	Check refrigerator for salad-making possibilities or try sliced cucumbers, tomatoes, and carrots.
3 cups	uncooked small pasta shells or noodles	Serve with rolls and pears.

Nutrition information for 1 cup

Exchanges/Choices: 2 1/2 Starch, 2 Lean Meat

Calories	280	Fat	3.5 g	Fiber	2.6 g	Sodium	465 mg	Total Carbohydrate	39 g
Calories from Fat	11%	Saturated Fat	1.1 g	Cholesterol	20 mg	Protein	22 g	Sugars	7 g

Lickety-Split Diabetic Meals

Lickety-Split Tip

**Want to create some fun and support
between you and your spouse?**

In a conspicuous place, hang 2 calendars side by side. Designate 1 for you and 1 for your spouse. Record your minutes of exercise each day. On Saturday or Sunday night, total up your minutes. The person with the least minutes gives a back-rub to the other. What competitive (and slightly romantic) fun!

Tantalizing Turkey Loaf Dinner

Hands-on – 20 min. Oven/Exercise – 60 min.

Serves 4

This dinner is a far cry from the traditional artery-clogging classic. It's fast and tasty, too! The applesauce replaces the moisture lost by using extra-lean ground turkey. Leftovers make great sandwiches!

Preheat oven to 350°.
Coat an 8" x 8" baking dish with cooking spray.

Menu
Tantalizing Turkey Loaf Dinner
Baked Potatoes
Broccoli

4	(4 oz each) baking potatoes or 2 (8 oz each) sweet potatoes	Scrub potatoes, pierce 3 or 4 times with a fork, wrap in foil, and place in oven.
1 small	onion	Chop and place in a medium bowl.
20 oz	extra-lean ground turkey breast	Add all to chopped onions and mix together thoroughly, using your hands if necessary. (Wash them first!) Form meat mixture into 4 equal-sized personal loaves and arrange in dish. (Can also make into 12 meat balls and bake for only 15 minutes. Serving size equals 3 meatballs per person.)
2 lg	egg whites	
1/2 - 1 tsp	Italian seasoning (children prefer less)	
1/4 tsp	red pepper flakes (opt)	
1/2 cup	applesauce, unsweetened	
1/2 tsp	salt (omit if bread crumbs are seasoned)	
1/2 cup	dry unseasoned bread crumbs	
2 T	grated Parmesan cheese	
1 cup	spaghetti sauce, no salt added (Eden)*	Pour sauce over top. Place in oven and set timer for 60 minutes. Head out for 50 or more minutes of exhilarating exercise.
4 cups	broccoli	After exercising, place into microwave-safe dish, cover, and cook on HIGH 5 minutes. Stretch! When oven timer goes off, it's time to eat!

Nutrition information for 1 turkey loaf, 1 4 oz potato, 1 cup broccoli

*See page 176 for an eye-opener about spaghetti sauce.

Exchanges/Choices: 2 1/2 Starch, 2 Vegetable, 4 Lean Meat

Calories	425	Fat	5 g	Fiber	8 g	Sodium	600 mg	Total Carbohydrate	52 g
Calories from Fat	8%	Saturated Fat	1 g	Cholesterol	58 mg	Protein	44 g	Sugars	13 g

Lickety-Split Diabetic Meals

Lickety-Split Tip

Relax away your high blood sugar! (Part 1)

While diet and exercise play significant roles in managing and preventing diabetes, new research suggests relaxation techniques can also help lower blood sugar. One study found that people with high stress and hostility levels are more likely to have insulin resistance, while other studies show meditation, yoga, and progressive muscle relaxation (PMR) help improve blood sugar control.

Yoga, anyone? Researchers in India found that when 20 people with diabetes practiced yoga daily for 40 days, there was a significant decrease in their fasting glucose levels and beneficial changes in insulin levels. Look for a class to join in your area or visit www.collagevideo.com to find a DVD/video you can do at home.

LaZonya

My lasagna has lots of veggies, low-fat cheese, and unboiled noodles (to save time). Double the recipe and freeze one pan for another time (freeze after baking). The sauce is so tasty, I have you make extra. Freeze it for a quick meal for topping a baked potato or pasta.

Menu

LaZonya

Tossed Salad

Whole-Wheat Garlic Cheese Toast (page 281)

9" x 13" baking dish   Preheat oven to 400°

1/2	each green and red bell pepper	**The Sauce...**
2	carrots	Clean veggies. Seed and chop peppers, chop or shred carrots, dice onions and slice mushrooms or zucchini, if using.
2 small	onions	
1 cup	sliced fresh mushrooms or zucchini (opt)	
1 T	olive oil	Heat oil over medium-high heat in your largest nonstick kettle and add garlic and vegetables.
1 tsp	minced garlic (2 cloves)	
1/4 cup	chopped fresh parsley	Chop. Reserve 1 to 2 T for later in recipe. Add to kettle.
20 oz	extra-lean ground turkey breast (opt)	Add turkey and/or tofu by crumbling it into the kettle (First-time tofu users, try 1/2 tofu and 1/2 turkey. Your guests will never tell the difference.) Add herbs. Cook, stirring frequently, for 5 minutes or until turkey is cooked through.
12 oz	firm tofu, crumbled (opt)	
1 tsp	dried oregano	
1/4 tsp	red pepper flakes	
2 jars	(26 oz each) spaghetti sauce, no-salt-added*	Add sauce and spinach. Simmer over medium heat while you prepare the cheese mixture. When ready, move sauce to assembly line.
1 box	(10 oz) frozen spinach	
1 tub	(15 oz) fat-free ricotta or nonfat cottage cheese	**The Cheeses...**
1/2 tsp	dried onion flakes	Mix together in a medium bowl. Divide into 3 equal parts (1 for each layer) for use during the LaZonya assembly process. Place a teaspoon in the bowl for scooping.
1 T	reserved chopped fresh parsley	
1 T	grated Parmesan cheese	
8 oz	reduced-fat shredded mozzarella†	

continued on next page...

Lickety-Split Diabetic Meals

Lickety-Split Tip

Relax away your high blood sugar! (Part 2)

Meditation. People who meditate regularly gain self-awareness, can sense stress reactions coming on, and can keep them from escalating. You can even perform meditation while walking, which provides a double bang for your buck because it's both physical and mental exercise. Try contacting a meditation specialist to learn proper deep breathing and to create a meaningful mantra to get you started. Or simply purchase an audio cd program to guide you.

Progressive muscle relaxation (PMR). PMR involves the tensing and relaxing of one muscle group at a time from head to toe until the entire body feels calmer. In *The Mind-Body Diabetes Revolution*, Duke University psychologist Richard Surwit, PhD, says that PMR is easy to learn and has been tested often with diabetes. A 2002 study of 108 people with type 2 diabetes found that those who practiced PMR in addition to receiving standard care, had lower glucose levels than those getting only standard care. Many meditation/relaxation audio programs include PMR. Be sure the one you get does.

1/2 cup	grated Parmesan cheese	Place opened bag in assembly line.
12 oz	whole-wheat lasagna	Place in bowl. Place a tablespoon in bowl for use in assembly line.
1/2 tsp	Italian seasoning	Place opened box in assembly line.

The Assembly...   Place in assembly line for sprinkling on top layer when assembly is complete.

1. Coat a 9" × 13" baking dish with cooking spray. Place 1¾ cups sauce in the bottom of dish.

2. Layer: 4 hard noodles; 1¾ cups sauce, spread evenly; 12 flat tsp ricotta cheese dropped evenly in a 3 × 4 pattern;
   1/2 cup mozzarella sprinkled evenly, and 2 T Parmesan cheese sprinkled evenly. Repeat layering 3 times.

3. After third Parmesan cheese sprinkle, complete the fourth and final layer with 4 hard noodles; 1½ cups sauce spread evenly;
   1/2 cup mozzarella sprinkled evenly; 2 T Parmesan cheese; and Italian seasoning sprinkled evenly over top.

Remember, there should be about 2 cups of leftover sauce for you to freeze for a quick meal later!

4. Pour 1/4 cup of water all around edges of dish. This provides needed steam to cook noodles.

5. Cover with aluminum foil, set timer and bake 45 minutes.

Capitalize on this time to get in a thorough resistance exercise workout.

6. Uncover and bake 10 minutes longer.

7. Prepare salad and garlic toast.

8. Allow 10 minutes to set before serving. Use this time to stretch and set the table!

*See page 176 for an eye-opener about spaghetti sauce.

†See reduced-fat cheese tip on page viii (Introduction).

Nutrition information for 1 square (1/12 of dish) made with ground turkey and tofu
Exchanges/Choices: 2 Starch, 1 Vegetable, 3 Lean Meat, 1/2 Fat

Calories	325	Fat	8 g	Fiber	8 g	Sodium	397 mg	Total Carbohydrate	40 g
Calories from Fat	19%	Saturated Fat	2 g	Cholesterol	26 mg	Protein	26 g	Sugars	10 g

Lickety-Split Diabetic Meals

Lickety-Split Tip

Be sure to stretch! It only takes a minute!

Benefits of stretching:

• Improves flexibility, mobility and range of motion.

• Helps prevent injuries.

• Promotes better circulation.

• Reduces tension.

• Helps prevent muscle stiffness and soreness after exercise.

Rules for stretching:

• Gently hold a stretch for about 20 seconds.

• Stretch only until you feel a comfortable stretch in the muscle.

• Breathe normally. Do not hold your breath.

• Never force a muscle to stretch too far when true pain is felt.

• Never bounce while stretching! You want a constant, steady stretch.

Mexican LaZonya

Hands-on — 30 min. Oven/Exercise — 20 min. **Serves 9**

(A.K.A. Bean and Vegetable Enchilada Bake) Teenagers will love how this dish resembles "Taco Bell."

Preheat oven to 375°. Note: If serving Cinnamon Butternut Squash, get it started first.

Menu

Mexican LaZonya

Cinnamon Butternut
Squash (page 279)

Low-Fat Ice Cream Cone

2 T	olive oil	Heat oil over medium-high heat in a large nonstick kettle. Add garlic and cook 1 minute.
1 tsp	chopped garlic (2 cloves)	
1 bag	(16 oz) California blend frozen vegetables	Add to the kettle and sauté until half-cooked, about 6 minutes.
1 bag	(16 oz) broccoli stir-fry frozen vegetables	
20 oz	extra lean ground turkey breast (opt)	Add to hot vegetables. Stir frequently until cooked through, about 6 minutes.
1 jar	(16 oz) salsa of your choice	Add to kettle and set timer for 5 minutes.
1 can	(16 oz) tomato puree	
2 T	Zippy Zonya Mexi Mix‡*	Stir into the simmering skillet. When the timer goes off, it's time to assemble. Optional step: Puree sauce in a food processor to disguise vegetables for picky eaters.
1 can	(15 oz) pinto, black, or kidney beans, rinsed and drained	
10-12	6" corn tortillas (flour tortillas work fine, too)	Assemble in a 9" × 13" baking dish, layering evenly: 1/3 of the sauce, 4 tortillas, and 1/2 cup cheese on top of tortillas (repeat 2 more times), but don't add last layer of cheese. Cover with aluminum foil and place in oven. Set timer for 25 minutes.
1½ cups	reduced-fat shredded cheddar cheese†	

How about jumping rope? Start with 5 minutes, working up to 20 when you can.

‡See recipe on page 40.
*If you have small children, you may want to reduce this by half.
†See reduced-fat cheese tip on page viii (Introduction).

Remove foil, add last layer of cheese, and bake 5 minutes. Serve with Cinnamon Butternut Squash.

Nutrition information for 1 square (1/9 of dish) using ground turkey and corn tortillas

Exchanges/Choices: 1 1/2 Starch, 1 Vegetable, 3 Lean Meat, 1/2 Fat

Calories	310	Fat	7 g	Fiber	8 g	Sodium	680 mg	Total Carbohydrate	34 g
Calories from Fat	20%	Saturated Fat	2 g	Cholesterol	33 mg	Protein	26 g	Sugars	5 g

Lickety-Split Diabetic Meals

Lickety-Split Tip

Calories burned during exercise

Don't get depressed when you think . . . I exercised for 20 minutes and all I burned was 160 calories??? Just remember the benefits of consistency over time:

Twenty minutes of exercise 3 times a week for a full year burns 24,960 calories, which translates into 7 pounds of fat burned in a year!

Thirty minutes of exercise 5 times a week for a year burns 62,400 calories, which translates into 18 pounds of fat burned in a year!

Forty-five minutes of exercise 5 times a week for a year burns 93,600 calories, which translates into 27 pounds of fat burned in a year!

As you can see, consistency pays!

Kickin' Chicken with Fries

Hands-on – 15 min. Oven/Exercise – 22 min. **Serves 4**

Check this out! You get your workout in and your family fed all in less than 45 minutes!
Your family will ask for this again and again!

Kids' Favorite!

Menu

Kickin' Chicken with Fries
Green Beans

Preheat oven to 450°. Arrange oven racks to accommodate both a baking sheet and a 9" × 13" baking dish.

1 cup	salsa or picante sauce	Mix together in a 2-cup measuring cup.
1 T	firmly packed brown sugar	
1/2 T	Dijon mustard	

4	(4 oz each) boneless, skinless chicken breasts	Place chicken in a 9" × 13" baking dish. Pour sauce over chicken. Put in oven.

1 bag	(24 oz) potato wedges*	Spread out on nonstick baking sheet. Place in oven. Set timer for 25 minutes.

1 bag	(16 oz) frozen green beans	Place in microwave-safe dish, cover, and cook on HIGH 12 minutes. (You will leave the vegetables sitting in microwave 10 minutes longer.)
2 T	water	

Jump on your treadmill or stationary bike for a quick 22 minutes.
(Take the first 2 minutes to warm up.)

At sound of timer, check chicken to see if it's done. Cook 5 more minutes if necessary.
It's Kickin' Chicken time!

* If you prefer, make homemade version of Oven Fries (page 277).

Nutrition information for 1 chicken breast, 1 cup fries, 1 cup green beans

Exchanges/Choices: 2 1/2 Starch, 2 Vegetable, 3 Lean Meat

Calories	393	Fat	5 g	Fiber	7 g	Sodium	355 mg	Total Carbohydrate	54 g
Calories from Fat	12%	Saturated Fat	1.3 g	Cholesterol	66 mg	Protein	33 g	Sugars	8 g

Lickety-Split Diabetic Meals

Lickety-Split Tip

How is it that people who can never find time to exercise can always find time to eat?

The wonder of 336.

You may find it interesting to learn that there are 336 30-minute time segments in **EVERY** week. You need **ONLY** 3 to 5 of these 30-minute time segments each week for exercise.

This requires less than 5% of your time each week!

(While eating, on the other hand, takes much more time, and we always find time for that!)

Delicate Baked Fish

Hands-on – 10 min. Oven/Exercise – 35 min.   **Serves 4**

The next time you walk by the fresh seafood counter, check out their fresh trout. My dear friend Jay Johnson taught me that the milk in this recipe keeps the flavor delicate and mild. (Not at all fishy!) Perfect for stronger-tasting fish as well as being a kids' favorite!

Menu
Delicate Baked Fish
Oven Fries
California Vegetables
9-Grain Rolls

Preheat oven to 350°.

1 bag	(24 oz) potato wedges*	Spread out on baking sheet. Place in oven.
1½ lbs	fresh cod, whitefish, perch, snapper, or trout fillet	Rinse clean and place in an 8" × 8" baking dish.
1/2	lemon, squeezed (or 1 T from a bottle)	Drizzle or pour over fish in order given.
1 tsp	oil (canola or olive)	
1 cup	skim milk	
1/8 tsp	salt	Sprinkle over top. Place in oven. Set timer and bake for 35 minutes.
6 grinds	fresh ground pepper	
3 dashes	paprika	
2 bags	(16 oz each) frozen California blend vegetables	Place in microwave-safe dish, cover, and let set in microwave.
1 T	water	Pop in an exercise video for 30 minutes of aerobic work. Remember to warm up.

*If you prefer, make homemade version of Oven Fries (page 277).

When timer goes off, cook vegetables in microwave on HIGH 10 minutes. Allow fish to continue baking until microwave finishes.

Step in place for 1 minute for a cool-down. Grab 2 soup cans and do bicep curls and overhead presses. Follow with some sit-ups and 2 minutes of stretching.

Set table. When vegetables are done, it's time to eat!

Nutrition information for 4 oz fish, 1 cup fries, 1½ cups vegetables
Exchanges/Choices: 2 1/2 Starch, 3 Vegetable, 4 Lean Meat

Calories	448	Fat	6 g	Fiber	9 g	Sodium	357 mg	Total Carbohydrate	57 g
Calories from Fat	12%	Saturated Fat	1.3 g	Cholesterol	74 mg	Protein	42 g	Sugars	9 g

Lickety-Split Diabetic Meals

Lickety-Split Tip

Nature's Popsicle: Frozen Grapes

If you haven't experienced frozen grapes yet, you don't know what you're missing!

• Take seedless grapes off their vine. (Use red, green, or both).

• **THOROUGHLY** wash the grapes and pat dry on a towel.

• Place in an airtight bowl or resealable baggie and freeze.

• Serve frozen or partially thawed.

• Enjoy 12 large or 15 small as a fruit serving, which serves as a dessert.

Icy, sweet, and delicious!

Super Time-Saving Tip

Skip prepping the potatoes and onion by using 4 cups of Ore Ida Potatoes O'Brien (a frozen hash brown product that I call for frequently). It has no fat (just chopped potatoes, onions, and peppers), tastes great, and saves you loads of time!

Chicken & Vegetables in Foil

A super-simple dinner that can be cooked indoors or on the outdoor grill. Your choice, Italian style or bar-becue. Best of all, there's no messy cleanup!

Menu
Chicken & Vegetables in Foil
Whole-Grain Bread
Frozen Grapes

Preheat oven to 400° or outdoor grill to medium heat.
Tear off 2 large pieces of foil just larger than the size of a baking sheet.

3/4 cup	**light or fat-free Italian dressing or bottled BBQ sauce**	Spread 1/2 the sauce in center of one piece of foil.
4	**(4 oz each) skinless, boneless chicken breast**	Layer on foil in order given. Spread on remaining sauce.
4 small	**(4 oz each) potatoes, scrubbed or peeled and thinly sliced***	
1 lg	**onion, sliced into rings***	
1 pkg	**(10 oz) frozen Brussels sprouts, cabbage wedges, or broccoli/ cauliflower mix**	Place in a strainer and run hot tap water over them for 1 minute. Drain and add to foil.
1 pkg	**(10 oz) frozen carrots**	
8 grinds	**fresh ground pepper**	Sprinkle over vegetables. Place other piece of foil on top. Seal with double folds. Place in oven and set timer for 75 minutes.

How about a nice long bike ride outdoors? Reserve the last 15 minutes for push-ups and sit-ups. (How many of those are you up to by now?) Stretch!

Carefully unseal foil package (watch out for steam) and serve with rolls and frozen grapes (see Nature's Popsicle above).

*See my Super Time-Saving Tip above.

Nutrition information for 1/4 of recipe using light Italian dressing (2 cups serving)
Exchanges/Choices: 1 1/2 Starch, 2 Vegetable, 3 Lean Meat, 1/2 Fat

Calories	331	Fat	6 g	Fiber	6 g	Sodium	535 mg	Total Carbohydrate	34 g
Calories from Fat	18%	Saturated Fat	1 g	Cholesterol	65 mg	Protein	32 g	Sugars	11 g

Lickety-Split Diabetic Meals

Lickety-Split Tip

Is your headache a sign of mild dehydration?

Do you ever arrive home with a headache? Did you know that this is often the first sign of dehydration?

Hydrating your body may relieve your headache. You need to be adequately hydrated in order to feel good and perform well, especially during your workout. The best habit is to drink fluids all day long. If you haven't, play catch-up and down a glass of water when you get home.

And always be sure to replace fluids after exercising!

Simple Baked Chicken & Rice

Hands-on – 10 min. Oven/Exercise – 60 min.

Serves 6

Got 10 minutes? That's all it takes to get this tasty favorite in the oven, leaving you with 1 whole hour of rejuvenating "all to yourself" exercise time.

Menu

Simple Baked Chicken & Rice

Tossed Salad

Apricot Halves

Preheat oven to 375°.

1 can	(10¾ oz) cream of mushroom or cream of chicken soup	Stir together in a 9" × 13" baking dish.
1 can	(14½ oz) reduced-sodium chicken broth, 1/3 less sodium	
1/3 cup	fat-free sour cream or nonfat plain yogurt	

1 bag	(16 oz) California blend frozen vegetables
1 can	(10 oz) cooked white meat chicken, rinsed and drained
1½ cups	whole-grain instant brown rice, dry
1 tsp	dried onion flakes
10 grinds	fresh ground pepper

Add to dish and stir.

Cover and put in oven to bake. Set timer for 45 minutes.

Tennis anyone? Remember to end with a thorough stretch session.

At sound of timer, uncover and continue baking 10 minutes.

Meanwhile, set table, grab a salad, and open the can of apricots. It's dinnertime!

Nutrition information for 1¼ cups

Exchanges/Choices: 2 1/2 Starch, 1 Vegetable, 1 Lean Meat

Calories	269	Fat	2 g	Fiber	5 g	Sodium	557 mg	Total Carbohydrate	47 g
Calories from Fat	9%	Saturated Fat	<1 g	Cholesterol	13 mg	Protein	13 g	Sugars	3 g

Lickety-Split Diabetic Meals

Lickety-Split Tip

Still wondering which exercise video to buy?

Call Collage Video at 800-433-6769 and ask for their free catalog entitled "The Complete Guide to Exercise Videos." It includes excellent descriptions of hundreds of the best videos on the planet. They even boast that their telephone video consultants have used the tapes themselves, so they can tell you the details. Now, that's service!

Better yet, visit their Web site at *www.collagevideo.com* where you can search options by type and view 30 seconds of each one right online. It's a great way to shop.

Chicken & Bean Enchiladas

Serves 10

My thanks to Stacy Rafalko for this neat recipe. Feel free to leave out the chicken or cheese if you prefer. These are easy and tasty!

Kids' Favorite!

Menu

Chicken & Bean Enchiladas

Green Beans

Sliced Cantaloupe, Honeydew, or Watermelon

Preheat oven to 350°.

2 cups	**Benito Bean Dip (page 27) or 1 (16 oz) can fat-free refried beans**	Gently combine in a medium bowl, enough to break up chicken.
1 can	**(10 oz) cooked white meat chicken, rinsed and drained**	
10	**6" flour tortillas**	Place 1/3 cup of bean mixture in a long single row on a tortilla. Roll up. Place in a 9" x 13" baking dish. Repeat with remaining 7 tortillas.
1 can	**(10 oz) enchilada sauce**	Pour over enchiladas.
1/2 cup	**reduced-fat shredded cheddar cheese†**	Sprinkle over top. Place in oven, uncovered. Set timer for 30 minutes.
		Throw on your sweatpants and a T-shirt and start your favorite exercise video.
		When timer sounds, allow enchiladas to cool a few minutes while you prepare green beans and slice melons. Try to stretch while you work.
10 T	**fat-free sour cream**	Serve enchiladas with 1 T of sour cream over each and optional onion and green pepper on top.
	minced fresh onion (opt)	
	chopped green bell pepper (opt)	†See reduced-fat cheese tip on page viii (Introduction).

Nutrition information for 1 enchilada with 1 T sour cream

Exchanges/Choices: 2 Starch, 1 Lean Meat

Calories	206	Fat	3.7 g	Fiber	4 g	Sodium	607 mg
Calories from Fat	16%	Saturated Fat	1 g	Cholesterol	7 mg	Protein	10.5 g

Total Carbohydrate	31 g
Sugars	2 g

Lickety-Split Diabetic Meals

Lickety-Split Tip

Do house guests cramp your exercise routine?

Why not invite them to join you? Make an early morning walk followed by a nutritious breakfast part of a perfect visit. It's amazing what a positive impact you can have on your family and friends!

Likewise, if you are the guest, look for opportunities to get your exercise in. Even if you go by yourself, it can provide a break for you and your host.

Creamy Chicken Enchiladas

Hands-on — 30 min. Oven/Exercise — 30 min.

Serves 10

Creamy, comforting, and "to die for" are the best ways to describe this.
My complete thanks to Diane Petersen for contributing this favorite recipe from her mom, Barb Filler.

Menu

Creamy Chicken Enchiladas

Cut Green Beans

Crinkle Cut Carrots

Apple Wedges

Kiwi Slices

Preheat oven to 325°.

6	**(4 oz each) skinless, boneless chicken breast, cut into strips**	Coat a large nonstick skillet with cooking spray and place over medium-high heat. Brown chicken, turning frequently. Add chilies during last 2 minutes.
1 can	**(4 oz) chopped green chilies**	
1 cup	**fat-free sour cream**	Meanwhile, in a medium saucepan, mix together and heat over medium-low heat.
1 can	**(12 oz) cream of chicken soup**	
1 can	**(10¾ oz) evaporated skim milk**	
1 can	**(2¼ oz) sliced black olives (opt)**	Place olives and cheese in assembly line. Spread 1/2 cup of soup mixture over bottom of 9" x 13" baking dish.
1 cup	**reduced-fat shredded cheddar cheese†**	
10	**6" flour tortillas**	Lay 5 tortillas on a clean countertop. Put 1 T soup mixture in a line down the center of each. Follow with: 2 T chicken, 1 T cheese, and 1 tsp olives. Roll up and place in dish. Repeat with remaining 5 tortillas. Pour remaining soup mixture over tortilla rolls. Sprinkle with remaining cheese. Place in oven and set timer for 20 minutes.
5 cups	**frozen cut green beans**	Place veggies in a large microwave-safe bowl. Cover and let set in microwave.
5 cups	**frozen crinkle cut carrots**	Is the weather nice? How about a nice nature walk? Otherwise, plug in an exercise video.
		When timer sounds, microwave vegetables 10 minutes on high. (Allow enchiladas to continue baking.) Do some sit-ups, push-ups, and stretches. Slice apples and kiwi. When vegetables are done — it's dinner time!

†See reduced-fat cheese tip on page viii (Introduction).

Nutrition information for 1 enchilada, 1 cup vegetables

Exchanges/Choices: 1 Starch, 1/2 Fat-Free Milk, 2 Vegetable, 2 Lean Meat, 1 Fat

Calories	320	Fat	8 g	Fiber	6 g	Sodium	610 mg	Total Carbohydrate	34 g
Calories from Fat	22%	Saturated Fat	2.8 g	Cholesterol	55 mg	Protein	26 g	Sugars	11 g

Lickety-Split Diabetic Meals

Lickety-Split Tip

Arriving home starved: What to do

If you arrive home starved, you'll need something to hold you over until dinnertime. For a snack that's great exercise fuel, it's hard to beat a piece of fruit or glass of fruit juice. Or try a few crackers, 1/2 a bagel, or 2 rice cakes. Be sure to chase it with a glass of water. This will give you energy and valuable hydration until dinnertime, while holding off hunger throughout your workout.

Encore! Leftover Spanish Rice Roll-up

Spoon leftover Spanish Red Beans & Rice (hot or cold) onto a whole-grain tortilla or lavash bread. Add extra salsa, lettuce, tomatoes, and roll it up. Delicious!

Spanish Red Beans & Rice

Hands-on – 10 min. Oven/Exercise – 55 min. **Serves 6**

Every household needs a Spanish red beans and rice dish! Feel free to make this with black beans if you prefer.

Menu

Spanish Red Beans & Rice

Tossed Salad

Pears

Preheat oven to 350°.

1 can	(15 oz) red, kidney, or black beans, rinsed and drained	Mix together in a 9" × 13" baking dish.
1 can	(14½ oz) diced tomatoes, no salt added	Cover and put in oven to bake. Set timer for 55 minutes.
1 cup	Uncle Ben's whole-grain instant brown rice, dry	
3/4 cup	salsa of your choice	
1 cup	water	
4 - 5 drops	Tabasco sauce (to taste)	The anticipation of this recipe puts me in the mood for 45 minutes of rollerblading. What strikes you?
1 tsp	ground cumin	
1/2 tsp	ground oregano	
1/2 tsp	salt (opt)	

1 cup	shredded reduced-fat cheddar cheese†	Upon return, scour fridge for salad fixins and make. When timer sounds, uncover, sprinkle cheese over top, and allow to melt in oven while you set the table.

Serve with a tossed salad and fresh or canned pears.

†See reduced-fat cheese tip on page viii (Introduction).

Nutrition information for 1 cup (including optional salt)

Exchanges/Choices: 2 1/2 Starch, 1 Vegetable

Calories	235	Fat	3 g	Fiber	5 g	Sodium	654 mg	Total Carbohydrate	41 g
Calories from Fat	11%	Saturated Fat	1.3 g	Cholesterol	8 mg	Protein	12 g	Sugars	7 g

Lickety-Split Diabetic Meals

Lickety-Split Tip

Exercise: A new way to get your quota

Long gone are the days that you **MUST** exercise 30–40 minutes **NONSTOP** to receive the benefits. Studies show that breaking your 30- to 40-minute exercise into 3 or 4 separate 10-minute segments has the same cardiovascular AND weight-loss benefits.

Now there is additional good news from the University of Pittsburgh, where researchers determined that at the end of 6 months, women on the short-bout program exercised 30 more minutes per week than the long-bout exercisers. That's an extra day's worth! They also lost 2 pounds more on average. Obviously, 10 minutes here and there is easier to stick to!

Also keep in mind:

• 10 minutes doesn't work up enough of a sweat to require a shower.

• Frequent 10-minute exercising breaks will do wonders for alleviating stress!

Ratatouille *

Hands-on – 20 min. Oven/Exercise – 2 hours   **Serves 6**

An especially excellent dish to make in the fall, or any time eggplant and zucchini are readily available. This makes a large batch and the flavor improves each day with reheating.

Preheat oven to 350°.

Menu

Ratatouille with Potatoes

Whole-Grain Bread or Surprise Pumpkin Pie (page 309)

1 small	eggplant unpeeled, cut into 1" cubes
4 small	(4 oz) potatoes, scrubbed clean, diced
1	red bell pepper, seeded and chopped
1	green bell pepper, seeded and chopped
2 small	zucchini (1 can be yellow crooked neck squash), sliced in half lengthwise and then into 1" slices
2 lg	onions, sliced

Prep vegetables and arrange in a 10" × 15" baking dish.

2 tsp	minced garlic (4 cloves)
1/2 cup	minced fresh parsley
1 tsp	dried basil, crushed
1½ tsp	salt
2 cans	(14.5 oz each) diced tomatoes, no salt added
3 T	olive oil

Mix together in a medium bowl, then pour over vegetables. Gently toss. Cover and bake 2 hours.

This allows ample time for a long fall hike. Aren't the colors beautiful? After exercising, you'll still have time to whip up the Pumpkin Surprise Pie and get it into the oven for 1 hour.

When timer sounds, remove Ratatouille and allow to set 30 minutes, still covered.

Meanwhile, do push-ups, sit-ups, and stretch.

grated Parmesan cheese (to taste)

Serve with a sprinkle of Parmesan cheese, and whole-grain bread or Surprise Pumpkin Pie.

*Option: Chicken Ratatouille

Nutrition information for 2¼ cups (without chicken)

Exchanges/Choices: 1 Starch, 3 Vegetable, 1 1/2 Fat

Place 6 skinless, boneless thighs or 4 skinless, boneless breasts under vegetables before baking.

Calories	223	Fat	7 g	Fiber	10 g	Sodium	653 mg	Total Carbohydrate	37 g
Calories from Fat	27%	Saturated Fat	1 g	Cholesterol	0 mg	Protein	5 g	Sugars	15 g

Lickety-Split Diabetic Meals

Lickety-Split Tip

Give foods a fun and tasty name

What would your kids rather eat, wild rice and squash or "Jack-in-the Pumpkin"? Being creative and thinking like a kid can help get your kids to try new foods they **THINK** they won't like. Kids don't think they like salads, but they know they love desserts, so the next time you make a salad, name it something that ends in "dessert." Also get your kids involved and let them help you make a special recipe. Being involved gives them a sense of pride and ownership so they'll want to make sure **EVERYONE** participates in eating it!

Jack in the Pumpkin

Hands-on – 60 min. Oven/Exercise – 75 min.   **Serves 6**

This delicious and hearty Mexican-style dish is baked in a hollowed-out pumpkin or squash, providing for the ultimate autumn holiday dish! It's also fun to use small pumpkins for single-serving bowls for each guest. This dish is equally good baked in a casserole dish.

Menu

Jack in the Pumpkin

Marinated Vegetable Salad (page 257)

Canned Peaches

Preheat oven to 375°.

1 cup	wild/brown rice mixed (1/4 wild, 3/4 brown), dry	Cook in a medium saucepan over medium heat about 45 minutes until done.
2 cups	water and/or broth, 1/3 less sodium	
1	onion, chopped	

1 med	pumpkin (pie pumpkin is best) or 2 lg buttercup squash

Meanwhile, wash and carefully carve open a lid that provides a fairly wide opening. Be sure to carve with your knife at an angle so the lid does not slip through opening after it bakes. (A saw-tooth pattern is especially attractive.) Scoop out all seeds and pulp and discard. Set aside bowl and lid.

1 T	oil (olive or canola)
1 tsp	minced garlic (4 cloves)
1/2	each red, green, and yellow bell pepper, seeded and chopped
2	onions, chopped

Heat oil in a large stir-fry pan over medium-high heat. Add garlic and vegetables and stir-fry a few minutes.

3/4 cup	medium or hot salsa (strain so salsa is thick)
2 cups	frozen corn
2 cans	(16 oz each) black beans, rinsed and drained
1/4 cup	chopped fresh parsley
2 tsp	cumin seed
1 tsp	dried oregano
1/8 tsp	cayenne
1/4 tsp	salt

Add to sauté along with cooked rice. Bring to a simmer for a few minutes. There should be minimal liquid.
Carefully spoon mixture into pumpkin. Place pumpkin on a baking sheet, with the lid alongside. Set timer for 1 hour and 15 minutes. Consider making a colorful Marinated Vegetable Salad.

How about a long fall bike ride? Use the extra time for toning exercises like sit-ups, push-ups, leg lifts, and, of course, stretching!

Nutrition information for approximately 1 cup, without pumpkin or squash

Exchanges/Choices: 3 1/2 Starch, 1 Vegetable, 1 Lean Meat

When timer goes off, remove from oven. Place pumpkin lid on top of pumpkin, if desired, and serve proudly. Meat from inside pumpkin will be tender and tasty to eat as well as its contents.

Calories	353	Fat	5 g	Fiber	12 g	Sodium	538 mg	Total Carbohydrate	64 g
Calories from Fat	13%	Saturated Fat	<1 g	Cholesterol	0 mg	Protein	15 g	Sugars	10 g

Lickety-Split Diabetic Meals

Lickety-Split Tip

Prepare for a lazy day tomorrow by building your own "Energy Bank" today

In the story of *Water with Lemon*, Fowler was an expert at capitalizing on his high-energy days by cooking extra batches and plopping "home-made frozen dinners" into his freezer or "energy bank." Why cook just enough chicken breasts or meat loaf or salmon fillets for the meal you're having today? Why not cook a double batch for a couple of evenings of sanity when you're dead tired or just don't feel like cooking? All you need is a little forethought to think in terms of "double batches" along with airtight containers and a permanent pen or grease pencil so you can date and label your "bank" deposits. The next time you have a stressful day, enjoy coming home and finding a delicious meal awaiting you, in your Energy Bank!

Spinach Veal Roll

Hands-on – 30 min. Oven/Exercise – 30 min.   **Serves 4**

Straight from the pages of Water with Lemon, this is the intriguing Veal Roll that Fowler makes for Karen while he explains one of his eight life-changing habits. Excellent for company or any day. (Fowler doubled this recipe since it freezes well for his Energy Bank!)

Menu
Spinach Veal Roll
Rice
Vegetables

2 cups	water	Place water in medium saucepan over medium-high heat. When it comes to a boil, add the rice and oil, stir, cover, and turn heat to medium-low. Simmer for 45 minutes.
1 cup	brown rice (not instant) (part wild rice opt)	
1 tsp	olive oil	

| 1 pkg | (10 oz) frozen chopped spinach | Place into a bowl and microwave on medium for 3 minutes. |

| 4 pieces | (1 lb total) thin-sliced (scaloppini) veal (or 4 turkey breast cutlets) | Place each veal piece on a large sheet of plastic wrap; cover veal with another sheet of plastic wrap. With the smooth side of a meat hammer, pound each piece vigorously to about 1/8" thick. Season with pepper. |
| 10 grinds | cracked pepper | |

Preheat oven to 375°.

2 tsp	olive oil	Remove spinach from microwave and squeeze out excess liquid. Sauté in a large skillet with onions, garlic, and spices. Remove pan from heat, let cool, stir in cheeses.
1 small	onion, finely chopped	
1 tsp	chopped garlic	
1 tsp	basil	
1/2 tsp	salt-free lemon pepper	

| 3/4 cup | nonfat cottage cheese | Spread spinach mixture evenly over veal pieces. Roll meat and mixture into individual meat rolls using the plastic wrap to help lift the meat. Transfer pieces to 9" × 12" baking dish, cover with foil, and bake for 30 minutes. |
| 1/2 cup | reduced-fat feta cheese | |

| 16 oz bag | frozen broccoli, cauliflower, and carrots | Place in microwave-safe dish, cover, and microwave 10 minutes on HIGH. Leave in microwave uncovered to stay warm. |

Spend extra 20 minutes going for a walk!

Serve with rice, vegetables, and a tossed salad on the side.

Nutrition information for 1 Spinach Veal Roll, ¾ cup rice, and 1 cup vegetables

Exchanges/Choices: 2 Starch, 2 Vegetable, 4 Lean Meat, 1 Fat

| Calories | 440 | Fat | 10 g | Fiber | 8 g | Sodium | 665 mg | Total Carbohydrate | 46 g |
| Calories from Fat | 20% | Saturated Fat | 3 g | Cholesterol | 93 mg | Protein | 39 g | Sugars | 7 g |

Lickety-Split Diabetic Meals

Lickety-Split Tip

When is the best time of day to exercise?

Just before breakfast? Or 1–2 hours after dinner? The beneficial effects on your blood sugar certainly differ, that's for sure. But the **BEST** time to exercise is whenever you can and will do it consistently, whether that's morning, noon, or night. To become a regular morning exerciser, or a regular before-dinner exerciser, or a regular after-dinner exerciser...the key word here is "regular." Consistency is the key for helping you keep your current blood sugars in target range and garnering the long-term effects of reduced cardiovascular disease risk. Remember to test your blood sugar before and after exercise, and carry a snack with you in case you experience low blood sugar. You will quickly learn how activity affects your blood sugar and what snacks, if any, are required. I recommend finding what time is **YOUR** best time, learning how it affects your blood sugar, and then being consistent with it.

Chili Cornbread Pie

Hands-on – 15 min. Oven/Exercise – 30 min. **Serves 9**

A simple one-dish meal that will make your kitchen smell awesome! Serve with carrot sticks, celery, and peppers.

Preheat oven to 375°.

Menu

Chili Cornbread Pie

Carrot sticks, Celery and Peppers

Chocolate Chip Bar Cookie (make ahead) (page 297)

2 cans	(15 oz each) chili beans (Eden)	
1 can	(16 oz) corn, no salt added	
1/2 med	onion, chopped (opt)	
1/4 cup	cilantro, chopped (opt)	
1 tsp	Zippy Zonya Mexi Mix‡	
1 can	(15 oz) diced tomatoes with chilies (Eden)	
1/2 tsp	salt*	

Combine in an 9" × 13" baking dish.

1 cup	yellow cornmeal
1 cup	all-purpose flour
1 T	baking powder
1 T	sugar
1/2 tsp	salt*

Combine in a medium bowl using a fork to be sure baking powder is evenly distributed.

1 cup	skim milk or soy milk
2 T	canola oil

Add to dry ingredients and stir just until blended.

Spoon 9 even spoonfuls of the batter in a 3 x 3 pattern onto the bean mixture.
Place in oven to bake. Set timer for 30 minutes.

Hop on your stepper for 30 minutes.

When the timer goes off, remove and allow to set 10 minutes while you prepare raw vegetables. It's time to eat!

‡See recipe on page 40.

*Omit salt if beans or corn have salt added.

Nutrition information for 1/9 of pie
Exchanges/Choices: 2 1/2 Starch, 2 Vegetable, 1/2 Fat

Calories	279	Fat	3.5 g	Fiber	7 g	Sodium	569 mg	Total Carbohydrate	53 g
Calories from Fat	11%	Saturated Fat	0 g	Cholesterol	<1 mg	Protein	11 g	Sugars	6 g

Lickety-Split Diabetic Meals

Lickety-Split Tip

"Growing up on the farm, both my husband and I were meat, potatoes, and white pasta lovers. After years (too many to advertise) of eating macaroni and cheese, spaghetti and marzetti dishes made with white pasta, we switched to whole-wheat pasta. Admittedly, we first tried it just because it was healthier, but soon realized that we actually liked the flavor better. It was also more filling than white pasta, so we ate smaller portions. We now use it exclusively and don't even like the gloppy white stuff anymore. We've even gotten our adult children to begin exploring with it. Changing from white pasta to whole-wheat pasta is a lot like our moving from the farm to the lake—a great move."

—Joy Smith

Community leader and long-time friend who's living it up at the lake and proving that we really can teach old dogs new tricks.

Pasta

Pasta is the "pre-game" meal of choice for athletes and a favorite among vegetarians. The nutritional plus from pasta comes from the fact that if you're eating a big plate of pasta, you're probably NOT eating a 12-ounce steak. This is good.

But what about all those carbohydrates? Don't they all just turn into a boatload of sugar? Not if you keep portion sizes smart and choose whole grains when you can. Remember that 1/2 cup of pasta equals a slice of bread. So it's imperative that your "scoop" doesn't turn into a 3 1/2 cup affair. (Don't laugh, this is the typical portion size served in restaurants.)

I asked a woman one time, "Do you realize that when you eat that entire portion of pasta served at a restaurant it's like eating seven slices of bread." She replied, "Oh no Zonya. I eat seven slices of bread with my pasta."

So it's certainly understandable why people have gotten high blood sugar readings after eating a meal of pasta and breadsticks. (Who came up with the idea to serve bread with pasta in the first place? Did they think the meal was a little shy of having enough carbohydrates?) If your meal plan says, "3 slices of bread or starch servings at dinner," then by all means, have 1 cup pasta and one slic garlic toast, or 1 1/2 cups pasta and no garlic toast. Always enjoy a giant salad first and choose a low-fat sauce (loaded with vegetables) over whole-grain pasta when you can. You'll be amazed to be able to enjoy pasta each and every week with a perfect blood sugar and weight to boot.

Lickety-Split Diabetic Meals

Lickety-Split Tip

But isn't pasta fattening and a killer for my blood sugar?

Following these 6 steps for perfect diabetic pasta meals:

1. Eat a large tossed salad first for appetite control.

2. Use a measuring cup to serve yourself, knowing every 1/2 cup is 15 grams of carbohydrate (or one bread/starch serving).

3. Use a low-fat recipe for the sauce (like the ones in this chapter).

4. Include as many vegetables in the sauce as you can.

5. Choose whole-grain pasta whenever possible for added fiber, vitamins, and minerals (like chromium, which is integral in carbohydrate metabolism).

6. Learn to eat only until your stomach says, "No longer hungry" instead of "full." This may take getting used to, but you will sleep better than going to bed "stuffed" like you did in the old days.

Veggie Sghetti

Hands-on – 30 min.   **Serves 8**

Occasionally we make this with turkey, but always with lots of vegetables. The vegetables replace the meat beautifully. Use any leftover sauce to top baked potatoes later in the week.

Menu

Veggie Sghetti

Tossed Salad

Whole-Wheat Garlic Cheese Toast (page 281)

Put a large pot of water on to boil.

4 cups	any combination of the following: chopped carrots, seeded and chopped green, red or yellow bell peppers, chopped zucchini, chopped mushrooms	Clean and chop or use all chopped frozen, to save time and energy.
1 pkg	(10 oz) frozen chopped broccoli, cauliflower, or spinach	

Delegate someone to make salad and garlic toast.

12 oz	spaghetti or any shape pasta (preferably whole-wheat)	As soon as water boils, stir in pasta and set timer for 10 minutes.

1 T	olive oil	Heat oil in a large nonstick saucepan over medium-high heat. Add onion, garlic, and chopped vegetables and sauté until just tender. (Also add turkey, if using, and brown.)
1 med	onion, cut into wedges	
1 tsp	chopped garlic (2 cloves)	
20 oz	extra-lean ground turkey breast (opt)	

1 jar	(26 oz) spaghetti sauce, no salt added*	Add to vegetables. Bring to a simmer. Optional step: Purée sauce in a food processor to disguise vegetables for picky eaters.
1 tsp	salt	Meanwhile, make a tossed salad and Whole-Wheat Garlic Cheese Toast.
2 tsp	dried oregano	When timer sounds, drain pasta and serve with sauce.
2 tsp	dried basil	
dash	red pepper flakes (to taste)	*See page 176 for an eye-opener about spaghetti sauce.

Nutrition information for about 1 cup sauce and veggies with turkey over 3/4 cup pasta

Exchanges/Choices: 3 Starch, 1 Vegetable, 2 Lean Meat

Calories	330	Fat	5 g	Fiber	4.5 g	Sodium	375 mg	Total Carbohydrate	48 g
Calories from Fat	14%	Saturated Fat	<1 g	Cholesterol	28 mg	Protein	26 g	Sugars	9 g

Lickety-Split Diabetic Meals

Lickety-Split Tip

When is pasta NOT good for you?

The following are all examples of a "bypass special" wearing the pasta disguise…

1. When the portion is so huge it makes you think, "Wow, I'm really getting my money's worth." (Immediately order a doggie bag and scoop up half for tomorrow. Your blood sugar, blood pressure, and waist will all thank you in the morning!)

2. Restaurant lasagna, including spinach lasagna and vegetarian lasagna (it's the truckload of cheese).

3. Restaurant fettuccine Alfredo (butter, oil, and cream—enough said).

4. When the pasta is tossed with lots of oil (restaurants commonly do this).

4. Most white sauces (unless it's a low-fat recipe like the one below).

Pasta Primavera

You and your guests will never believe that this cream sauce is practically fat-free. Do you want chicken, shrimp, or vegetables only? I use the shrimp or chicken options when entertaining and vegetables only for every day.

Menu

Pasta Primavera

Cranberry Salad (page 267)

Brownie Banana Split (page 321)

Make the Cranberry Salad ahead, if serving.
Put a large pot of water on to boil.

10 cups	fresh or frozen vegetables — any combination of the following: chopped broccoli, chopped carrots, chopped cauliflower, seeded and chopped, green, red, or yellow bell pepper, chopped zucchini, chopped yellow squash, chopped mushrooms, pea pods	Clean and chop, or use all chopped frozen to save time. Set aside.
12 oz	pasta (fettuccine or linguine)	As soon as water boils, stir in pasta and set timer for 10 minutes. When timer sounds, drain and keep warm.
1 T	olive oil	Heat oil in a large nonstick skillet or wok over medium-high heat.
1 lg	onion, cut into wedges	Add garlic and onion. Cook 1 minute.
1 - 2 tsp	minced garlic (2–4 cloves)	
4	(4 oz each) skinless, boneless chicken breasts, cubed (opt)	Add chicken to pan and sauté 5 minutes (or skip this step). When chicken is almost finished cooking, add vegetables and stir. Sauté until vegetables are just tender.

continued on next page...

Lickety-Split Diabetic Meals

Lickety-Split Tip

When is pasta **NOT** good for you? (continued)

More examples of a "bypass special" wearing the pasta disguise …

6. When the marinara sauce is made with so much oil you can't sauté the vegetables.

7. When the "sprinkled" Parmesan cheese exceeds a sprinkle.

8. When the recipe includes sausage and other artery-clogging meats.

9. When the pasta portion itself is too much. The right amount is 1 cup for most people. Since most restaurants serve 3 times this amount, make sure you're taking home a doggie bag for 2 more days of pasta meals!

Pasta Primavera (continued)

1 cup	(1/2 can) chicken broth, 1/3 less sodium	Meanwhile, in a small bowl, mix the 1/2 cans of chicken broth and evaporated skim milk. (Combine the remaining broth and milk in an airtight container, label, and freeze for the next time you make this.)
3/4 cup	(1/2 can) evaporated skim milk	
1/4 cup	cornstarch	Add to broth mixture and stir well.
1/2 cup	white wine	
12 oz	frozen cooked shrimp, peeled and deveined (opt)	Remove tails if necessary. Add to vegetables (or skip this step). Add the broth mixture to the vegetables. Simmer until thick and bubbly.
1 tsp	dried basil	Add seasonings and cheese, followed by the cooked, drained pasta. Toss gently. Serve with Cranberry Salad and remember to save room for Brownie Banana Split.
2 tsp	dried oregano	
10 grinds	fresh ground pepper	
1/4 tsp	salt	
1/2 cup	grated Parmesan cheese	

Nutrition information for about 1 cup sauce & shrimp (no chicken) over 3/4 cup pasta

Exchanges/Choices: 2 1/2 Starch, 2 Vegetable, 2 Lean Meat

Calories	331	Fat	5 g	Fiber	4 g	Sodium	340 mg	Total Carbohydrate	48 g
Calories from Fat	14%	Saturated Fat	1 g	Cholesterol	70 mg	Protein	21 g	Sugars	8 g

Lickety-Split Diabetic Meals

Lickety-Split Tip

True or False

Eating 3 cups of regular pasta (not a whole-grain variety) is like eating 6 slices of white bread.

Depressing, but TRUE.

Most pasta is made from refined wheat and does not contain the fibrous bran or the nutrient-dense germ (similar to the white flour used for white bread). We all know it's better to eat WHOLE-GRAIN bread, so why not have this rule apply to pasta as well? Whole-grain pasta fills you up on a smaller portion size, saving you calories while providing numerous added nutrients like chromium to help fight type 2 diabetes.

And if you're saying, "But I tried whole-grain pasta once and I didn't like it," studies show that people generally accept a new food by the 11th try. So, persistence pays!

Southwest Chili Pasta

Hands-on – 25 min.

Serves 5

A delicious and colorful "south of the border" pasta dish. And it is quick!

Menu
Southwest Chili Pasta
Tossed Salad
Fudgesicle

Put a large pot of water on to boil.

1	green bell pepper	Seed and chop pepper and set aside.
		Open cans called for below. Drain beans, reserving liquid.
5 oz	pasta (preferably whole-wheat), any size or shape	As soon as water boils, stir in pasta and set timer for 10 minutes.
1 T	olive oil	Heat oil in large nonstick saucepan over medium-high heat, then sauté garlic and chopped
2 tsp	minced garlic (4 cloves)	pepper for 1 minute.
1½ tsp	cumin seeds or 1 tsp ground cumin	Add and sauté 10 seconds longer.
1 can	(15 oz) black beans, rinsed and drained	Add to pan and simmer 10 minutes. If chili becomes too thick, thin it slightly with reserved bean liquid.
1 can	(15 oz) kidney beans, rinsed and drained	When timer sounds, drain pasta and serve with chili over top.
1 can	(14½ oz) diced tomatoes, no salt added	Serve with tossed salad.
2–3 tsp	chili powder (or to taste)	

Nutrition information for about 1 cup of beans and sauce over 1/2 cup pasta

Exchanges/Choices: 2 1/2 Starch, 1 Vegetable, 1 Lean Meat

Calories	270	Fat	4 g	Fiber	13 g	Sodium	453 mg
Calories from Fat	13%	Saturated Fat	<1 g	Cholesterol	0 mg	Protein	13 g

Total Carbohydrate 50 g
Sugars 8 g

Lickety-Split Diabetic Meals

Lickety-Split Tip

Great ideas for first-time whole-wheat pasta users

1. Serve with lots of chunky tomato sauce.

2. Toss the pasta and sauce in the kitchen so the children will not speculate why the pasta is brown.

3. Try cooking half white and half whole-wheat until you are used to it.

4. Try the 60% pastas now available from Eden. These products are delicious and you really can't tell they are made with whole wheat! Eden offers fine 100% whole-wheat pasta as well. Look in your health food store or health food section of your grocery store. If it's not there, ask for it.

Herbed Italian Sausage over Pasta

Here's a tasty change from the traditional spaghetti dinner and yet another use for your Homemade Turkey Sausage (page 13).

(page 13)

Menu

Herbed Italian Sausage over Pasta

Crunchy Tossed Salad

Whole-Wheat Garlic Cheese Toast (page 281)

Put a large pot of water on to boil.

1 lg	onion	Slice onion into small wedges and vegetables into thin strips or however you'd like.
1 each	green and yellow bell pepper	
10	baby carrots, chopped (opt)	
1 small	zucchini, cut in half and sliced (opt)	

8 oz	pasta (preferably whole-wheat), any size or shape	As soon as water boils, stir in pasta and set timer for 10 minutes.

1 T	oil (olive or canola)	Add oil to a hot nonstick skillet and sauté vegetables for 2 minutes. Add turkey sausage, breaking up into crumbles. Cook until done.
4	(2 oz each) Homemade Turkey Sausage patties (page 13)	

1 jar	(26 oz) spaghetti sauce, no salt added*	Add to skillet and bring to a simmer.
1 tsp	Italian seasoning	When timer sounds, drain pasta. Pour sauce over pasta to serve.
1 tsp	salt (opt)	Don't forget the tossed salad and Whole-Wheat Garlic Cheese Toast.

*See page 176 for an eye-opener about spaghetti sauce.

Nutrition information for about 1 cup sauce & veggies over about 1 cup pasta (including optional salt)

Exchanges/Choices: 3 Starch, 1 Vegetable, 1 Lean Meat, 1/2 Fat

Calories	325	Fat	7 g	Fiber	5 g	Sodium	525 mg	Total Carbohydrate	50 g
Calories from Fat	19%	Saturated Fat	<1 g	Cholesterol	19 mg	Protein	21 g	Sugars	13 g

Lickety-Split Tip

Selecting a Healthy Spaghetti Sauce

What's better than sliced bread? Ready-made spaghetti sauce in a jar! As the Lickety-Split queen, you can bet I have an entire shelf dedicated to jars of spaghetti sauce, plus one open in the fridge nearly all the time. The challenge is, picking a healthy one. We need to watch out for the salt and sugar that is commonly added because once they're in, there's no taking them out!

Spaghetti sauce is a very competitive market. They want you to **LOVE** the taste of their sauce, and want it to lack **NOTHING** over any of their competitors. Unfortunately, garlic, basil, and oregano are not the only secret weapons they use to win over your taste buds.

Salt and sugar are high on the list. And yes, they do add salt to the tune of about ¼ teaspoon for every ½ cup, and sugar to the tune of about 1 teaspoon per ½ cup. Quite frankly, this is too much for both of these!

So why not buy spaghetti sauce that's no salt and no sugar added? It certainly seems logical to me! Even though there are very few brands that offer no salt added currently on the market (I actually have only found one), I strongly believe it is well worth it. See my tip on page 336 for a comparison chart of popular brands, along with the brand that is forever housed on my shelves.

Parmesan Turkey Cutlets over Angel Hair

When you're serving pasta once a week, it's nice to vary the presentation. My thanks to Connie and Rich Bloom for this neat find. If you don't have angel hair, any pasta will do.

Menu

Parmesan Turkey Cutlets over Angel Hair

Where's the Lettuce? Salad (page 255)

Put a large pot of water on to boil.

1 jar	**(26 oz) spaghetti sauce, no salt added***	Place in a small nonstick saucepan over medium-low heat.
1/4 cup	**grated Parmesan cheese**	Mix together in a small bowl.
1/4 tsp	**Italian seasoning**	
5 grinds	**fresh ground pepper**	
3/4 tsp	**salt (opt)**	
12 oz	**angel hair pasta**	As soon as water boils, stir in angel hair and set timer for 7 minutes.
1 lb	**skinless turkey breast cutlets (6 slices, 1/4" thick each)**	Heat oil in a large nonstick skillet over medium heat. Coat each turkey cutlet with cheese mixture on both sides and place in skillet. Cook 2 minutes on each side, until cooked through. Be careful not to overcook.
1 T	**olive oil**	

When timer sounds, drain pasta.

To serve, place 1 cup pasta on each plate, top with 1 turkey cutlet and 1/2 to 3/4 cup sauce over top.

Serve with Where's the Lettuce? Salad.

*See page 176 for an eye-opener about spaghetti sauce.

Nutrition information for 1 small turkey cutlet, 1 cup pasta, 1/2 cup sauce (including optional salt)

Exchanges/Choices: 3 1/2 Starch, 3 Lean Meat

Calories	403	Fat	7.5 g	Fiber	4 g	Sodium	405 mg	Total Carbohydrate	54 g
Calories from Fat	17%	Saturated Fat	<1 g	Cholesterol	34 mg	Protein	29 g	Sugars	8 g

Lickety-Split Tip

Is fat an issue in spaghetti sauce?

Sometimes people ask me if they should be worried about the fat in ready-made spaghetti sauce. The answer is no.

Spaghetti sauce varies from 2–6 grams of fat per ½ cup. As long as they use olive oil (which most do), it's actually a good thing. Studies show that the oil actually helps the absorption of the beneficial lycopenes found in tomatoes. So some fat is actually better than zero! As long as it isn't from Parmesan cheese or other saturated fat sources.

White Beans & Penne Pasta

Hands-on – 35 min.

Serves 6

My thanks to neighbors Eric & Anne Tooley for sharing this family favorite. While the topping of oil with rosemary seems fattening, the numbers still come out healthy and the taste is exceptional.

Menu

White Beans and Penne Pasta

Tossed Salad

1 T	olive oil	Sauté 3 or 4 minutes in a large nonstick pan over medium-high heat.
1 lg	onion, cut into wedges	
1 tsp	minced garlic (2 cloves)	

2 cans	(14½ oz each) diced tomatoes, no salt added	Add and simmer 10 minutes. Use this time to put together a tossed salad.
2 cans	(14½ oz each) chicken broth, 1/3 less sodium	
2 cans	(15 oz each) Great Northern beans, rinsed and drained	
1/4 tsp	salt (opt)	

6 oz	penne pasta, dry	Stir in and set timer for 10 minutes. Meanwhile, make tossed salad.

2 T	olive oil	Mix together in small microwave-safe bowl. Warm in microwave on HIGH 30 seconds.
1 tsp	dried rosemary or 1 T fresh	Ladle the servings of pasta in individual bowls and drizzle rosemary oil over each serving. Top with Parmesan cheese, if desired. Don't forget the salad.

Nutrition information for about 1½ cups (including optional salt)

Exchanges/Choices: 3 Starch, 1 Vegetable, 1 Lean Meat, 1 Fat

Calories	340	Fat	8 g	Fiber	10 g	Sodium	695 mg	Total Carbohydrate	55 g
Calories from Fat	21%	Saturated Fat	<1 g	Cholesterol	0 mg	Protein	14 g	Sugars	10 g

Lickety-Split Diabetic Meals

Lickety-Split Tip

What is tamari?

Tamari (sometimes called shoyu) is very similar to reduced-sodium soy sauce, but is lighter in color and flavor. Both tamari and shoyu are popular in natural food recipes because they are made the more natural and traditional way with long fermentation. Soy sauce, on the other hand, is a general term for the dark brown flavoring liquids with a soybean base. Soy sauce is prepared unfermented from hydrolyzed vegetable protein, corn syrup, caramel color, and salt.

I suggest looking for tamari or shoyu for both their "natural product" quality and delightful taste. If you cannot find them, use reduced-sodium soy sauce in their place.

Oriental Noodle Toss with Black Beans

Hands-on – 20 min.

Serves 6

The sesame oil really makes this. Excellent as a main dish or as a side dish to grilled or broiled salmon steak. Serve warm or at room temperature.

Menu

Oriental Noodle Toss with Black Beans

Tossed Salad with Crunchy Vegetables

Raspberry Sorbet

Put a large pot of water on to boil.

1 T	sesame oil	Stir together in a medium-large serving bowl.
2 T	tamari or soy sauce, reduced-sodium	
1/2 tsp	ginger (fresh grated is best)	

8 oz	thin spaghetti or other noodles	As soon as water boils, stir in pasta and set timer for 6 minutes (9 minutes if not using a thin pasta.)

1 can	(15 oz) black beans, rinsed and drained	Add to bowl.
3	green onions, tops and bottoms chopped	

1 pkg	(10 oz) frozen pea pods or snow peas	When timer sounds, add pea pods or snow peas to boiling noodles for 1 minute. Drain. Toss with beans and sauce.

It's mealtime!

Nutrition information for about 1 cup

Exchanges/Choices: 2 1/2 Starch, 1 Lean Meat

Calories	253	Fat	3.5 g	Fiber	5.5 g	Sodium	360 mg	Total Carbohydrate	41 g
Calories from Fat	12%	Saturated Fat	0 g	Cholesterol	0 mg	Protein	10 g	Sugars	4 g

Lickety-Split Diabetic Meals

Lickety-Split Tip

What's it like being married to a nutritionist?

"Most awesome."

—My husband, Scott Foco

Maintaining a 20-pound weight loss since 3 months after we met.

Pizza

What's America's favorite food? Pizza! And what food often gets blamed for raising blood sugars, clogging arteries, and adding body fat? Pizza! But NOT anymore!

At first you would think pizza, made healthy and fast at home, would be a complete oxymoron. But thanks to the convenience of pita bread (which makes great portion- and carb-controlled individual pizza crusts) or ready-made whole-grain crusts, convenient low-sodium sauces, and low-fat cheese, you can make your own healthy pizzas at home. And all in much less time than it takes to get pizza delivered!

The following recipes use ready-made sauces, lean meat (if any), low-fat cheese, and ample vegetable toppings, which make the pizzas nutritionally smart. So stock up on your supplies. They're all on the grocery list in the back of this book.

You will notice that some of the recipes instruct you to sauté the vegetable toppings first before placing on the pizza. Other recipes instruct you to place the toppings on raw (leaving them a little "more crunchy" when finished). It will not take long before you decide if more or less crunchy is your family's favorite. Simply add the sauté step if your preference is less crunchy.

Lickety-Split Diabetic Meals

Lickety-Split Tip

Pita: The perfect ready-made pizza crust

If you haven't used pita bread for pizzas yet, you haven't lived! Pitas allow everyone to make individual "custom" pizzas with the convenient ready-made "crusts." (Forget about the "pocket" and just lay them flat.) Be sure to look through all the recipes in this chapter, because you can adapt any of them to make a pita pizza in seconds.

You may be pleasantly surprised to learn that opting for the pita bread over the ready-made pizza crust saves 250 mg of sodium per serving, and the built-in portion control of a single serving helps curb carbohydrates and calories.

P.S. Buy several packages of pitas for the freezer so you'll always have them on hand.

P.P.S. Be sure to involve the kids! They will love making their own pizzas!

Pita Pizza

Hands-on – 15 min. Oven – 10–12 min. **Serves 2**

A quick and easy meal that both kids and adults will love. Also works great using whole wheat tortillas or English muffin halves for the crust. When you have more time, let the kids assemble their own pizzas.

Menu

Pita Pizza
Salad or Raw Vegetables
Sliced Fruit

Turn oven on to broil. Position oven rack 6" from heating element. Leave the oven door ajar.

2	whole-wheat pitas	Lay flat on a baking sheet.
6 T	spaghetti sauce, no salt added*	Spread 1/2 of sauce onto each pita.
1/4 tsp	dried oregano	Sprinkle 1/2 on top of each pita.
1/4 tsp	dried basil	
1/2 oz	98% fat-free ham	Dice and sprinkle 1/2 on top of each pita.
1/4	green bell pepper, seeded and sliced	Layer 1/2 onto each pita as desired.
1/4 small	onion, sliced	
3	fresh mushrooms, sliced	
1/2 cup	reduced-fat shredded mozzarella cheese†	Complete pizzas by sprinkling 1/2 onto each pita.
2 T	grated Parmesan cheese	Broil 2 to 4 minutes, until cheese is melted and beginning to brown.
dash	red pepper flakes (as desired)	Serve with tossed salad and fruit for dessert.

*See page 176 for an eye-opener about spaghetti sauce.

†See reduced-fat cheese tip on page viii (Introduction).

Nutrition information for 1 pita pizza

Exchanges/Choices: 2 Starch, 2 Lean Meat, 1/2 Fat

Calories	272	Fat	6.5 g	Fiber	7 g	Sodium	747 mg	Total Carbohydrate	37 g
Calories from Fat	20%	Saturated Fat	2 g	Cholesterol	16 mg	Protein	21 g	Sugars	6 g

Lickety-Split Diabetic Meals

Lickety-Split Tip

Pizza AND cookies?
Are you sure this is a diabetic cookbook?

The only thing better than pizza is pizza and cookies. The secret here lies in portion control and timing. Limit yourself to one serving or two slices of pizza, go outside and play Frisbee, and you can justify heading back to the kitchen for some dessert.

Chocolate No-Bakes (page 301) are fast, and even just one of them (with a glass of milk, perhaps) really hits the spot!

Garden Vegetable Pizza

Hands-on – 15 min. Oven – 10–12 min.   **Serves 4**

Pre-steaming the broccoli florets turns them bright green and keeps them from drying out. If you prefer your onion and peppers soft versus a little crunchy, microwave them along with the broccoli, adding 1 minute.

Menu

Garden Vegetable Pizza

Where's the Lettuce Salad (page 187)

Chocolate No-Bake Cookies (page 301)

Preheat oven to 425°.

4	whole-wheat pitas or 1 ready-made pizza crust	Spread sauce evenly over pitas or crust.
1 cup	(or more) spaghetti sauce, no salt added*	

1½ cups	bite-size broccoli florets	Rinse, drain, and place in a microwave-safe dish. Cover and cook on HIGH 1 minute.

1 small	onion, thinly sliced into rings	Prep vegetables and neatly arrange over pitas or crust.
5	fresh mushrooms, sliced, or 1 can (4 oz) sliced mushrooms, drained	Top with broccoli.
1/2	red bell pepper, seeded and cut into strips	
1/2	green bell pepper, seeded and cut into strips	
1	ripe tomato, thinly sliced	

2 T	grated Parmesan cheese	Sprinkle evenly over pitas or crust in order given.
1 cup	reduced-fat shredded mozzarella cheese†	Bake until cheese is melted, 10 to 12 minutes.
4 dashes	red pepper flakes (to taste)	Meanwhile, make Where's the Lettuce? Salad.
4 sprinkles	Italian seasoning	Serve one pita per person or cut pizza into 8 slices. Serve with salad and Chocolate No-Bake Cookies.

*See page 176 for an eye-opener about spaghetti sauce.

†See reduced-fat cheese tip on page viii (Introduction).

Nutrition information for 1 pita or 2 slices

Exchanges/Choices: 2 Starch, 2 Vegetable, 2 Lean Meat

Calories	294	Fat	6 g	Fiber	10 g	Sodium	643 mg	Total Carbohydrate	45 g
Calories from Fat	18%	Saturated Fat	1.5 g	Cholesterol	10 mg	Protein	21 g	Sugars	9 g

Lickety-Split Diabetic Meals

Lickety-Split Tip

Solution to typical pizza problem #1,
CHEESE and LOTS of it

Making pizza at home means you can select part-skim mozzarella mixed 50–50 with the fat-free variety, for 3 grams of fat per ounce, and use just 4 ounces (1 cup) of cheese for an entire pizza. This makes an incredibly low-fat pizza!

Hot & Spicy Pizza with Sausage

Hands-on – 20 min. Oven – 10–12 min.

Serves 4

Here's another reason for making the Homemade Turkey Sausage (page 13). The sausage offers great flavor and convenience. Note, vegetarians: Even without the sausage, this recipe is very delicious.

Menu

Hot & Spicy Pizza with Sausage

Where's the Lettuce Salad (page 255)

Preheat oven to 425°.
Spray nonstick pan with nonstick spray.

2	(2 oz each) Homemade Turkey Sausage patties (page 13)	Sauté until sausage is done, break up and crumble the patties.
1 small	onion, thinly sliced	
1/2	red pepper, sliced into strips	
1/2	green pepper, sliced into strips	
4	whole-wheat pitas or 1 ready-made pizza crust	Meanwhile, spread sauce evenly over pitas or crust. Spread sausage mixture over sauce.
1 cup	(or more) spaghetti sauce, no salt added*	
8–12	jalapeño or hot pepper rings to taste (opt)	Place evenly over top.
4 dashes	red pepper flakes (or to taste)	Sprinkle over pitas or crust.
1 T	grated Parmesan cheese	Bake until cheese is melted, 10 to 12 minutes.
1 cup	reduced-fat shredded mozzarella cheese†	Meanwhile, make Where's the Lettuce? Salad. Serve one pita per person or cut pizza into 8 slices.

*See page 176 for an eye-opener about spaghetti sauce.

†See reduced-fat cheese tip on page viii (Introduction).

Nutrition information for 1 pita or 2 slices (without hot pepper rings)

Exchanges/Choices: 2 Starch, 1 Vegetable, 3 Lean Meat

Calories	304	Fat	6 g	Fiber	8 g	Sodium	685 mg	Total Carbohydrate	40 g
Calories from Fat	18%	Saturated Fat	1.5 g	Cholesterol	23 mg	Protein	26 g	Sugars	9 g

Lickety-Split Tip

What is chutney?

Chutney is the relish that traditionally accompanies Indian food, and is made of chopped fruits and spices like ginger, allspice, and cinnamon, or garlic, vinegar, and hot pepper. Yes, it does contain sugar, but when used sparingly as a thin spread across the crust, the flavor is unbelievable and the carbs can be accounted for. Look for it in the specialty section of your grocery store. Trust me, it's a delicious spicy-sweet dynamo.

Chicken Chutney Pizza

Hands-on – 20 min. Oven – 10–12 min.   **Serves 4**

*My husband ordered this in a restaurant once. I said, "What? Are you crazy?"
And yes, crazy we both are now for Chutney Pizza! This stuff is really great!*

Menu

Chicken Chutney Pizza
Tossed Salad

Preheat oven to 425°.

1	(4 oz) chicken breast, cut into small chunks (opt)	Coat a medium nonstick skillet with cooking spray. Sauté together over medium-high heat until chicken is no longer pink.
1 small	onion, sliced into rings	
1/2	red bell pepper, seeded and cut	
1/2	green bell pepper, seeded and cut	
4	whole-wheat pitas or 1 ready-made pizza crust	Meanwhile, spread chutney evenly over pitas or crust. When chicken is done, spread chicken mixture over chutney.
1/3 cup	mango, pineapple or peach chutney	
1 can	(8 oz) pineapple tidbits, in its own juice, drained	Place on pitas or crust.
1 cup	reduced-fat shredded mozzarella cheese[†]	Sprinkle over pitas or crust. Bake until cheese is melted 10 to 12 minutes. Meanwhile, make tossed salad. Serve one pita per person or cut pizza into 8 slices.

[†]See reduced-fat cheese tip on page viii (Introduction).

Nutrition information for 1 pita or 2 slices

Exchanges/Choices: 2 Starch, 1/2 Fruit, 1 Vegetable, 2 Lean Meat

Calories	300	Fat	4 g	Fiber	7 g	Sodium	660 mg	Total Carbohydrate	48 g
Calories from Fat	10%	Saturated Fat	1 g	Cholesterol	24 mg	Protein	23 g	Sugars	10 g

Lickety-Split Tip

Solution to typical pizza problem #2, Fatty toppings

I probably don't have to tell you how bad pizza toppings like pepperoni (a.k.a. pig fat puddles) are for you. Saturated fat, sodium, preservatives . . .YUK!!! You'll notice that I've included a meat topping that will surprise you: sautéed chicken breast strips. I have to admit, it sounded weird at first, but give it a try! In the meantime, for the true hard-core pizza traditionalists, try this:

1. Opt for just 1 meat topping.

2. Choose leaner meat toppings like ham or Canadian bacon.

3. Select as many vegetable toppings as possible.

Other pizza ordering tips ...

4. Ask for regular or thin crusts (more "dry") instead of deep dish, which is often more starchy and greasy ... notice the shine on your fingers?

5. Refrain from extra cheese (you can do it!) and request "half the cheese you usually put on, please."

Southwest Chicken Pizza

Hands-on – 25 min. Oven – 5–10 min.

Serves 4

Since we like to have pizza once a week, this gives us some nice variety. Enjoy!

Menu

Southwest Chicken Pizza
Tossed Salad
Fresh Orange Sections

Preheat oven to 425°. Spray 2 cookie sheets with nonstick spray.

8	**6" corn tortillas**	Bake 8 minutes until slightly crisp.
2	**(4 oz each) skinless, boneless chicken breasts, diced**	Meanwhile, coat a medium nonstick skillet with cooking spray. Sauté together over medium-high heat until chicken is no longer pink.
1 small	**zucchini, sliced lengthwise, then crosswise 1/4" thick**	
1 small	**onion, thinly sliced**	
4-5 drops	**Tabasco**	
2 tsp	**Zippy Zonya Mexi Mix‡**	
1/2 cup	**thick salsa***	Meanwhile, spread 1 T salsa evenly over each corn tortilla.
		Spread cooked chicken mixture over salsa.
1 cup	**reduced-fat shredded cheddar cheese†**	Sprinkle over tortillas in order given.
5	**black olives, sliced**	Bake until cheese is melted, 5–10 minutes.
		Meanwhile, prepare tossed salad and orange sections.
1/3 cup	**fat-free sour cream**	Serve 2 tortilla pizzas per person with one rounded tsp of sour cream on each.

*If your salsa is thin, use a slotted spoon to lift out the thick parts.

†See reduced-fat cheese tip on page viii (Introduction).

‡See recipe on page 40.

Nutrition information for 2 tortilla pizzas with sour cream
Exchanges/Choices: 2 Starch, 1 Vegetable, 3 Lean Meat

Calories	304	Fat	6 g	Fiber	4 g	Sodium	520 mg	Total Carbohydrate	35 g
Calories from Fat	17%	Saturated Fat	2.4 g	Cholesterol	35 mg	Protein	27 g	Sugars	5 g

Lickety-Split Diabetic Meals

Lickety-Split Tip

Solution to typical pizza problem #3: Pizza is usually the only food choice served at the meal

I know what you're thinking. Pizza contains all of the necessary food groups, right? Yes, but **NOT** in the right proportions to provide enough fiber and cancer-fighting nutrients to balance out all of the cheese fat. I remind you in each recipe that a serving of pizza is two slices (three or four slices for very active people). In addition to this, you should serve it with salad or vegetables and fruit. With this strategy, you can include pizza in a healthy diet every single week! TGIF!

Polynesian Pizza

This pizza features the unexpected, BBQ sauce! Now, I know what you're thinking, but be brave. Try it!

Menu

Polynesian Pizza

Crunchy Apple Salad (page 261)

Preheat oven to 425°.

4	whole-wheat pitas or 1 ready-made pizza crust	Spread sauce evenly over pitas or crust.
1/3 cup	BBQ sauce	
1 small	onion, thinly sliced into rings	Layer on pitas or crust. Reserve pineapple juice for another use.
1/2	red bell pepper, seeded and cut into strips	
1/2	green bell pepper, seeded and cut into strips	
1 can	(8 oz) pineapple tidbits, in its own juice, well drained	
1 cup	shredded reduced-fat mozzarella cheese†	Sprinkle evenly over pitas or crust. Bake until cheese is melted, 10 to 12 minutes. Meanwhile, make Crunchy Apple Salad. Serve one pita per person or cut pizza into 8 slices.

†See reduced-fat cheese tip on page xi (introduction).

Nutrition information for 1 pita or 2 slices

Exchanges/Choices: 2 Starch, 1/2 Carbohydrate, 1 Lean Meat

Calories	250	Fat	4 g	Fiber	7 g	Sodium	750 mg	Total Carbohydrate	42 g
Calories from Fat	14%	Saturated Fat	1 g	Cholesterol	8 mg	Protein	16 g	Sugars	12 g

Lickety-Split Diabetic Meals

Lickety-Split Tip

Is seafood high in cholesterol or not?

Contrary to what you may have heard, shrimp, scallops, lobster, and crab (as long as they are not fried or sautéed in lots of fat) can definitely be part of a healthy diet. Here's what you need to know about seafood:

1. Seafood is naturally very low in total fat, including saturated fat.

2. Ounce for ounce, seafood has about the same amount of cholesterol as chicken.

3. Seafood contains the beneficial omega-3 fatty acids (see pages 116 and 118 for more information).

4. Stick with **MODERATE** portions (3 ounces or 7 medium shrimp) and avoid those "all you can eat" buffets.

5. Dip lobster in lemon, not butter.

6. Avoid fried shrimp or broiled scampi or scallops swimming in butter!

7. Ask for "dry broiled" or steamed seafood.

8. Of course, include lots of vegetables with your meal.

Shrimp Pizza

Hands-on – 25 min. Oven – 8–10 min. **Serves 4**

Yet another delicious way to enjoy pizza at home. For a great appetizer idea, use mini pitas (2" round) to build tasty single-serving appetizers, with one shrimp on each. Select your brand of cocktail sauce carefully, as brands may vary in sodium content by as much as four times the amount.

Menu

Shrimp Pizza

Sunshine Carrot-Raisin Salad (page 259)

Preheat oven to 425°.

4	English muffins	Spread sauce evenly over muffin halves.
4 T	seafood cocktail sauce	
1/2	green bell pepper, seeded and cut into strips	Arrange evenly over sauce.
5	fresh mushrooms, sliced	Sprinkle evenly over vegetables.
1 cup	reduced-fat shredded mozzarella cheese[†]	Arrange shrimp over cheese. (If using frozen cooked shrimp, run warm water over them to quick-thaw, then drain. Remove tails, if necessary.)
4 oz	(about 18 medium) cooked shrimp (frozen works well)	Bake 8 to 10 minutes.

Meanwhile, make Sunshine Carrot-Raisin Salad.

Serve each person 2 English muffin halves.

[†]See reduced-fat cheese tip on page viii (Introduction).

Nutrition information for 2 English muffin halves

Exchanges/Choices: 2 Starch, 2 Lean Meat

Calories	250	Fat	4 g	Fiber	2 g	Sodium	748 mg	Total Carbohydrate	32 g
Calories from Fat	14%	Saturated Fat	1.3 g	Cholesterol	50 mg	Protein	20 g	Sugars	5 g

Lickety-Split Tip

Great ideas from people like you!

As a 25-year veteran of the Michigan State Police, who always passes the annual physical fitness test at the highest (gold) level, how do you do it?

"I receive added motivation from reading books like *Personal Best* by George Sheehan. He refers to the Latin term 'Arête, which is 'functioning as one should.' His analogy for being fit is 'being a good animal.' My training run is an exercise for my body, but even more, an exercise for my mind. I find it an unequalled haven for concentration, creativity, and problem solving."

—My brother, Clif Edwards

25-year veteran of the Michigan State Police, never lost a race that really counts (chasing criminals).

Stir-Fry

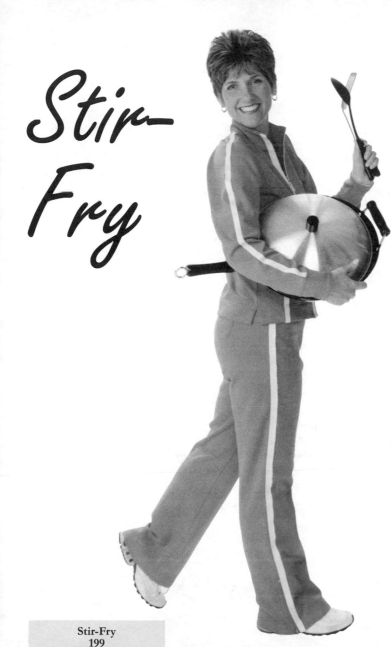

I highly recommend woking once a week.

Not to be confused with walking, of course, which should be done much more often!

There are 3 complaints I hear quite often from clients:

• "4 ounces of meat looks **SO** tiny on my plate!"

• "Vegetables are boring without butter and salt."

• "If you want me to eat rice, I want a nice sauce to go over it."

Well, there's an easy way to end all 3 complaints in a hurry, and that's with a stir-fry!

But doesn't that sound like a lot of work? Don't you need special equipment? How do you make a nice flavorful sauce? Aren't commercially prepared sauces high in sodium? Can't you walk to China in the time it takes to chop all those vegetables?

As you're about to find out, stir-frying is a fast and simple way to get a delicious, vegetable-packed meal on the table. You'll love how just a small amount of beef, chicken or pork (or no meat at all!) can flavor the entire dish. (Even meat lovers are fooled by the small meat portions!)

You can use your largest nonstick frying pan or pick up a nonstick wok. You can vary the vegetables you use according to what's in season and what your family likes. You can use frozen vegetables to eliminate time-consuming chopping. And yes, you can shop for commercially made sauces that don't break the sodium rules (see page 338).

Perhaps the best part is, you can select a different type of stir-fry each week, so "Saturday night stir-fry nights" are never boring. Happy woking!

Lickety-Split Diabetic Meals

Lickety-Split Tip

Make healthy eating a habit

The goal is to achieve a healthy eating style that's natural to you, or second nature. Whether you are dining out, at a party, buying groceries, or just snacking, it should be a natural habit for you to choose healthy foods and appropriate portions. When this becomes a habit, it works as an invisible force in keeping the weight off.

The Easiest Stir-Fry Ever!

Looking for a "Stir-Fry for Dummies"? Here you go! Absolutely no chopping and no sauce making.
Make it with or without chicken.

3/4 cup	whole-grain instant brown rice, dry	Place rice and water in a medium nonstick saucepan. Cover, bring to a boil, and reduce heat to medium-low. Set timer for 5 minutes. When timer sounds, remove from heat and allow to sit, covered.
1¹/₃ cups	water	
1 small	onion	Meanwhile, cut onion into wedges and chicken into strips.
3	(4 oz each) skinless, boneless chicken breasts (opt)*	
1 T	oil (canola or sesame)	Heat in a nonstick wok over medium-high heat. Add onion and chicken. Stir-fry until chicken is browned.
2 bags	(16 oz each) frozen mixed stir-fry vegetables	Add to wok (no need to thaw). Cook 11 to 13 minutes to desired tenderness. (It's ready when the water from the vegetables evaporates.)
1 jar	(10 oz) sweet and sour sauce	Stir in. Let cook 2 more minutes, then serve over brown rice.
1/2 cup	slivered almonds or chopped walnuts or cashews	Save room for dessert.

*As another option, 12 oz extra-firm tofu cut into strips works great instead of chicken.

Nutrition information for scant 1 cup stir-fry (with chicken) over 1/2 cup rice
Exchanges/Choices: 2 Starch, 1/2 Carbohydrate, 1 Vegetable, 2 Lean Meat, 1/2 Fat

Calories	347	Fat	9 g	Fiber	8 g	Sodium	338 mg	Total Carbohydrate	44 g
Calories from Fat	23%	Saturated Fat	<1 g	Cholesterol	33 mg	Protein	20 g	Sugars	15 g

Lickety-Split Diabetic Meals

Lickety-Split Tip

Isn't 800 mg of sodium too much?

For a cup of soup, or a half cup of Rice-a-Roni, yes.

For a complete entree, no. Keep in mind these sodium facts:

• 2,000 to 3,000 mg are allowed each day.

• While 800 mg sounds like a lot, as an entire entree it fits into your day quite easily.

• Even two slices of bread contain 400 mg of sodium!

Sweet & Sour Stir-Fry

Hands-on – 40 min.   **Serves 4**

Chicken, pork tenderloin, or tofu—it's up to you! The pineapple and nuts really make this dish.

Menu

Sweet & Sour Stir-Fry

Brown Rice

1–2 Fig Newtons or Fortune Cookies

1/2 cup	whole-grain instant brown rice, dry	Combine in a microwave-safe dish.
1 cup	water	Cover and cook on HIGH 7 minutes, until tender.
8 oz	pork tenderloin or 2 skinless, boneless chicken breasts or 12 oz tofu (or try 1/2 meat, 1/2 tofu)	Meanwhile, trim meat. Slice into strips or cube tofu. Set aside.
1	onion	On a clean cutting board, cut vegetables into small pieces, keeping piles separate.
1 bunch	broccoli	
2 cans	(8 oz each) pineapple tidbits, in its own juice, drained	Drain juice into a 2-cup measuring cup. Add water to equal 3/4 cup of liquid.
1 T	cornstarch	Stir into pineapple juice. Set mix aside.
2 T	soy sauce, reduced-sodium	
1 T	oil (canola or sesame)	Heat a large nonstick skillet or wok over medium-high heat. Add oil, garlic, and ginger, then add meat or tofu and onion. Stir-fry 4 minutes until meat is cooked through.
1 tsp	minced garlic (2 cloves)	
1 tsp	ginger (fresh grated tastes best)	Stir pineapple juice mix and add to wok, stirring to mix.
3 T	slivered almonds or chopped almonds or cashews	Add the pineapple, broccoli, and nuts.
		Cover and let simmer over medium-low heat 3 to 4 minutes.
		Serve immediately over rice, while broccoli is still bright green.

Nutrition information for 1 cup stir-fry (using pork) over 1/2 cup rice

Exchanges/Choices: 2 Starch, 1 Fruit, 1 Vegetable, 2 Lean Meat, 1 Fat

Calories	365	Fat	11 g	Fiber	7 g	Sodium	383 mg	Total Carbohydrate	51 g
Calories from Fat	27%	Saturated Fat	1.5 g	Cholesterol	38 mg	Protein	21 g	Sugars	19 g

Lickety-Split Diabetic Meals

Lickety-Split Tip

Create a support system

Remember the "buddy" system in school? Well, creating a support system to help you reach and maintain healthy habits works the same way. This can be sharing weekly fitness goals with a spouse, friend, counselor, personal trainer, or coach. Being accountable to someone pays off with big rewards. It's also excellent to have an exercise buddy. Even simple encouragers like people at work who cover for you while you walk are important contributors to your success.

Easy Pepper Steak Stir-Fry

Hands-on — 30 min.   **Serves 4**

A great way to pacify hard-core meat eaters with a small 3-oz serving of steak.

Menu

Easy Pepper Steak Stir-Fry

Brown Rice

Raspberry Sorbet

1/2 cup	whole-grain instant brown rice, dry	Combine in a microwave-safe dish. Cover and cook on HIGH 10 minutes or until tender. (Steam squash separately, if you prefer.)
1 cup	water	
1 small	zucchini, sliced into 1/2" rounds	
1 small	yellow crooked neck squash, sliced into 1/2" rounds	

1 lb	top round steak, well trimmed of fat	Slice "across the grain" into very thin strips. Set aside.

1 can	(14½ oz) beef broth, 1/3 less sodium	Mix together in medium bowl. Set aside.
3 T	cornstarch	
1 T	soy sauce, reduced-sodium	

1 T	oil (sesame)	After slicing onion and peppers, heat oil in a large nonstick frying pan or wok over medium-high heat. Add vegetables and stir-fry 2 minutes. Add beef and cook 2 minutes or until done.
1 tsp	minced garlic (2 cloves)	Stir the broth and add to wok. Stir until thick and bubbly.
1	onion, cut into wedges	Serve over rice. Clean your palate with a scoop of rasberry sorbet.
1	red bell pepper, seeded and cut into strips	
1	green bell pepper, seeded and cut into strips	
1	yellow bell pepper, seeded and cut into strips	

Nutrition information for 1¼ cups stir-fry over 1/2 cup rice and 1 cup zucchini

Exchanges/Choices: 2 Starch, 2 Vegetable, 2 Lean Meat

Calories	390	Fat	9 g	Fiber	5 g	Sodium	437 mg	Total Carbohydrate	40 g
Calories from Fat	21%	Saturated Fat	2.3 g	Cholesterol	77 mg	Protein	37 g	Sugars	9 g

Lickety-Split Diabetic Meals

Lickety-Split Tip

Dining out tips for a Chinese restaurant

1. Order the plain steamed rice versus the fried rice, and eat only half. You will save about 13 grams of fat, 30 grams of carbohydrates, and 250 calories!

2. Order a dish that's full of vegetables.

3. For a 15-gram fat savings, skip the egg roll.

4. Eat just half the order and save the rest for tomorrow.

5. Say, "Steam the chicken and vegetables, please, and add no sesame oil at the end."

6. Be brave and try a tofu dish. The Chinese know how to do tofu!

7. Ask that your meal be made without MSG.

Saucy Almond Chicken Stir-Fry

You'll love all the extra sauce, which thoroughly smothers the rice.
The crunch of the almonds and water chestnuts makes for a delightful contrast.

Menu

Saucy Almond Chicken Stir-Fry over Brown Rice

Sliced Apples, Kiwi, and Oranges

3/4 cup	whole-grain instant brown rice, dry	Combine in a microwave-safe dish. Cover and cook on HIGH 9 to 10 minutes or until tender.
1¹/₃ cups	water	

1 can	(14½ oz) chicken broth, 1/3 less sodium	Stir together in a medium bowl. Set aside.
1 T	sugar	
2 T	vinegar (cider)	
1/4 cup	cornstarch	
1/4 cup	soy sauce, reduced-sodium	

1 T	sesame oil	Heat oil and garlic in a large nonstick skillet or wok over medium-high heat. Add chicken and almonds. Cook until chicken is cooked through and almonds are golden brown, about 5 minutes.
1 tsp	minced garlic (2 cloves)	
1/2 cup	slivered almonds	
4	(4 oz each) skinless, boneless chicken breasts, cut into 1/2" pieces	

1	red bell pepper, cut into 3/4" pieces	Meanwhile, cut pepper into 3/4" pieces and open containers. Add to stir-fry when chicken is done. Cook 3 to 4 minutes.
2	boxes (10 oz each) frozen pea pods or whole green beans	Stir the broth mixture and pour in. Cook and stir until thick and bubbly.
1 can	(8 oz) sliced water chestnuts, drained	Serve over rice with fruit on the side.

Nutrition information for 1 cup stir-fry over 1/2 cup rice

Exchanges/Choices: 2 Starch, 2 Vegetable, 2 Lean Meat, 1 Fat

Calories	345	Fat	10 g	Fiber	6 g	Sodium	604 mg	Total Carbohydrate	43 g
Calories from Fat	24%	Saturated Fat	1 g	Cholesterol	44 mg	Protein	26 g	Sugars	6 g

Lickety-Split Diabetic Meals

Saucy Almond Chicken Stir-Fry

Lickety-Split Tip

Master your emotional well-being

Learn to identify stress eating, boredom eating, or emotional eating and replace this with a more healthful coping response. Find out what constitutes your "plunge into oblivion" that is something other than food or drink. Learn to listen and respond correctly to your internal appestat, which tells you when you are hungry and when you are satisfied. It's amazing how many times you don't really need food; you just need the "escape into oblivion."

"Unfried" Rice Dinner

Hands-on – 30 min.   **Serves 4**

Although initially you may want to serve this as a side dish, you will soon discover that it is a satisfying one-dish meal. Perfect for a light supper.

Menu
"Unfried" Rice
Orange & Kiwi Slices

Note: If you don't have leftover cooked rice on hand, put 3/4 cup Uncle Ben's whole-grain instant brown rice in a microwave-safe dish with $1^{1}/_{3}$ cups water. Cover and microwave 7 minutes on **HIGH** while you prep vegetables.

1 cup	shredded or finely chopped carrots (about 15 baby carrots)	Prep vegetables. For speed, use food processor to coarsely shred or finely chop carrots.
3	green onions, tops and bottoms, chopped	
1/2	green bell pepper, seeded and chopped	
1 can	(7 oz) sliced mushrooms, drained	

Great use for leftover cooked rice.

2 tsp	sesame oil	Heat in a nonstick skillet over medium-high. Add above vegetables, and stir-fry 1 to 2 minutes.
1/2 tsp	ginger (fresh grated tastes best)	
1/2 tsp	minced garlic (1 clove)	

3 cups	cooked whole-grain brown rice	Stir in and cook 5 minutes.
1 cup	frozen peas	
3 T	soy sauce, reduced-sodium	

2	eggs	In a small cup, beat eggs with a fork. Push rice mixture to side of skillet and add eggs and pepper to open side. Allow eggs to set thoroughly. Cut the cooked eggs into rectangular bites.
5 grinds	fresh ground pepper	

Gently combine eggs with rice and serve with orange and kiwi slices.

Nutrition information for 1¼ cups

Exchanges/Choices: 2 Starch, 1 Vegetable, 1 Fat

Calories	245	Fat	6 g	Fiber	5 g	Sodium	633 mg	Total Carbohydrate	38 g
Calories from Fat	21%	Saturated Fat	1 g	Cholesterol	106 mg	Protein	10 g	Sugars	5 g

Lickety-Split Diabetic Meals

Lickety-Split Tip

"Every morning I weigh myself. I have a 4-pound window in which I vary. The day I go one pound over that window, a switch goes on in my brain that says, 'Cut back on what you're eating, and put in a longer run.'"

—My mom, Grace Owens, maintaining 123 lb for 42 years.

Soups

No doubt about it, winter or summer, rain or shine, soup satisfies. The 30 or so minutes required to make a steamy pot of soup can yield high rewards. Just take a look at all the benefits of making soup at home:

• A tasty way to eat lots of healthy vegetables and beans.

• You control the sodium and fat content.

• Weight-loss aid (soup before dinner can suppress your appetite).

• A pot can be stored in the refrigerator and single servings reheated all week.

• Individual servings can be frozen for another day.

So, if you think you don't have time to make soup from scratch, take a peek through this chapter. The time spent on a Saturday or Sunday afternoon will be well worth it!

Lickety-Split Diabetic Meals

Lickety-Split Tip

Weight-loss tip: Eat negative-calorie foods

Think "cooked and raw vegetables" every day. There's no science to this recommendation, it's just a reminder to eat 2 healthy doses of vegetables every day. When it comes to losing weight, you will want to have lots of these "negative-calorie foods" (foods that require more calories to digest than they yield) at each meal. Each serving of Miracle Soup will take care of the "cooked" vegetable goal. Remember, almost all vegetables are negative-calorie foods, so enjoy, enjoy, enjoy!

Miracle Soup

Hands-on – 15 min. Simmer – 20 min.   **Serves 16**

Ever heard of a negative-calorie food? That's a food that takes more calories to burn than it yields. Hence, the name "Miracle," because this soup is great for weight loss. Enjoy a bowl with lunch and dinner! A pot lasts several days.

Menu

Miracle Soup

Low-Fat Whole-Wheat Crackers or a Sandwich

Sliced Fruit

6 cups	water	Place in a large soup pot over medium-high heat.
4 cups	low-sodium vegetable juice	

3 lg	onions	Meanwhile, chop vegetables into bite-sized pieces.
1	green bell pepper, seeded	
6	celery stalks	
10	carrots	

2 cans	(14½ oz each) diced tomatoes, no salt added
4 cups	cored and shredded cabbage*
1/2 cup	salsa
1/4 tsp	garlic powder
1/4 tsp	pepper
1/2 tsp	red pepper flakes (opt)
1 tsp	dried basil
1 tsp	salt (opt)
2 tsp	dried oregano
1 envelope	dry onion or vegetable soup mix
5 dashes	Tabasco (or to taste)

Toss vegetables and other ingredients into pot. Simmer until the vegetables are as done as you like, about 20 minutes.

Serve hot off the stove with crackers or a sandwich and fruit.

Miracle Soup keeps in the refrigerator for up to 5 days and also freezes well.

*Use your food processor or buy pre-shredded.

Nutrition information for about 1½ cups (including optional salt)

Exchanges/Choices: 3 Vegetable

Calories	70	Fat	0 g	Fiber	4 g	Sodium	470 mg	Total Carbohydrate	16 g
Calories from Fat	0%	Saturated Fat	0 g	Cholesterol	0 mg	Protein	2 g	Sugars	10 g

Lickety-Split Diabetic Meals

Lickety-Split Tip

Have a cold?

"The main objective of natural remedies is to stimulate a person's inherent ability to heal themselves."

—*My homeopath, Caroline Smoyer*

I keep the following items in my medicine cabinet, in case a cold strikes:

1. Studies have shown that zinc gluconate lozenges (containing 13.3 mg of zinc), taken every 2 hours at the onset of a cold, help decrease the duration from seven days down to four. The brand that the studies used was "Cold-Ease." (Since zinc can interfere with copper absorption, do not exceed six days of use.)

2. The herbal remedy echinacea has also been determined to help boost immune functioning, which in turn reduces the severity of a cold. (Do not take echinacea routinely, as it loses its effectiveness.) Medical experts recommend buying the extract for purity.

3. Taking vitamin C during a cold may also help alleviate the severity and symptoms. I keep 500-mg tablets on hand and take 1 or 2 tablets twice a day, until the cold is gone.

Lentil Spinach Soup

Hands-on – 10 min. Simmer – 50 min. **Serves 6**

If lentils aren't a favorite of yours yet, just give them time, they will be! I love this refreshing, easy-to-make soup any time of the year, including summer. It keeps in the refrigerator for up to 5 days and also freezes well.

Menu

Lentil Spinach Soup

Cornbread (page 283), Crackers, or Popcorn

Tossed Salad

Applesauce

2	onions	Chop into bite-size pieces.
2	carrots	
1 T	olive oil	Sauté with vegetables in a medium soup pot for 2 minutes.
1/2 tsp	minced garlic (1 clove)	
4 cups	water	Add water and lentils to pot. Cover and bring to a boil, then simmer for 45 minutes. (Feel free to make some Cornbread and a salad now!)
1¼ cups	dried lentils (1/2 pound), rinsed and picked over for stones	
1 can	(14½ oz) diced tomatoes, no salt added	
1 pkg	(10 oz) frozen spinach	Meanwhile, take out of freezer to begin thawing. Add to the soup after the 45-minute simmer.
1 T	lemon juice	Add to soup and simmer 5 minutes longer.
1 tsp	grated lemon peel or 2 tsp red wine vinegar (opt)	Serve with Cornbread, crackers, or popcorn, salad, and applesauce.
1 tsp	salt (opt)	

Nutrition information for about 1½ cups (including optional salt)

Exchanges/Choices: 1 1/2 Starch, 2 Vegetable, 1 Lean Meat

Calories	215	Fat	3 g	Fiber	9.5 g	Sodium	508 mg	Total Carbohydrate	35 g
Calories from Fat	11%	Saturated Fat	<1 g	Cholesterol	0 mg	Protein	14 g	Sugars	10 g

Lickety-Split Diabetic Meals

Lickety-Split Tip

Make exercise your middle name

Adopt a set routine that your neighbor can "set a clock to." Aside from losing 15 pounds in a year, exercising four or more hours a week cuts your risk for breast cancer by 65 percent!

Creamy Cauliflower Soup

Hands-on – 15 min. Simmer – 50 min. **Serves 6**

A great way to enjoy cancer-fighting cauliflower, this creamy, low-fat soup is delicious.
(Please note that the marjoram and savory make this soup, so substitutions are not recommended.)

Menu

Creamy Cauliflower Soup

Saltines or French Bread

Tossed Salad

2 cans	(14½ oz each) chicken broth, 1/3 less sodium	Bring to a boil in a medium soup pot.
2	(8 oz each) potatoes	Meanwhile, peel and cut into chunks. Add to pot and simmer 20 minutes.
2	celery stalks	Meanwhile, chop celery and cauliflower. After 20 minutes, add everything to pot and simmer 30 more minutes.
1 head	cauliflower	
1 tsp	dried marjoram	
1 tsp	dried savory	
1/2 tsp	salt (opt)	
1 T	olive oil	Meanwhile, chop onion. Sauté all for 2 minutes, then add to simmering soup.
1 medium	onion	Purée soup in a food processor or blender (in small batches if required).
1/2 tsp	minced garlic (1 clove)	Serve with crackers or French bread and tossed salad.

Nutrition information for about 1½ cups (including optional salt)

Exchanges/Choices: 1 Starch, 2 Vegetable, 1/2 Fat

Calories	150	Fat	2.6 g	Fiber	7 g	Sodium	587 mg	Total Carbohydrate	26 g
Calories from Fat	15%	Saturated Fat	<1 g	Cholesterol	0 mg	Protein	8 g	Sugars	8 g

Lickety-Split Diabetic Meals

Lickety-Split Tip

Fat-reducing trick for ground beef: Rinse that fat away!

According to a study in the *Journal of the American Dietetic Association*, nutrition researchers found that simply rinsing cooked ground beef reduced the fat content by as much as 50 percent! The steps below can help cut the fat in your favorite recipes that call for cooked ground beef. Try this for your chili, spaghetti, pizza topping, and tacos. This technique will allow you to take advantage of lower-priced, higher-fat ground beef and still enjoy the benefits of a leaner product.

1. Brown ground beef in a skillet over medium heat 8 to 10 minutes or until no longer pink. Stir occasionally to break beef into small pieces (about 1/4 inch).

2. Transfer the cooked beef crumbles to a lined mesh strainer or colander and set it on a half-quart (or larger) sturdy bowl to catch the dripping grease. It's best if the bulk of the grease does not go down your sink.

3. Pour hot tap water (the study used water that was 150 degrees) over beef to rinse fat. Drain 5 minutes.

4. Proceed as your recipe directs. If your recipe calls for browning ground beef with onion or garlic, begin that step now. Add seasonings and herbs at this time as well.

I bet you're wondering if this removes any of the important nutrients. The answer is good news again! Rinsing does not substantially reduce the amount of protein, iron, zinc, or vitamin B-12. And what about the taste? Of course fat does add flavor, but as long as the sauce you are using is flavorful and you're adding the onions, garlic, and herbs, this defatted version tastes great. And it's a teeny compromise with a big health bonus.

Remember, for recipes where rinsing is not feasible (as in meatloaf or stuffed peppers), it is best to use extra lean (95%) ground beef or ground turkey.

3-Bean Turkey or Vegetarian Chili

Hands-on – 15 min. Simmer – 15–20 min.

Serves 10

This very fresh and light chili is a wonderful change from the heavy flavor of traditional chili loaded with fat.

Menu

3-Bean Chili

Whole-Wheat Crackers or Cornbread (page 283)

Raw Vegetables

2	onions	Cut vegetables into small wedges.
1	red bell pepper, seeded	
1	green bell pepper, seeded	
4	carrots or 1 cup shredded carrots	

1 T	olive oil	Heat oil in your largest kettle over medium-high heat. Add garlic, chopped vegetables, and turkey. Sauté 5 minutes.
1 tsp	minced garlic (2 cloves)	
20 oz	extra-lean ground turkey breast (opt)	

1 can	(15 oz) kidney beans	While the vegetables are sautéing, open all the beans. Toss in a colander, rinse, drain, and add to sauté.
1 can	(15 oz) garbanzo or pinto beans	
2 cans	(15 oz each) black beans	

Great for football parties!

2 T	cumin seeds or 1 T ground cumin	Add to sauté.
1 T	chili powder	
1 tsp	oregano	
1/4 tsp	red pepper flakes (opt)	
3 shakes	cayenne pepper (opt)	
1/4 cup	jalapeño or hot pepper rings from a jar (opt)	

8 cups	low-sodium vegetable juice	Stir into pot and bring to a simmer for 10 to 20 minutes.
1 can	(14½ oz) diced tomatoes, no salt added	Serve with crackers or Cornbread and raw vegetables.

Nutrition information for about 1½ cups including ground turkey

Exchanges/Choices: 2 Starch, 1 Vegetable, 2 Lean Meat

Calories	290	Fat	3.5 g	Fiber	12 g	Sodium	629 mg	Total Carbohydrate	42 g
Calories from Fat	11%	Saturated Fat	<1 g	Cholesterol	22 mg	Protein	23 g	Sugars	14 g

Lickety-Split Diabetic Meals

Lickety-Split Tip

New tastes take 11 times!

If your child doesn't like a new food the first time you serve it, don't give up. Studies have shown that it takes up to 11 times to get used to a new taste. So get creative and serve it different ways. After the 10th time, your child will have a new favorite. Works on husbands, too!

Secret Weapon:

Try using whole-grain alphabet pasta (available from Eden at *www.EdenFoods.com* instead of rice in this Speedy Minestrone soup. Call it Alphabet Adventure Soup and watch your younger eaters learn to love it!!!

Speedy Minestrone with Rice

Hands-on – 15 min.   **Serves 8**

No idea what to have for dinner? How about this 15-minute soup? It's as close to a homemade soup as a busy person can get. Enjoy!

Menu
Speedy Minestrone with Rice
Popcorn or Crackers
Sliced Fruit or Frozen Yogurt

2 cans	(14½ oz each) chicken broth, 1/3 less sodium	In a large saucepan, bring to a boil over medium-high heat.
1 cup	water	
2 cans	(14½ oz each) diced tomatoes, no salt added	

3/4 cup	Uncle Ben's whole-grain instant brown rice, dry	Stir in remaining ingredients. Return to boil.
1 can	(15½ oz) kidney beans, rinsed and drained	Reduce heat to low, cover, and simmer 5 minutes.
1 pkg	(10 oz) frozen mixed vegetables	Remove from heat and let stand 3 minutes while you set the table.
1/2 tsp	dried oregano	
1/4 tsp	pepper	
3 dashes	Tabasco (or to taste)	

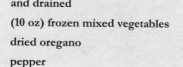

Remember—
You want your evening meal to be the smallest meal of the day!

1/2 cup	grated Parmesan cheese (1 T per serving)	Sprinkle servings with cheese if desired.
		Serve with popcorn or whole-wheat crackers, and fruit or frozen yogurt for dessert.

Nutrition information for about 1½ cups

Exchanges/Choices: 1 1/2 Starch, 1 Vegetable, 1 Lean Meat

Calories	185	Fat	2 g	Fiber	6 g	Sodium	515 mg	Total Carbohydrate	34 g
Calories from Fat	10%	Saturated Fat	<1 g	Cholesterol	4 mg	Protein	10 g	Sugars	8 g

Lickety-Split Diabetic Meals

Lickety-Split Tip

Popcorn Facts—True or False?

Air popping your popcorn is always better than oil popping.

Answer: TRUE, with one exception.

What do you put on top? Do you add melted butter or margarine to go on top? How much do you use? I bet you didn't know that if you're using 2 T or more of margarine to put on top, you'd be better off popping your corn in 1 T of OIL. (Because, yes, oil is better for you than margarine.) 1 T oil in popping goes a lot further than does 1 T margarine dribbled on top.

The solution: Air-pop and use a product like I Can't Believe It's Not Butter spray, lightly on top, or oil-pop 1/4 cup of kernels in 1 T of canola or olive oil. (Serves 2 or more.)

Quick Creamy Tomato Soup

For those of you especially keen on the health benefits of soy, here's a surprisingly delicious way to sneak it in.

Menu

Creamy Tomato Soup

Tossed Salad with Reduced-Fat Cheese

Whole-Wheat Garlic Cheese Toast (page 281) or Popcorn

3 Gingersnap Cookies

1 jar	(26 oz) spaghetti sauce, no salt added*	Process in a food processor or blender until creamy.
6 oz	silken soft tofu	
1/2 tsp	dried oregano, basil, or Italian seasoning	
1/2 tsp	salt	

1 can	(14½ oz) chicken broth, 1/3 less sodium	Add and process again to thin the consistency.

Heat the desired amount in the microwave or over medium heat.

Serve with a salad and Whole-Wheat Garlic Cheese Toast or popcorn. Treat yourself to 3 gingersnap cookies for dessert.

*See page 176 for an eye-opener about spaghetti sauce.

Makes a great sauce over pasta or mashed potatoes.

Nutrition information for about 1 cup

Exchanges/Choices: 1 Starch, 1 Medium-Fat Meat

Calories	150	Fat	5 g	Fiber	4.5 g	Sodium	545 mg	Total Carbohydrate	19 g
Calories from Fat	29%	Saturated Fat	<1 g	Cholesterol	0 mg	Protein	8 g	Sugars	9 g

Lickety-Split Diabetic Meals

Lickety-Split Tip

Trade white pasta for whole-grain pasta

The higher fiber, vitamin, and mineral content in whole-grain pasta will help you feel full on half the portion size. Done twice a week, this habit alone will melt 5 pounds in a year while helping you ward off diabetes and heart disease. Include unique wholesome and high-protein grains like quinoa, buckwheat, spelt, rye, and kamut.

Hearty Bean & Pasta Stew

Hands-on – 20 min. Simmer – 12 min. **Serves 12**

Have you always thought beans required some sort of meat for flavoring? This recipe is a good example of how beans can taste great without meat. You must try this!

Menu
Hearty Bean & Pasta Stew
Tossed Salad
Whole-Grain Bread
Sliced Kiwi and Oranges

2 med	onions	Chop into pieces.
1	green bell pepper, seeded	
2 T	olive oil	Heat in a large nonstick pot. Add onion and pepper. Sauté for 3 minutes on medium.
1 tsp	minced garlic (2 cloves)	
1 can	(14½ oz) diced tomatoes, no salt added	Meanwhile, open cans and vegetable juice jar. Add to pot.
1 can	(14½ oz) chicken broth, 1/3 less sodium	
4 cups	low-sodium vegetable juice	
2 cups	water	
1 can	(15 oz) each pinto beans, garbanzo beans, and kidney beans	Open cans. Rinse and drain in colander. Add to pot.
2 T	low-sodium chicken bouillon	Add and mix thoroughly. Bring pot to a boil.
1 T	dried oregano	
2 tsp	dried basil	
1/4 tsp	red pepper flakes (opt)	
25 grinds	fresh ground pepper	
4 cups	whole-wheat small pasta shells, macaroni, or corkscrews, dry	Add to pot. Set timer for 12 minutes. Meanwhile, make a salad and slice whole-grain bread.
12 T	reduced-fat shredded mozzarella cheese†	Sprinkle 1 T mozzarella and 1 tsp Parmesan cheese on top of individual servings.
12 tsp	grated Parmesan cheese	†See reduced-fat cheese tip on page viii (Introduction).

Nutrition information for 1 cup serving with mozzarella and Parmesan

Exchanges/Choices: 2 1/2 Starch, 2 Vegetable, 1 Lean Meat, 1/2 Fat

Calories	300	Fat	5 g	Fiber	9 g	Sodium	480 mg	Total Carbohydrate	52 g
Calories from Fat	15%	Saturated Fat	1 g	Cholesterol	4 mg	Protein	15 g	Sugars	10 g

Lickety-Split Diabetic Meals

Lickety-Split Tip

"When it was our turn to host our couples' golf league for dinner, some of the guests asked if it was going to be **HEALTHY,** knowing that I work for Zonya. Like **HEALTHY** would somehow compromise the taste and enjoyment! Well, I fixed a triple recipe of Zonya's Crock-Pot Fajitas for 20 people, and then watched all 20 devour the entire meal while raving about taste! Besides having a great meal ready for a hungry group immediately after playing a round of golf, this healthy recipe changed more than one person's notion of 'healthy **AND** delicious' that night."

—Deb Wise, ZHI Marketing and Operations Director, and my friend for over 35 years.

Slow-Cooking

A slow cooker (or crockery cooker or Crock-Pot®) is simply a must for a busy family. Do you experience high-stress, just-home-from-work, what's-for-dinner chaos? Well, coming home to a house filled with a delicious aroma completely takes care of that!

The question is, where is your slow cooker right now? Is it where it can be easily used each week? Or is it way back in some forgotten cupboard with an inch of dust on it?

Get ready to unearth it, because low-fat, easy-to-load recipes are all right here. If you think slow-cooking "all tastes the same" or "only has high-fat recipes," this section will come to the rescue.

Since coming home to a nice stuffed slow cooker makes for a completely stress-free easy dinner, I suggest Monday as your slow-cooker day. You can do the loading the night before (store it in the refrigerator) and simply plug it in on Monday morning for a complete "no cook" day!

It's time to get slow-cookin'. You're going to love coming home to the delicious aroma of dinner!

Lickety-Split Diabetic Meals

Lickety-Split Tip

Secrets to successful slow-cooked meat and vegetables

Some slow-cooker recipes recommend adding frozen meat to the crock, to help vegetables get a head start on cooking. This assures that the meat is tender but not overcooked when the vegetables are done.

Dense vegetables such as carrots, potatoes, and rutabagas take longer to cook than many meats. When combining ingredients in a slow cooker, place root vegetables on the bottom of the pot; then add meats, seasonings, other vegetables, and liquid. This keeps vegetables moist during cooking, and cooks them more evenly.

Turkey Vegetable Stew

Hands-on – 12 min. (a.m.) and 8 min. (p.m.) **Serves 8**

Here's my favorite way to serve stew. Look for turkey tenderloins in the fresh poultry section of your grocery store. Freeze them when you get home. Add them frozen to the slow cooker to prevent the meat from becoming overcooked before the vegetables are done.

Menu

Turkey Vegetable Stew

Crunchy Apple Salad (page 261)

Whole-Wheat Rolls

6 med	(6 oz each) potatoes	7 to 11 hours before serving: Thoroughly wash and scrub, or peel if not organic potatoes. Quarter them and place in slow cooker.
6	carrots	Peel and cut into chunks. Add to potatoes.
2	onions	
2	skinless, boneless, turkey tenderloins, frozen (about 1½ lb total)*	Place in slow cooker while still frozen.
1 cup	each of frozen peas and corn	Place ingredients in slow cooker in order listed. Mix slightly.
1 tsp	dried oregano	Cook on HIGH 7 hours or on LOW 10 to 11 hours.
1 tsp	salt (opt)	Before serving, break tenderloins into bite-sized chunks.
1/2 tsp	hot pepper flakes (opt)	
1/2 jar	(about 13 oz) spaghetti sauce, no salt added†	8 minutes before serving: Whip up a quick Crunchy Apple Salad and serve with rolls.
2 cups	water	

*Skinless chicken breasts can be substituted.

†See page 176 for an eye-opener about spaghetti sauce.

Nutrition information for about 1½ cups (including optional salt)

Exchanges/Choices: 2 Starch, 1 Vegetable, 2 Lean Meat

Calories	275	Fat	2.5 g	Fiber	6 g	Sodium	410 mg	Total Carbohydrate	37 g
Calories from Fat	8%	Saturated Fat	0 g	Cholesterol	35 mg	Protein	27 g	Sugars	11 g

Lickety-Split Diabetic Meals

Lickety-Split Tip

Who has time in the morning to load the slow cooker?

If this is your attitude, try this 1-minute super-easy recipe. If that still seems like too much work, keep in mind that you can load the slow cooker the night before (and simply store in the refrigerator overnight). And remember, a 1-minute investment now means a **GREAT** reward later.

Come on! You can find 1 minute!

Tortellini Stew

Hands-on — 3 min. (a.m.) and 5 min. (p.m.)   **Serves 8**

You can load the crockpot in less than a minute with this recipe! Popular with small kids, although you may want to serve the green beans on the side.

Menu

Tortellini Stew with Green Beans

Whole-Wheat Garlic Cheese Toast (page 281)

Canned Peaches

1 bag	**(16 oz) frozen cheese tortellini***
1 bag	**(16 oz) frozen cut green beans**
1 jar	**(26 oz) spaghetti sauce, no salt added†**
1/2 jar	**(13 oz) water**
1 tsp	**salt (opt)**

4 to 7 hours before serving:

Place in slow cooker in order listed. Mix slightly.

Cook on HIGH 4 hours or on LOW 6 to 7 hours.

10 minutes before serving:

Prepare Whole-Wheat Garlic Cheese Toast.

Serve with sliced peaches.

Kids' Favorite!

*If frozen tortellini isn't available, simply freeze refrigerated tortellini at home.

†See page 176 for an eye-opener about spaghetti sauce.

Nutrition information for 1¼ cup serving (including optional salt)

Exchanges/Choices: 2 1/2 Starch, 1 Vegetable, 1/2 Fat

Calories	244	Fat	6 g	Fiber	5 g	Sodium	533 mg	Total Carbohydrate	39 g
Calories from Fat	21%	Saturated Fat	2 g	Cholesterol	33 mg	Protein	11 g	Sugars	8 g

Lickety-Split Diabetic Meals

Lickety-Split Tip

Slow-cooker buying tips

Size: Slow cookers range in size from 1 to 6 quarts, with the most common being the mid-range. Which size you select is up to you and depends on the size of your family and whether or not you enjoy leftovers.

Removable inside crock: I like this feature because it's easier to clean, prettier to serve, and when you load it the night before, it fits in the refrigerator much more easily.

Side-versus-bottom heating elements: Most slow-cooking cookbooks use an appliance with the side element. In this design, the heat element stays on continuously, while the designs with a bottom element "cycle" on and off. My recipes have been tested with both types.

Buffet Bonus

Slow cookers are handy for buffets. Simply keep the pot on **LOW** and the food will be just as warm for the last guest as it was for the first.

Mexican 5-Bean Soup

Hands-on – 10 min. (a.m.) **Serves 10**

Here's a delicious bean soup. I know what you're thinking—"Can I just drink the beer with the soup, instead?"

Menu

Mexican 5-Bean Soup

Cornbread (make ahead; page 283) or Crackers

Tossed Salad

Raspberry Sorbet

1 can	(15 oz) red kidney beans	5 to 10 hours before serving:
1 can	(15 oz) garbanzo beans	Rinse and drain beans thoroughly in a colander.
1 can	(15 oz) navy beans	Place in slow cooker.
1 can	(15 oz) black beans	
1 lg	onion	Dice and place in slow cooker.
1 can	(4 oz) green chilies, undrained	
1 pkg	(10 oz) frozen cut green beans	Place in slow cooker and stir.
4 tsp	Zippy Zonya Mexi Mix‡	Cook on HIGH 5 to 6 hours or on LOW 9 to 10 hours.
1½ tsp	dried basil	Just before serving:
1/2 tsp	dried oregano	Ladle into serving bowls.
1/4 tsp	Tabasco	
3 cups	water	
2 cans	(14½ oz each) chicken broth, 1/3 less sodium	
1 can	(12 oz) beer, or 12 oz water	
1¼ cups	(2 T per soup bowl) reduced-fat shredded cheddar cheese or mozzarella cheese†	Sprinkle on top of soup. Serve with crackers or Cornbread and tossed salad.

†See reduced-fat cheese tip on page viii (Introduction).

‡See recipe on page 40.

Nutrition information for about 1 cup

Exchanges/Choices: 1 1/2 Starch, 2 Vegetable, 2 Lean Meat

Calories	225	Fat	3 g	Fiber	9 g	Sodium	795 mg	Total Carbohydrate	32 g
Calories from Fat	11%	Saturated Fat	1 g	Cholesterol	6 mg	Protein	16 g	Sugars	4 g

Lickety-Split Diabetic Meals

Lickety-Split Tip

Beat the heat and save electricity!

A slow cooker:

• Does not heat the kitchen like your oven does—a real bonus during summer months.

• Saves energy by using very little electricity, since the wattage is low.

You may also like to know:

• The low-heat setting cooks foods in 8 to 10 hours, while the high-heat setting cooks foods in 5 to 6 hours.

• Exact timing with slow-cooking is not critical. If you are working a little late or delayed in traffic, another hour of extra cooking time won't make a big difference to most recipes that are cooking on **LOW.**

Split Pea Soup

Hands-on – 15 min. (a.m.) and 5 min. (p.m.)   **Serves 10**

Want a good reason to try split pea soup? One serving provides more than half the fiber you need in a day! This soup thickens as it cools, and I love it thick. Tasty, quick, and a good money-saving recipe as well.

Menu

Split Pea Soup

Cornbread (make ahead; page 283) or Crackers

Tossed Salad

Frozen Yogurt

3½ cups	dried split peas	**8 to 11 hours before serving:** Rinse in a colander, pick over for stones and place in slow cooker.
3	celery stalks	Chop and place in slow cooker.
3	carrots	
1 lg	onion	
4 cups	water	Place in slow cooker and mix.
2 cans	(14½ oz each) chicken broth, 1/3 less sodium	Cook on HIGH 8 to 9 hours or on LOW 10 to 11 hours.
1 tsp	poultry seasoning	
20 grinds	fresh ground pepper	
2 oz	lean ham (opt)	**30 minutes before or just before serving:** Cut ham into small cubes. Add in the last 1/2 hour of cooking. Serve with crackers or Cornbread, tossed salad and low-fat frozen yogurt for dessert.

Nutrition information for about 1 cup with ham

Exchanges/Choices: 2 1/2 Starch, 1 Lean Meat

Calories	256	Fat	1 g	Fiber	18 g	Sodium	290 mg	Total Carbohydrate	44 g
Calories from Fat	4%	Saturated Fat	0 g	Cholesterol	3 mg	Protein	19 g	Sugars	7 g

Lickety-Split Diabetic Meals

Lickety-Split Tip

No peeking allowed!

A slow cooker makes foods moist and flavorful. Meat and vegetable juices blend together, creating a delicious combination of flavors.

Resist the temptation to lift the lid to take a quick peek or stir frequently. Slow-cooking depends on the heat that builds up in the crock itself and takes quite a bit of time to reheat. Stirring is not required unless noted in the recipe.

Beef Barley Soup

Did you know barley has even more cholesterol-lowering powers than oat bran? Yes, we should eat more of it. And this soup, made with lean beef, is a great place to start.

Menu

Beef Barley Soup

Crackers

Lite Fruit Cocktail

1½ lb	sirloin steak, well trimmed of fat	**4 to 12 hours before serving:** Cut meat into 1" cubes. Place in slow cooker.

1 cup	thinly sliced carrots	Prep and place in slow cooker.
1 cup	sliced celery	
1 med	onion, chopped	
1	green bell pepper, seeded and chopped	

2 cans	(14½ oz each) beef broth, 1/3 less sodium	Add to slow cooker. Cover and cook on HIGH 4 to 5 hours or on LOW 10 to 12 hours.
1 can	(14½ oz) diced tomatoes, no salt added	**Just before serving:**
1 cup	spaghetti sauce, no salt added*	Skim off any fat.
1/2 cup	quick-cooking or pearl barley, dry	Serve with crackers and fruit cocktail.
1½ tsp	dried basil	
1/2 tsp	salt (opt)	*See page 176 for an eye-opener about spaghetti sauce.
1/4 cup	fresh parsley, chopped	
dash	pepper	

Nutrition information for about 1½ cups (including optional salt)

Exchanges/Choices: 1/2 Starch, 2 Vegetable, 2 Lean Meat, 1/2 Fat

Calories	225	Fat	7 g	Fiber	4 g	Sodium	467 mg	Total Carbohydrate	18 g
Calories from Fat	27%	Saturated Fat	2.3 g	Cholesterol	42 mg	Protein	23 g	Sugars	6 g

Lickety-Split Diabetic Meals

Lickety-Split Tip

Slow cooker tips for dried beans

• They cook very well in the slow cooker.

• Pre-soaking is usually not necessary.

• They cook best on the high setting and will require 4 to 6 hours of cooking.

• This is a great way to save money over buying canned beans.

Gypsy Stew

Hands-on – 20 min. (a.m.) and 8 min. (p.m.)   **Serves 8**

Choose from chicken, pork, or go meatless. The sweet potatoes and Spanish flavors are terrific together.

Menu

Gypsy Stew

Broccoli Salad with Dried Cherries (page 265)

Whole-Wheat French Bread

2 cans	**(15 oz each) garbanzo or navy beans,** rinsed and drained
1 pkg	**(10 oz) frozen spinach**
1 lb	**pork tenderloin or skinless, boneless, chicken breasts** (opt)
2 cans	**(14½ oz each) chicken broth,** 1/3 less sodium
1 cup	**water**
1 can	**(14½ oz) diced tomatoes, no salt added**
1 lg	**(18 oz) sweet potato (peeled and cubed)**
1 lg	**onion, chopped**
1	**red or yellow bell pepper, seeded and chopped**
2 tsp	**paprika**
2 tsp	**ground cumin**
1/4 tsp	**ground cinnamon**
1 tsp	**dried basil**
1/4 tsp	**salt** (opt)
8 grinds	**fresh ground pepper**
8 dashes	**cayenne** (opt)

5 to 11 hours before serving:

Add to slow-cooker.

Cover and cook on LOW 10 to 11 hours or on HIGH 5 to 6 hours until beans are tender.

Just before serving:

For a delicious side dish, consider making Broccoli Salad with Dried Cherries.

Serve with whole-wheat French bread.

Note: Add 1 to 2 tsp sugar to smooth flavors, if desired.

Nutrition information for about 1½ cup serving made with pork (including optional salt)

Exchanges/Choices: 1 1/2 Starch, 1 Vegetable, 2 Lean Meat, 1/2 Fat

Calories	260	Fat	4.5 g	Fiber	8.5 g	Sodium	640 mg	Total Carbohydrate	34 g
Calories from Fat	15%	Saturated Fat	1 g	Cholesterol	37 mg	Protein	21 g	Sugars	8 g

Lickety-Split Diabetic Meals

Lickety-Split Tip

Snacking from a Veggie Tray

It's amazing what you learn while living with friends. My husband and I had this opportunity for 6 weeks when the completion of our new home was taking longer than expected. In our friends' refrigerator, I couldn't help but notice on the upper shelf was this 8" x 4" glass relish plate. It would mysteriously be replenished daily with sliced peppers (green and red), carrots, cucumbers, or whatever was on hand. The plate would join the table during the preparation of every lunch and dinner (and sometimes breakfast, too!). Everyone was invited to munch until the meal was served, as well as throughout the meal. Talk about a super way to increase the family's vegetable consumption. It really worked!

—*Lesson learned from my friend Jay Johnson*

Mother of two girls who adore sliced red and green peppers, practicing what she learned from her mother, Carita Rick.

Super Time-Saving Tip:

Whenever bell peppers and onion are called for, use 1 bag or more of pepper stir-fry, found in the freezer section.

Crock-Pot Fajitas

Hands-on – 20 min. (a.m.) and 10 min. (p.m.)   **Serves 12**

*You want chicken fajitas—use chicken. You want beef fajitas—use beef! Vegetarian?
Got that covered, too. These fajitas are a family favorite. OLÉ!*

Menu
Crock-Pot Fajitas
Raw Vegetables and Dip
Fresh Sliced Cantaloupe

1 lb	beef top round steak, skinless, boneless chicken breast, pork tenderloin, or 24 oz. firm tofu	**4 to 8 hours before serving:** Trim meat well of fat and cut into 6 portions. (Crumble or cube tofu.) Place in slow cooker.
1 lg	onion	Cut vegetables into strips and place in slow cooker.
1	green bell pepper, seeded	
1	red bell pepper, seeded	
1	yellow bell pepper, seeded	
3/4 tsp	salt	Add to slow cooker and mix well.
12	jalapeño or hot pepper rings from a jar	Cook on HIGH 4 to 5 hours or on LOW 7 to 8 hours.
1 can	(15 oz) pinto, kidney, or black beans, drained and rinsed	**Just before serving:**
2 T	lime juice or 2 envelopes True Lime crystallized lime	Break meat into bite-sized chunks.
4-5 T	Zippy Zonya Mexi Mix‡	
12	6" flour tortillas	Warm tortillas in microwave. Use tongs or a slotted spoon to remove contents from slow cooker. Assemble fajitas with toppings of your choice.
3	ripe tomatoes, chopped	Serve 1 fajita per person with raw veggies, dip, and fruit for dessert.
1 cup	shredded lettuce	Note: Expect about 1 cup of liquid left in the crockpot. Makes an excellent soup starter.
3/4 cup	fat-free sour cream (1 T per fajita)	‡See recipe on page 40.

Nutrition information for 1 fajita using 1/2 cup beef mixture, with tomatoes, lettuce, and sour cream

Exchanges/Choices: 1 1/2 Starch, 2 Vegetable, 1 Lean Meat, 1/2 Fat

Calories	235	Fat	4 g	Fiber	4 g	Sodium	440 mg	Total Carbohydrate	32 g
Calories from Fat	15%	Saturated Fat	1 g	Cholesterol	25 mg	Protein	17 g	Sugars	4 g

Lickety-Split Diabetic Meals

Lickety-Split Tip

Gourmet Taste Tip for Cumin Seed

Try "toasting" the cumin seeds to intensify the flavor. Place in a small dry saucepan over medium-high heat until toasty and the seeds begin to pop. Then add to the beans. This will take you less than 2 minutes to do and really boosts the flavor!

Encore! For Mexican Black Beans

Serve heated leftovers over rice or over a baked potato. Also superb as nachos.
Pour hot beans over baked tortilla chips, top with low-fat cheese, and pop in the oven to melt. Mmmm!

Mexican Black Beans

Thick, hearty, and awesome! By minimizing the liquid, we intensify the flavor.
My thanks to Lynne DeMoor, M.S., R.D., for discovering this winner.

Menu

Mexican Black Beans

Cornbread (page 283),
Crackers, or Baked Tostitos

Raw Vegetables & Dip

1 lb	(2½ cups) dried black beans
6 cups	water

4 to 13 hours before serving:

Rinse beans in a colander and pick over for stones.
Put drained beans in slow cooker with water. Cook on HIGH 5 hours,
or LOW 12 to 13 hours.

1/2	green bell pepper, seeded and chopped*
1/2	yellow bell pepper, seeded and chopped*
1/2	red bell pepper, seeded and chopped*
1 lg	onion, chopped*
1 T	olive oil
1 tsp	minced garlic (2 cloves)

1 hour before serving:

Towards end of cooking time, prep vegetables and sauté in medium skillet about 5 minutes. While veggies are sautéing, place a strainer over a bowl. Pour entire slow cooker full of beans into strainer, retaining 1 cup of bean water. Return beans to slow cooker. (Discard remaining bean water or save for another use.)

Add sautéed vegetables to slow cooker.

**Note:
Recipe can be made on top of the stove in 2½ hours. Can also be doubled and freezes well.**

1 T	cumin seeds (or 2 tsp ground cumin)
1 T	dried oregano
1 tsp	salt (opt)
2 tsp	paprika
1/4 tsp	cayenne (opt)
10	jalapeño or hot pepper rings (from a jar), chopped
1 can	(14½ oz) diced tomatoes, no salt added

Add to cooker and mix well. Allow to cook on HIGH 30 minutes to 1 hour longer. Use this time to make Cornbread if you'd like.

Serve with crackers, Baked Tostitos or Cornbread, and crunchy raw veggies on the side.

*See my super time-saving tip on page 240.

Nutrition information for about 1½ cups (including optional salt)

Exchanges/Choices: 2 Starch, 1 Vegetable, 1 Lean Meat

Calories	240	Fat	2.5 g	Fiber	10 g	Sodium	375 mg	Total Carbohydrate	42 g
Calories from Fat	9%	Saturated Fat	<1 g	Cholesterol	0 mg	Protein	13 g	Sugars	5 g

Lickety-Split Diabetic Meals

Lickety-Split Tip

After-Dinner Exercisers—True or False

It is OK to exercise soon after eating dinner.

Answer: TRUE!

You should be able to do mild exercise like walking without discomfort. If not, that "full stomach feeling" is telling you that you have eaten TOO MUCH. The difference lies in finishing your meal NOT when you are "full," but when you are "no longer hungry." This simple habit will do wonders for your evening energy level and for weight control!

Remember that your **EVENING** meal should be your **SMALLEST MEAL** of the day!

Low-Fat Slow-Cooking

When using meat in a slow cooker, stick to the exceptionally lean choices such as skinless chicken and turkey, beef sirloin or round steak, pork tenderloin, and lean ham, AND trim well. Otherwise, all the fat that cooks out of the meat ends up in the surrounding food and then on you!

Beef Stroganoff over Noodles

Hands-on – 15 min. (a.m.) and 22 min. (p.m.)

Serves 10

Delicious down-home creamy taste. Hard to believe this finds a place on a healthy menu!

1 can	(10¾ oz) cream of mushroom soup	**4-1/2 to 10 hours before serving:** Combine in slow cooker.
1 can	(14½ oz) beef broth, 1/3 less sodium	
1 can	(4 oz) sliced mushrooms, drained	
3 T	cornstarch	
3/4 tsp	dried thyme	
1/4 tsp	garlic powder	
1/3 cup	Marsala wine (opt)	
1/2 tsp	salt (opt)	

1 lg	onion, thinly sliced	Add and slightly mix to cover meat in sauce.
2½ lb	lean top round or sirloin steak, well trimmed of fat, cubed	Cover and cook on LOW 9 to 10 hours or on HIGH 4½ to 5 hours.

Place a large pot of water on to boil.

22 minutes before serving:

1½ cups	fat-free sour cream	Stir sour cream into slow-cooker mixture. Beef should easily break apart.

12 oz	egg noodles, preferably whole wheat	Add to boiling water. Set timer for 9 minutes. Meanwhile, see if you can find some raw salad fixings and set table.

12 oz	frozen carrots	When timer goes off, add to bubbling noodles. Set timer for 1 minute.
12 oz	frozen green beans	Drain noodles and vegetables. Serve beef-and-mushroom sauce over top, with a salad on the side

Nutrition information for 1 cup beef and sauce over 1 cup noodles & vegetables (including optional salt and wine)

Exchanges/Choices: 2 1/2 Starch, 1 Vegetable, 4 Lean Meat

Calories	396	Fat	6 g	Fiber	6 g	Sodium	492 mg	Total Carbohydrate	44 g
Calories from Fat	13%	Saturated Fat	2 g	Cholesterol	78 mg	Protein	39 g	Sugars	8 g

Lickety-Split Diabetic Meals

Lickety-Split Tip

Pork, "The Other White Meat"

Chicken. Chicken. Fish.

Chicken. Chicken. Fish.

Many of you may feel you are about to grow feathers and gills. But did you know today's pork averages 31% less fat than it did 10 years ago? We can thank farmers for raising leaner hogs and butchers for trimming leaner cuts. The following cuts of pork are as low in fat content as a skinless chicken breast, or only slightly higher than.

• Pork tenderloin

• Boneless pork sirloin chop or top loin chop

• Boneless pork loin roast or sirloin roast

• Pork loin chop

• Canadian bacon

As always, trim well, and keep the serving size to 3 to 4 ounces (the size of a deck of cards or the palm of your hand).

Cranberry Pork Roast over Noodles

Hands-on – 5 min. (a.m.) and 25 min. (p.m.)

Serves 8

Guests will rave about this unique and tender roast! You'll love it because it's so simple.

Menu
Cranberry Pork Roast
Noodles
Broccoli and Carrots
Tossed Salad

2 lb	pork tenderloin, frozen (one long roast or cut into 8 thick slices)	**8 hours before serving:** Place in slow-cooker.
1 can	(16 oz) jellied cranberry sauce	In a medium bowl, mix together (mashing cranberry sauce). Pour over roast.
1/2 cup	orange juice	Cook on LOW 8 hours, or on HIGH 4 hours.
1 tsp	dry mustard	
1/4 tsp	ground cloves	
1 bag	(8 oz) whole-wheat egg noodles, dry	20 minutes before serving, put a large pot of water on to boil. Add to boiling water, set timer for 10 minutes or according to package directions.
1 head	broccoli (2 or 3 stalks), cut into florets	Place in microwave-safe dish, cover, and cook on HIGH 7 minutes.
1 bag	(1 lb) baby carrots	Drain 2 cups of juice from roast. Skim off any fat (if there is any, pork tenderloin is so lean). Add water if necessary, to make 2 cups. Pour into a small saucepan.
1 T	water	Bring to boil over medium heat.
2 T	cornstarch	In a small cup, mix together and pour into boiling juice while whisking. Cook 1 minute until thick and bubbly.
2 T	water	Drain noodles and serve sauce over the sliced pork and noodles, with vegetables on the side.

Nutrition information for 3 oz pork, 1/2 cup noodles, 2 T gravy, 1 cup broccoli & carrots
Exchanges/Choices: 2 Starch, 1 Carbohydrate, 2 Vegetable, 3 Lean Meat

Calories	406	Fat	7 g	Fiber	8 g	Sodium	150 mg	Total Carbohydrate	56 g
Calories from Fat	16%	Saturated Fat	2 g	Cholesterol	75 mg	Protein	30 g	Sugars	23 g

Lickety-Split Diabetic Meals

Lickety-Split Tip

Is it true that carrots are high in sugar?

The glycemic index is a measurement of how quickly 50 grams of carbohydrate in a food raises a person's blood sugar. No matter what the food is, the portion is always 50 grams worth of carbohydrate. (It's a scientifically "fair" test.) Do you know how many carrots it takes to make a 50-gram carbohydrate sample? One and one-half pounds! A typical serving of carrots is 3 ounces. Therefore, the glycemic index reading should be divided by 8 for an accurate comparison to other foods. In fact, the new terminology to watch for is "the glycemic load," which takes the portion size into consideration.

Popular diet books, including *Enter The Zone, Sugar Busters!,* Suzanne Somers' *Somersizing* and *The South Beach Diet* are to blame for disseminating this misleading information about carrots.

How did this happen? They read the glycemic index reports at face value, and never thought about the implication of, "What's a typically consumed portion?" Although the authors consist of medical doctors, PhD's, and an award-winning actress, they have one thing in common. They have not been trained in dietetics the way registered dietitians are, and we always ask, "What's the portion typically consumed?" (When an author makes this kind of mistake, does it make you wonder about the book's accuracy overall?)

So please erase this false information from your brain stores, and have fun setting your friends straight when they try to tell you that the nutritious carrots on your plate are loaded with sugar!

Chicken Cacciatore

Hands-on – 15 min. (a.m.) and 15 min. (p.m.)   **Serves 12**

Once again, a family favorite that's so easy to make. Feel free to substitute other vegetables like bell pepper strips for the zucchini and yellow crooked neck squash.

Menu

Chicken Cacciatore

Corkscrew Pasta

Tossed Salad

Applesauce Dumplings (page 319) or Hot Fudge Brownie Cake (page 317)

2½ lb	boneless, skinless chicken thighs or boneless, skinless chicken breasts (still frozen is fine)	4 to 10 hours before serving: Place in slow cooker.
4 med	zucchini or yellow crooked neck squash, cut in 1/2 lengthwise and sliced into 1" pieces	Add to slow cooker.
1 med	onion, cut into wedges	
1 jar	(26 oz) spaghetti sauce, no salt added*	Pour over all and stir. Cook on HIGH 4 to 5 hours or on LOW 8 to 10 hours.
1 tsp	salt	

Put a large pot of water on to boil.

12 oz	corkscrew (or any shape) whole-wheat pasta	15 minutes before serving: When water boils, add pasta. Set timer for 10 minutes. Meanwhile, put together a salad and set table. When timer sounds, drain pasta. Serve chicken over pasta with salad on the side.

Note: Stick with light portions and, after an evening walk, enjoy a bit of homemade dessert.

*See page 176 for an eye-opener about spaghetti sauce.

Nutrition information for 1 cup of the recipe using chicken thighs over 1/2 cup pasta

Exchanges/Choices: 1 1/2 Starch, 1 Vegetable, 3 Lean Meat

Calories	260	Fat	5.5 g	Fiber	5 g	Sodium	285 mg	Total Carbohydrate	30 g
Calories from Fat	19%	Saturated Fat	1 g	Cholesterol	78 mg	Protein	24 g	Sugars	5 g

Lickety-Split Diabetic Meals

Lickety-Split Tip

6 Keys to Your Lowest Blood Pressure Ever!

Do you have high blood pressure?

1. If you're at all overweight, lose weight. Even losing just 5 or 10 pounds can have a very positive effect on your blood pressure.

2. Enjoy regular exercise! A lifestyle with regular exercise definitely helps lower your blood pressure. (As always, check with your doctor first!) See page 130 for suggestions.

3. EAT MORE foods high in potassium, calcium, and magnesium. These work in opposition to sodium in the body, therefore lowering blood pressure. Include your 5 to 9 (or more!) fruits and vegetables per day, plus nonfat and low-fat dairy foods, whole grains, and dried beans.

4. Limit your sodium intake to 2,000 mg or fewer per day. Keep in mind that the salt shaker is only 1/4 of the problem. The major culprit is processed foods—and not just the ones that taste salty.

5. Avoid or limit alcohol. There is increasing evidence of a link between high blood pressure and alcohol consumption.

6. Find ways to relax and release stress from your body. How about yoga? Also, always make time for your favorite hobbies that are relaxing.

Sweet & Sour Chicken

Hands-on — 10 min. (a.m.) and 10 min. (p.m.)   **Serves 8**

Please be aware that LaChoy also makes a larger jar of sweet & sour for stir-fry, but it's higher in sodium, so shop carefully.

Menu

Sweet & Sour Chicken over Brown Rice

Broccoli

8	(4 oz each) skinless, boneless chicken breasts (still frozen is fine)	**4–9 hours before serving:** Place in slow cooker, in the order given.
1 can	(8 oz) pineapple tidbits, in its own juice, drained (reserve juice for another use)	
1 bag	(16 oz) frozen pepper stir-fry (green, red, yellow bell peppers and onions)	
24	baby carrots, left whole	

Kids' Favorite!

2 jars	(10 oz each) sweet & sour sauce	Pour over all. Cook on LOW 8 to 9 hours or on HIGH 4 to 5 hours.

3/4 cup	whole-grain instant brown rice, dry	**10 minutes before serving:** Place in microwave-safe dish.
1 1/3 cups	water	

1 head	broccoli, cleaned and cut into florets	Add to rice. Cover and microwave 9 minutes on HIGH.

1 tsp	fresh grated ginger root (opt)	Portion each plate with 1 cup of rice and broccoli, one chicken breast, and 1/2 cup sauce with peppers and pineapple. Then sprinkle each portion with a "dusting" of fresh grated ginger root before serving. (I keep fresh ginger root in the freezer at all times. It's always "fresh" and available, and grates easily.) Return unused ginger root to freezer promptly.

Nutrition information for approx. 1/2 cup rice, 1/2 cup broccoli, one chicken breast, and 1/2 cup sauce with peppers and pineapple

Exchanges/Choices: 1 Starch, 2 Carbohydrate, 2 Vegetable, 2 Lean Meat

Calories	375	Fat	4.5 g	Fiber	4 g	Sodium	335 mg	Total Carbohydrate	56 g
Calories from Fat	11%	Saturated Fat	<1 g	Cholesterol	65 mg	Protein	29 g	Sugars	30 g

Lickety-Split Diabetic Meals

Lickety-Split Tip

"Because cancer-fighting compounds in my foods are of utmost importance to me, I focus on dried beans, whole grains, fruits, vegetables, and plenty of soy foods, including a pound of tofu every week. I ensure this with my ritual morning shake, consisting of tofu, soy milk, carrots, fruit, fruit juice, wheat bran, wheat germ, and flax seeds. I developed this shake after my third cancer, as a way to get as many phytochemicals in my diet as possible."

—*Diana Dyer, MS, RD, CNSD Dietitian*
Vibrant and healthy 3-time cancer survivor.

P.S. To follow an example for creating your own cancer recovery and healing program, order Diana's book, *A Dietitian's Cancer Story: Information and Inspiration for Recovery and Healing from a 3-Time Cancer Survivor.* From diet to meditation, exercise, supplements, and alternative and conventional cancer therapies, Diana shares it all in this wonderful and personal book.

Available by calling 800-843-8114 or visiting *www.CancerRD.com.*

Salads and Sides

I've forgotten to mention…be SURE to eat LOTS and LOTS of isothiocyanates, indoles, dithiolthiones, limonene, allyl sulfides, and saponins. Oh, and don't forget the caffeic acid, ellagic acid, ferulic acid, and phytic acid.

What in the world am I talking about? These are just a few of the hundreds (perhaps thousands) of phytochemicals. (And you thought chemicals were bad?) While these sound like chemicals made in a lab, they are as natural as natural can be. They happen to be manufactured within the walls of plants, hence their name phyto (plant) chemicals. So what's the big deal about plant chemicals? They're big cancer fighters, that's what! New studies indicate that these compounds seem to play an important role in the production of enzymes that help dispose of potential carcinogens. For the past 20 years, scientists all over the world have consistently found that people who eat greater amounts of fruits and vegetables have lower rates of most cancers. Of course, fruits and vegetables are already rich in life-saving folacin, vitamin C, and beta carotene, (not to mention being low calorie, low carb, and completely wasit friendly) but these newly discovered compounds now add even more gold to the pot.

This chapter is full of tasty ways to enjoy more fruits and vegetables! Many of these salads can be made ahead (like on the weekend) and enjoyed over the next several hectic weekdays.

Lickety-Split Diabetic Meals

Lickety-Split Tip

The Leafy Facts

Many people eat an iceberg lettuce salad with a tomato fragment and think, "I got my fiber in for the day!"

But just how nutritious is iceberg lettuce, compared to darker greens like romaine or spinach? Just as its color indicates, it pales in comparison, with less than half the fiber and valuable nutrients. To get more from your salads, try these suggestions:

1. Choose darker greens like romaine and spinach. Mix them 50–50 with iceberg until your family adjusts.

2. Buy the ready-to-eat dark green salad mixes for a real timesaver.

3. If you choose to buy bulk lettuce and clean it yourself, buy a salad spinner. This allows you to wash and spin your lettuce dry in seconds.

4. Always chop as many vegetables as you can to go on top of the salad. The vegetables pack more nutrition and fiber than the greens do.

5. Or, just skip the lettuce altogether and hit the veggies, as in Where's the Lettuce? Salad.

Where's the Lettuce? Salad

Out of lettuce? No problem! All you need are vegetables, and any combination of what you find in your refrigerator will do.

Tastes great with:

Any main dish that's a little low on vegetables, like Tortellini Stew (page 231), or Hungarian Chicken Paprikash (page 113)

Scrounge through the refrigerator for whatever vegetables you can find.

4 cups	**any of the following:** • **green, red, or yellow bell peppers, (seeded and chopped)** • **chopped celery** • **chopped tomatoes** • **chopped onions** • **fresh parsley (chopped fine)** • **sliced carrots** • **chopped cauliflower** • **chopped broccoli**	Place in a medium bowl.
1 can	**(15 oz) garbanzo beans, drained and rinsed (opt)**	Add to bowl.
1 can	**(15 oz) beets, drained (opt)**	
1/3 cup	**lower fat dressing of your choice (Thousand Island, Honey French, etc.)**	Toss with dressing and serve, or let guests dress their own.

Nutrition information for about 1 cup, including the garbanzo beans and beets (with Thousand Island dressing)

Exchanges/Choices: 1/2 Starch, 2 Vegetable

Calories	99	Fat	2 g	Fiber	4 g	Sodium	308 mg	Total Carbohydrate	17 g
Calories from Fat	19%	Saturated Fat	0 g	Cholesterol	0 mg	Protein	4 g	Sugars	7 g

Lickety-Split Diabetic Meals

Lickety-Split Tip

Fruits & Vegetables: Zonya's favorite way to get 10 to 11 a day

Breakfast	Cereal with 2 T raisins and 1 orange	2
Snack	4 oz juice diluted in 8 oz water and ice (sparkling water is great!)	1
Lunch	1/4 of a cantaloupe	1
	1 whole tomato (2 slices on my sandwich and I eat the rest)	1
	6 baby carrots	1
Snack	1 kiwi	1
	4 oz. juice diluted in 8 oz water and ice	1
Dinner	1½ cups mixed vegetables or stir-fry, or a huge green salad with lots of vegetables on top, or 1½ cups Marinated Vegetable Salad	2–3

10–11 servings!

Marinated Vegetable Salad

A colorful dish to bring to potlucks and picnics.

Tastes great with:

Grilled Turkey Burgers or Chicken Breasts

3	carrots, sliced diagonally	
2 cups	broccoli florets	
2 cups	cauliflower florets	

1–3 hours before serving:

Clean and prep vegetables, and place in a microwave-safe dish with 2 tsp water.

Cover and microwave on HIGH 4 minutes, or until vegetables just begin to get tender. Transfer to a colander and rinse with cold water to halt cooking process.

1/2 each	green, red, and yellow bell pepper, seeded
2	green onions
1/2 cup	light or fat-free Italian dressing
1 tsp	dried oregano

Cut peppers into 1" slices and chop onions. Combine everything with cooked vegetables in medium bowl and toss.

Allow to marinate 1 to 3 hours in refrigerator and serve.

Note: This salad does not keep longer than 1 day. The vegetables begin to wilt, due to the salt in the dressing.

Canned sliced beets, drained, are also nice in this salad.

Nutrition information for about 1 cup

Exchanges/Choices: 2 Vegetable

Calories	65	Fat	2 g	Fiber	3.6 g	Sodium	220 mg	Total Carbohydrate	11 g
Calories from Fat	28%	Saturated Fat	0 g	Cholesterol	0 mg	Protein	2 g	Sugars	5 g

Lickety-Split Diabetic Meals

Lickety-Split Tip

What color is on your plate?

Let's talk food colorings: reds, oranges, yellows, purples, and greens. I'm not talking about the dyes made in a lab, but the natural colors produced by plant cells. How colorful is your diet? In addition to the fine vitamins and minerals present in vegetables and fruits, the colors alone (called bioflavonoids) of peppers, carrots, sweet potatoes, etc., nourish your cells with powerful agents to fight disease (and brighten your menu).

How often do you serve carrot-raisin salad? I'm warning you that once you make this, your family will want it on the menu 30 times a year!

Sunshine Carrot-Raisin Salad

This salad is a great way to get loads of beta-carotene and tastes like candy!
Toss this together 30 minutes before your main dish is done.

Tastes great with:

Turkey Joes (page 91) or Broiled Orange Roughy (page 117)

Kids' Favorite!

1/3 cup	plain nonfat yogurt	In a medium-sized bowl, mix together to form the dressing.
1 T	sugar	
3 T	Miracle Whip Light	
1/4 tsp	vanilla extract	
3 dashes	ground cinnamon	
2 dashes	ground nutmeg	
1/2 cup	raisins	
1 can	(8 oz) pineapple tidbits, in its own juice, drained	Reserve juice for another use. Mix pineapple into dressing.
3 cups	(10 oz bag) shredded carrots (about 5 medium or 45 baby carrots)	Buy pre-shredded carrots or use a food processor to shred carrots. Stir into dressing to coat well. Chill salad until ready to serve.

Optional additions:

2 T	sweetened shredded coconut (less than 2 grams fat per serving)	For a nice variation, add one of these as an option.
	or	
1 T	peanut butter	

Nutrition information for about 1/2 cup without optional additions

Exchanges/Choices: 1/2 Carbohydrate, 1 Vegetable

Calories	75	Fat	1.2 g	Fiber	1.5 g	Sodium	78 mg	Total Carbohydrate	16 g
Calories from Fat	14%	Saturated Fat	0 g	Cholesterol	0 mg	Protein	1.5 g	Sugars	13 g

Lickety-Split Diabetic Meals

Lickety-Split Tip

Pineapple juice works like lemon juice

Did you know that pineapple juice works just as well as lemon juice to keep sliced apples from turning brown? Remember this the next time you make a fresh fruit salad with sliced apples or pears. (We call this a Fruit Explosion.) Simply stir in a can of pineapple chunks, along with the juice, to prevent browning (and also to avoid that tart lemon taste)!

Crunchy Apple Salad

Hands-on – 8 min.   Serves 8

Do you have apples in your fruit bowl that are, well, shall we say, "past their prime"?
Let this recipe resuscitate them back to life. It only takes about 8 minutes to put this together.

Tastes great with:

Polynesian Pizza
(page 195)

or

Turkey Vegetable Stew
(page 229)

1/3 cup	plain nonfat yogurt	Whisk together in a medium bowl.
1 T	sugar	
1 T	Miracle Whip Light	
1/4 tsp	vanilla extract	
3 dashes	ground cinnamon or Chinese 5-spice powder	
2 T	walnuts or raisins or both	

Kids' Favorite!

2 lg	(10 oz each) apples, preferably 1 red and 1 green	Slice, core, and cut into chunks. Add to bowl.

1 can	(8 oz) pineapple tidbits, in its own juice, drained	Drain pineapple, reserving juice for another use. Add to bowl and toss gently to coat well.
		Chill salad until ready to serve.

Nutrition information for 1/2 cup with walnuts

Exchanges/Choices: 1/2 Fruit, 1/2 Carbohydrate

Calories	75	Fat	1.75 g	Fiber	2 g	Sodium	27 mg	Total Carbohydrate	15 g
Calories from Fat	21%	Saturated Fat	0 g	Cholesterol	0 mg	Protein	1 g	Sugars	12 g

Lickety-Split Diabetic Meals

Lickety-Split Tip

5-a-day (at least!) for better health: more matters!

So, how does your plate rate? Americans in general average 2.1 servings per day of fruits and vegetables combined. The Center for Science in the Public Interest has for years recommended 5–9 servings per day. The American Cancer Institute is so convinced of the cancer-fighting abilities of fruits and vegetables that they've been recommending 9–11 servings each day. And the 2005 federal dietary guidelines call for as many as 13 half-cup servings of fruits and vegetables.

So what about the "5-a-day" campaign that we've been hearing for years? It was created by the Produce for Better Health Foundation in partnership with the Centers for Disease Control. Since Americans were eating so few, they figured it was a realistic goal. But with all the added studies showing more is better, as of

March 2007, their new campaign is to encourage Americans to eat more with, "Fruits & Veggies—More Matters." So just think of 5-a-day as a good starting point, but push yourself as far as you can go!

I also recommend to first aim for 5-a-day **WITHOUT** counting juice servings, since juice does not contain important fiber. Also, if you can achieve 5-a-day and then drink 8 ounces of juice a day (2 fruit servings), this will get you up to 7 servings. Double your "token" portion of vegetables at dinner and you're up again. Also think of a fruit or vegetable at every snack time. While it may seem tough at first, just take it one meal and one snack at a time and remember, more matters!

Veggie Pasta Salad

Hands-on – 30 min.

Serves 32**

Keep this delicious salad in mind for lunch, dinner, and potlucks!
Please note: This is an intentionally large batch, as it will keep for 3 days.

Tastes great with:

Soup or sliced fruit

Put a large pot of water on to boil.

1 box	(16 oz) dry whole-wheat pasta of your choice	While you wait for water to boil, begin steps below. As soon as water is ready, add pasta and set timer according to directions on box.

2 cups	diagonally sliced carrots	Cut carrots diagonally. Cut broccoli into bite-size florets. Seed and cut peppers into small chunks.
1 large	bunch broccoli	
1 each	red, yellow, and green pepper	At the sound of the timer, quickly toss carrots and broccoli into boiling water with pasta. Set timer for 1 minute. When timer goes off again, quickly drain and rinse in cold water to halt cooking process. (This step brightens the vegetables while taking the edge off their rawness.)
3/4 cup	low-fat dressing of your choice (perhaps Italian, Honey French, or Ranch)	Transfer pasta to a large bowl that has a tight-fitting lid. Add peppers and dressing. Mix to coat evenly.

2	tomatoes*	Chop tomatoes. Prepare dishes for immediate serving. Add chopped tomatoes and serve.

*Adding chopped tomato to the large batch in this recipe will not allow it to be kept for 3 days. So each time you are ready to serve the dish, just add more chopped tomato.

**Serves 8 as a main dish (1½-cup servings)

Nutrition information for 1/2 cup side dish (using light Italian dressing)

Exchanges/Choices: 1/2 Starch, 1 Vegetable

Calories	70	Fat	1 g	Fiber	2.5 g	Sodium	64 mg	Total Carbohydrate	15 g
Calories from Fat	11%	Saturated Fat	<1 g	Cholesterol	0 mg	Protein	2.5 g	Sugars	2 g

Lickety-Split Diabetic Meals

Lickety-Split Tip

Eat a fruit or vegetable at EVERY meal and snack

This drives down calories while skyrocketing the nutrients you need. Trade pre-dinner snacks of cheese and crackers for raw veggies and light dip. This daily 300-calorie savings will help you shed 31 pounds in a year, while helping you control diabetes and fight heart disease and cancer.

Broccoli Salad with Dried Cherries

Hands-on – 8 min. **Serves 10**

I bet you're surprised to see such a high-fat salad in my book. I figure the price of the pecans and dried cherries will assure that you make it on special occasions only. As I always say, "With moderation and balance, all foods can fit!"

Tastes great with:
Slow-cooked dishes like:
Tortellini Stew (page 231) or
Gypsy Stew (page 239)

1 bunch	broccoli, cut into bite-sized florets	Combine in a large, attractive serving bowl.
1/4	red onion, thinly sliced, then chopped	
1/2 cup	chopped pecans	
1 cup	dried cherries	

1/2 cup	**Miracle Whip Light**	Whisk together in a small bowl.
1/2 cup	plain nonfat yogurt	Pour over broccoli mixture, toss gently and serve.
1/4 cup	grated **Parmesan** cheese	
1 T	sugar	
1 T	vinegar (cider or any variety)	
1/2 tsp	ground cinnamon	

Nutrition information for 1/2 cup

Exchanges/Choices: 1 Fruit, 1 Vegetable, 1 1/2 Fat

Calories	146	Fat	7 g	Fiber	2 g	Sodium	155 mg	Total Carbohydrate	20 g
Calories from Fat	40%	Saturated Fat	<1 g	Cholesterol	4 mg	Protein	2 g	Sugars	17 g

Lickety-Split Diabetic Meals

Lickety-Split Tip

Hunger versus thirst

Many people mistake feelings of mild thirst for hunger. (Confusing these feelings is especially common if you are fatigued.) Eating when you are thirsty can put on unwanted pounds. If weight control is important to you, drink a glass of water first before nibbling.

Cranberry Salad

A festive and popular holiday and potluck favorite. Simple, low calorie, and delicious.

Tastes great with:

Thanksgiving Dinner or everyday sandwiches

1 lg pkg	(0.6 oz) sugar-free strawberry gelatin	4 hours before serving or night before:
2 cups	boiling water	Place gelatin in a large decorative serving bowl.* Dissolve with boiling water.

1½ cups	cold water	Add to bowl and stir.
1	(8 oz) apple, cored and chopped	
2 cans	(8 oz each) pineapple tidbits, in its own juice, undrained	
1/3 cup	chopped pecans or walnuts	

1 package	(12 oz) fresh cranberries (can be frozen or partially thawed)	Place in a food processor and process until partly chunky, mostly smooth. Add to salad and stir well. Refrigerate at least 4 hours before serving.

*Decorative Ring Mold option:

Prepare salad in a bowl, then transfer to a decorative ring mold or bundt pan to chill.
To serve, dip pan in sinkful of warm water and invert onto serving platter.
Fill center with red and green grapes.

Nutrition information for 1/2 cup

Exchanges/Choices: 1/2 Fruit

Calories	40	Fat	1 g	Fiber	2 g	Sodium	33 mg
Calories from Fat	24%	Saturated Fat	0 g	Cholesterol	0 mg	Protein	<1 g

Total Carbohydrate	7 g
Sugars	4 g

Lickety-Split Diabetic Meals

Lickety-Split Tip

Which picnic would your heart rather have?

Typical Picnic "A"

1 oz potato chips

1 charbroiled bratwurst on a bun

1/2 cup traditional coleslaw

1 cup traditional potato salad

Another 1 oz potato chips

2 chocolate brownies

This meal contains 1,485 calories, 90 grams of fat, and 150 grams of carbohydrate!

That's equal to 6 tablespoons (over 1/3 cup) of shortening or lard!

Picnic "B"

4 carrot sticks

4 oz skinless, boneless chicken breast

2 T BBQ sauce

1/2 cup Potato Salad (below)

1 cup 5-Bean Salad (page 271)

Fresh fruit for dessert

This meal contains only 525 calories, 12½ grams of fat, and 70 grams of carbohydrate! What a BIG FAT DIFFERENCE!

Knowledge is power and we have choices!

Potato Salad

Hands-on – 45 min.

Serves 16

Traditional-tasting potato salad at half the fat and calories!

Tastes great with:

Turkey or
Salmon Burgers (page 119)

Put both a large and small pot of water on to boil.

8	(8 oz each) redskin potatoes, scrubbed clean and cubed	Add to large pot of boiling water.
4	eggs	Add to small pot of boiling water. Set timer for 10 minutes.
1 small	red or yellow onion	Meanwhile, mince onion and dice celery. Place in a large serving bowl.
3	celery stalks	When timer sounds, drain eggs and rinse with cold water. Set timer for 20 additional minutes (to finish potatoes). Crack and peel eggs. Chop and add to bowl.
		When timer sounds, drain potatoes and cool slightly before adding to bowl.
1/2 cup	light coleslaw-type dressing	Gently mix with potatoes.
1/4 cup	Miracle Whip Light	
10 grinds	fresh ground pepper	
1/4 tsp	salt (opt)	
2 T	prepared mustard (plain or Dijon)	
2	fresh tomatoes (opt)	Garnish with tomato wedges.

Nutrition information for about 1/2 cup with 1 tomato wedge and optional salt

Exchanges/Choices: 1 1/2 Starch, 1/2 Fat

Calories	140	Fat	4 g	Fiber	2 g	Sodium	196 mg	Total Carbohydrate	23 g
Calories from Fat	25%	Saturated Fat	<1 g	Cholesterol	58 mg	Protein	4 g	Sugars	4 g

Lickety-Split Diabetic Meals

Lickety-Split Tip

Beans: Flavorful cholesterol sponges

Cooking from this book means that you'll be eating meals that will help lower your cholesterol because they are low in fat, high in fiber, and moderate in carbohydrates.

In addition to using these recipes, be sure to choose several (2 to 4) bean recipes each week. Why? Beans are particularly high in the gummy, gooey, spongy fiber that sops up that nasty cholesterol.

Other great tips for lowering your cholesterol:

1. Limit saturated fat even more by selecting cheeses that are fat-free instead of low-fat.

2. Include 2–3 tablespoons of ground flax seed, ideally every day that you don't eat fish. Flax is the dynamo high-fiber plant source of omega-3 fatty acids that are as beneficial as fish, without the mercury and PCB's. Mix into your yogurt, cereal, baked goods, etc.

3. Control your weight. Dropping a few pounds can have a very positive effect on both your blood pressure and cholesterol level.

4. Control your blood pressure. This is about more than just limiting your sodium intake, but about increasing calcium, potassium, and magnesium, too. Sources include low-fat dairy products, fruits, vegetables, and whole grains.

5. EXERCISE! The physical benefits of exercise are well known. The American Heart Association now recognizes physical inactivity as a major risk factor of the development of coronary heart disease, yet
   only one in five Americans engages in regular physical activity.

For more tips on lowering your cholesterol, see the Index.

5-Bean Salad

Hands-on — 10 min.

Serves 20

Why stop at 3-bean salad? This has triple the cholesterol-lowering power of 3-bean salad, and a lot less oil. This makes a big batch, so plan on enjoying it all week long.

Tastes great with:

Grilled Chicken or Fish

1 can	(15 oz) butter beans	
1 can	(15 oz) kidney beans	
1 can	(15 oz) garbanzo beans	
1 can	(16 oz) wax beans	
1 can	(16 oz) green beans	

4 hours before serving:

Open cans and rinse and drain beans thoroughly in a colander. Transfer to a large bowl with a tight-fitting lid.

1 small	red or white onion, sliced into rings
1	green bell pepper, chopped

Stir into beans.

1/2 cup	balsamic vinegar
1/4 cup	water
2 T	sugar
1/4 cup	oil (canola or olive)
1 tsp	oregano
1/2 tsp	chopped garlic (1 clove)

Mix together in a 2-cup measuring cup. Pour over beans and toss to coat evenly.

Best if allowed to marinate 4 or more hours

If you wish to make only 1/2 this batch, simply reserve 1/2 the beans for an upcoming batch of chili.

Nutrition information for 1/2 cup

Exchanges/Choices: 1 Starch

Calories	85	Fat	3 g	Fiber	3 g	Sodium	305 mg	Total Carbohydrate	13 g
Calories from Fat	29%	Saturated Fat	0 g	Cholesterol	0 mg	Protein	3.5 g	Sugars	4 g

Lickety-Split Diabetic Meals

Lickety-Split Tip

Attention, ladies: Exercise helps prevent breast cancer

Researchers at the University of Southern California* found that 1 to 3 hours of exercise per week during the reproductive years cuts breast cancer risk by 30%.

Four or more hours of exercise each week cuts risk by 60%!

How many hours have you gotten in so far this week?

*Bernstein, L; Henderson, BE; Hanisch, R; Sullivan-Halley, J; Ross, RK. Physical exercise and reduced risk of breast cancer in young women. *J National Cancer Inst* 1994; 86:1403-08.

Creamy Tuna Twist

Hands-on – 25 min. Serves 16*

Great for picnics and potlucks. Also makes a great lunch box main dish salad to fight sandwich boredom. Simply up the portion size to one cup.

Tastes great with:

A bowl of vegetable soup and fruit

Put a medium-size pot of water on to boil.

2 cans	(6 oz each) water-packed tuna (rinsed and drained)	Place in a large bowl with a tight-fitting lid.
3	celery stalks, chopped	Mix with tuna.
1 small	red onion, chopped	
3 cups	dry corkscrew or shell pasta	When water is boiling, add pasta. Set timer for 8 minutes.
3/4 cup	Miracle Whip Light	Whisk together in a 2-cup measuring cup. Mix well with tuna.
1/2 cup	nonfat plain yogurt	
1 T	vinegar (cider)	
1 T	dill weed	
10 grinds	fresh ground pepper	
2 cups	frozen peas	When timer sounds, add peas to boiling pasta. Set timer for 2 minutes.

When timer sounds, quickly drain and rinse both pasta and peas in cold water. Toss well with tuna mixture. Serve chilled.

*Serves 8 as a main dish (1 cup servings)

Nutrition information for about 1/2 cup

Exchanges/Choices: 1 Starch, 1 Lean Meat

Calories	115	Fat	3 g	Fiber	1 g	Sodium	180 mg	Total Carbohydrate	16 g
Calories from Fat	21%	Saturated Fat	0 g	Cholesterol	6 mg	Protein	7 g	Sugars	4 g

Lickety-Split Diabetic Meals

Lickety-Split Tip

The wonder of cruciferous vegetables

How often do you eat cabbage? Brussels sprouts? Kale?

Important studies show cruciferous vegetables (the cabbage family) appear to protect you against colorectal, stomach, and respiratory cancers. Cruciferous vegetables include: broccoli, Brussels sprouts, cabbage, cauliflower, collards, kale, kohlrabi, mustard greens, bok choy, and turnip greens.

Please take a hard look at this list. How many of these cabbage family vegetables do you eat in a week? How can you increase that number? You guessed it! Pasta Slaw comes to the rescue. It's both low calorie and full of cancer fighters.

Enjoy!

Produce Shopping the European Way

The Europeans make it an after-work ritual to stop at a corner produce market so they can enjoy the freshest ingredients for dinner. Have you considered this habit for your family? If you find huge grocery stores too overwhelming, maybe it's time to break out of your grocery store rut and find a more intimate place to shop.

Pasta Slaw

Serves 16

You know how salads are great for helping you lose weight? Well, so is this. I make this up whenever my clothes are fitting snug. I then include a serving with lunch and dinner. Just think of it as a negative-calorie food (see tip on page 212)!

Tastes great with:
Grilled Chicken or Fish

Put a medium-size pot of water on to boil.

2 cups	shredded cabbage	Buy already shredded, or shred using a food processor. Place in a large serving bowl.
2 cups	shredded carrots	
2 oz	whole-wheat spaghetti, dry (1 cup cooked)	When water is boiling, add pasta. Set timer for 10 minutes.
1	green bell pepper, chopped	Add to cabbage and carrots.
1	red bell pepper, chopped	
1/2	red onion, or 4 green onions, chopped	
1 T	lemon juice (preferably fresh squeezed)	Mix together in a small bowl.
2 T	balsamic vinegar (or red wine)	At sound of timer, drain pasta and add to vegetables while still hot.
1/2 tsp	salt	Toss all together with dressing. Serve warm or chilled.
1/2 tsp	oregano	
1 T	oil (olive or canola)	
1/2 tsp	chopped garlic (1 clove)	
dash	pepper (to taste)	

Nutrition information for 1/2 cup

Exchanges/Choices: 1 Vegetable

Calories	34	Fat	1 g	Fiber	1 g	Sodium	85 mg	Total Carbohydrate	6 g
Calories from Fat	25%	Saturated Fat	0 g	Cholesterol	0 mg	Protein	1 g	Sugars	2 g

Lickety-Split Diabetic Meals

Lickety-Split Tip

Eat the skin on your potato because it's good for you … Or is it?

While nutritionists have recommended eating the potato skin because of its extra vitamins, minerals, and fiber, new findings are causing a second look at this advice. These days most commercial potatoes have been sprayed to slow their sprouting and extend their shelf life. This spray has raised safety concerns. Therefore, the advice to "eat the skin on your potato because it's good for you," holds true only for potatoes bought at your local farmers market or organically grown. There is still good nutrition throughout the potato even without the skin.

Oven Fries

Hands-on – 10 min. Oven – 50 min.   **Serves 4**

I can't begin to tell you how much my husband loves these! They're easy to make, inexpensive, and a delicious low-fat version of the high-fat American favorite. I'll leave it up to you to decide what to serve them with. Perhaps baked chicken legs and steamed vegetables?

Tastes great with:

Baked Chicken Legs or Turkey Joes (page 91)

Steamed Vegetables

Preheat oven to 375°.
Coat a nonstick baking sheet with cooking spray.

4 med	**(6 oz each) baking potatoes (also try sweet potatoes, they're great!)**	Thoroughly wash and scrub—peel if non-organic potatoes. (See tip above.) Cut lengthwise into wedges. Place in bowl.
1 T	**oil (canola or olive)**	Drizzle over potatoes and toss.
1/2 tsp	**Mrs. Dash or Spike seasoning (salt-free) or any seasonings you like**	Sprinkle over potatoes and toss. Spread seasoned potato wedges over baking sheet. Set timer and bake 50 minutes or until tender. At the sound of the timer, transfer to a serving dish.
	salt, pepper, and ketchup	Sprinkle lightly with salt and pepper to taste. Serve with ketchup.

Note: Ore Ida now makes frozen potato wedges, which are almost exactly the same as these. Buying their product will save you from scrubbing and slicing potatoes (about 10 minutes).

Husbands and kids love these!

Nutrition information for 1/2 cup, without ketchup, salt and pepper

Exchanges/Choices: 2 Starch, 1/2 Fat

Calories	164	Fat	3.5 g	Fiber	2 g	Sodium	8 mg	Total Carbohydrate	31 g
Calories from Fat	19%	Saturated Fat	0 g	Cholesterol	0 mg	Protein	4 g	Sugars	1 g

Lickety-Split Diabetic Meals

Lickety-Split Tip

Antioxidants

You've been hearing this word a lot lately. What is it again? The best example is to slice an apple and watch what happens. In only a few minutes the milky white flesh turns brown. This is "oxidation." Every good cook knows that lemon juice will slow the browning process. The vitamin C in the lemon juice is the "antioxidant." Here are some examples of oxidation in the human body:

Cataracts: Eye fluids normally contain large amounts of vitamin C, but with aging these levels decline. As that happens, proteins in the lens oxidize, making the lens more susceptible to clouding and the development of cataracts.

Cancer: Many scientists believe that some cancers result from oxidative damage to cells, therefore reducing their resistance to carcinogens.

Heart disease: Scientists are now concerned not only with the presence of "bad" LDL (low density lipoprotein) cholesterol in the blood stream, but at what rate it oxidizes with the artery wall to create plaque.

Therefore, eating a diet high in antioxidants becomes increasingly important to fight the onset of common diseases.

Cinnamon Butternut Squash is LOADED with the powerful antioxidant beta carotene, as well as tons of phytochemicals. Make it often!

Cinnamon Butternut Squash

Hands-on – 5 min. Oven – 60 min. **Serves 8**

Train yourself to make this delicious side dish frequently.
Winter squash is one of the best anti-aging foods around!

Tastes great with:

Mexican LaZonya (page 141)

Preheat oven to 375°.

2 med	(2 lb each) butternut squash

Slice squash in half lengthwise, and scoop out the seeds.

10 sprinkles	ground cinnamon

Sprinkle cinnamon into the squash.

Place cut side down on a cookie sheet and add about 1/2 cup of water to the pan. (This helps keep it moist without having to add butter to the squash.)

Bake 1 hour.

Scoop squash out and into a bowl. Mash with a fork.
Sprinkle with additional cinnamon if desired.

(Brown sugar can be added, but taste it first.
Sometimes the squash is so naturally sweet, it doesn't need it!)

Nutrition information for about 1/2 cup mashed squash

Exchanges/Choices: 1 Starch

Calories	50	Fat	0 g	Fiber	2 g	Sodium	5 mg	Total Carbohydrate	13 g
Calories from Fat	0%	Saturated Fat	0 g	Cholesterol	0 mg	Protein	1 g	Sugars	3 g

Lickety-Split Diabetic Meals

Lickety-Split Tip

To serve bread or not to serve bread...that is the question!

Why is it that some meals are served with bread and some aren't? Back in the days of working on the farm, bread or rolls were served with every meal. Let's face it, up at the crack of dawn, farm hands needed that extra energy. And thus, the "bread with every meal" tradition was born!

But do we all need that much bread? What if we have a rather sedentary job? And what if we have diabetes? What if we want to **LOSE** weight and control our blood sugars?

A slice of whole-grain bread, garlic toast, or a roll is best included when the meal has just one starch serving or just a little, such as broiled fish, broccoli, and a small baked potato.

Similarly, adding whole-grain crackers or a slice of crusty-whole-grain bread would fit nicely with a meal of vegetable soup.

Examples of meals containing 2 starch servings are: potatoes and corn or rice and beans. It's up to you if you add a third starch. Active individuals who burn a great deal of calories, and many men, need the third and fourth serving of carbohydrate calories. So let them eat bread at every meal!

For people with sedentary lifestyles or those seeking to lose weight or control their diabetes, their blood sugar control, I recommend that you either pass on the bread or halve your portions of corn or potatoes.

Whole-Wheat Garlic Cheese Toast

Throughout my recipes, I call for serving dishes with garlic toast. Here's what I make that's healthy and fast.

Tastes great with:

Soups

Any moderate-serving pasta dish

Position oven rack 6" away from heating element. Turn oven on to broil. Remember to leave door ajar.

4 slices	whole-wheat bread	Place bread on a nonstick baking sheet.
16 sprays	olive oil spray or **I Can't Believe It's Not Butter spray**	Spray bread with 4 sprays each slice.

4 dashes	oregano (or as desired)	Sprinkle evenly over bread.
4 dashes	garlic powder (or as desired)	Broil 1 to 2 minutes. Set the timer, as they can burn quickly! I usually just broil one side, but flip the bread and toast another minute if desired.
4 dashes	grated Parmesan cheese (or as desired)	For serving, cut toast diagonally in each direction to make 4 triangles per slice.

Nutrition information for 4 triangles (1 slice of bread)

Exchanges/Choices: 1 Starch

| Calories | 60 | Fat | 1 g | Fiber | 2 g | Sodium | 145 mg | Total Carbohydrate | 12 g |
| Calories from Fat | 15% | Saturated Fat | 0 g | Cholesterol | 0 mg | Protein | 3 g | Sugars | 5 g |

Lickety-Split Diabetic Meals

Lickety-Split Tip

Margarine vs. butter, the slippery debate

Think butter is "natural" and therefore better for you than margarine? Think again.

Butter is more saturated than lard. You are better off putting lard on your bread than butter! Margarine, on the other hand, is not picture perfect, either. It's hydrogenated (which makes it thick and spreadable) and may contain troublesome trans-fatty acids.

What should you do?

1. At breakfast, opt for low-sugar jams, jellies, apple butter, honey, and/or natural peanut butter instead of habitually spreading on margarine.

2. When sautéing, use nonstick cooking spray or 1 T of oil instead of butter or margarine.

3. When making grilled cheese sandwiches or garlic toast, lightly brush on oil instead of spreading on margarine.

4. In baking, use applesauce or other mashed fruit, and use small amounts of oil when necessary.

5. Use a product like I Can't Believe It's Not Butter spray for popcorn and baked potatoes.

6. Buy a small tub of light margarine that states, "zero grams of trans fat." Store it in the back of your refrigerator and use it rarely. (Following steps 1–5, you should not need to use this more than twice a week.)

P.S. Try honey on this cornbread instead of the "habitual" margarine!

Cornbread

Even as a child, I loved cornbread. I can mix this up in 5 minutes and pop it in the oven for 20 minutes. This gives me time to whip up a main dish. Remember to make a double batch while you're at it! This recipe uses oil instead of shortening and less of it.

Tastes great with:

Chili (page 219) or Lentil Spinach Soup (page 215) or Hearty Bean & Pasta Stew (page 225)

Preheat oven to 425°.

Coat a 9" pie plate, 8" × 8" pan or 10-cup muffin tin with cooking spray.

1 cup	yellow, whole-grain cornmeal	Mix together in a bowl using a fork.
1 cup	flour (whole-wheat pastry flour if you like)	Be sure baking powder is well distributed.
1/4 cup	sugar	
1 T	baking powder	

1 cup + 2 T	skim milk	Add to dry ingredients and mix until blended.
1 T	canola oil	Pour into sprayed baking pan.
2	egg whites or 1 egg	Bake 20 minutes (15-17 minutes for muffins) or until a toothpick comes out clean.

Nutrition information for 1/10 of pan or one muffin

Exchanges/Choices: 1 1/2 Starch, 1/2 Fat

Calories	135	Fat	2 g	Fiber	1 g	Sodium	185 mg	Total Carbohydrate	25 g
Calories from Fat	13%	Saturated Fat	<1 g	Cholesterol	0 mg	Protein	4 g	Sugars	6 g

Lickety-Split Diabetic Meals

Lickety-Split Tip

"For many years now I have loved the Peanut Buster Parfait at Dairy Queen. With my new commitment to healthy eating, I decided to substitute fat-free frozen yogurt for the ice cream and chocolate syrup for the hot fudge. I also order the small instead of the medium. The result: I am just as satisfied without feeling at all deprived."

—Stacey W., celebrating the 6th month of her new healthy lifestyle.

Congratulations, Stacey! You've successfully saved 200 calories and 25 grams of fat, while not feeling deprived. This is what it's all about!

Sweet Treats

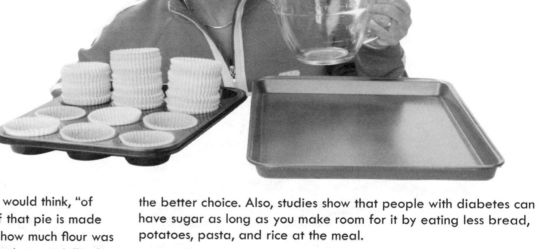

What is the better choice for the person with diabetes?

1. a sugar-free slice of pie

2. a whole-grain, low-fat oatmeal cookie made with half the sugar?

This is a tricky question to answer. Most people would think, "of course the answer is the sugar-free pie!" Even if that pie is made with artificial sweetener (making it sugar free,) how much flour was used? How much fat was used? (After all, the number one killer for people with diabetes is heart disease.) What are the total calories, carbohydrates, and fat grams?

Just because it's a sugar-free dessert, it may still be high in carbohydrates from the white flour used, may contain fats that are not good for your heart, and may have a higher calorie content. All of these factors guarantee that you'll pack on additional pounds. A small cookie made from wholesome ingredients may actually be

the better choice. Also, studies show that people with diabetes can have sugar as long as you make room for it by eating less bread, potatoes, pasta, and rice at the meal.

The following sweet treats are wholesome and demonstrate the use of sugar in moderation. They use fruits to sweeten them as much as possible, and call for half the sugar of the conventional recipe. They sport high-fiber, whole-grain flours and have virtually no saturated fat or trans fat. Every recipe gives the calorie, fat, and carbohydrate count so you can see how it fits into your daily allotment. While baking Splenda can be substituted to bring the carbs down a bit more, it's not a must. Portion control remains the biggest key to keeping blood sugars controlled.

Lickety-Split Diabetic Meals

Lickety-Split Tip

Do you suffer from sweet cravings?

How much fruit have you been eating? Chances are, you've been missing the mark. Your brain requires simple carbohydrates to function. Fruit is very high in simple carbohydrates. When you don't get enough, your brain sends you a fruit craving. The problem is you misinterpret the signal as "sweets" or "chocolate" cravings!

Zonya's Sweet Craving Cure: Enjoy 3 servings of fruit throughout your day at meals and snacks, along with a glass of water—no more sweet cravings.

P.S. A slice of my Simple Summer Fresh Fruit Pie counts as 1 fruit serving!

Simple Summer Fresh Fruit Pie

Here's a simply gorgeous (and easy!) dessert. One summer weekend at the lake, my husband suggested we eat the pie first, since it looked so good. Everyone agreed. It was so light and delicious!

1 lg pkg	(0.6 oz) sugar-free strawberry gelatin	3 hours before serving or night before:
2 cups	boiling water (as called for on box)	Place gelatin in a medium bowl, add boiling water and stir to dissolve. (You will not be adding the cold water as called for on the box.)

1 lg pkg	(5.1 oz) instant vanilla pudding	In a large bowl, mix together with an electric mixer. It will be thicker than usual.
1½ cups	skim milk (instead of 3 cups called for on package)	Add the dissolved gelatin and mix until smooth.

2 regular	(6 oz each) reduced-fat graham cracker crusts,	Place fruit attractively to fill crust, using in order listed.
1 quart	fresh strawberries, cleaned and left whole	Pour 1/2 of the pudding mixture over each pie. The pudding mixture will seep between each piece of fruit.
2 medium	bananas, sliced	Refrigerate until firm, about 2 hours.
4	fresh peaches or nectarines, sliced into wedges	Serve proudly and prepare for rave reviews.
1 pint	fresh blueberries, washed and drained	

Nutrition information for 1 slice (1/8 of pie)

Exchanges/Choices: 2 1/2 Carbohydrate, 1/2 Fat

Calories	195	Fat	4 g	Fiber	3 g	Sodium	270 mg	Total Carbohydrate	37 g
Calories from Fat	18%	Saturated Fat	1.1 g	Cholesterol	0 mg	Protein	3 g	Sugars	22 g

Lickety-Split Diabetic Meals

Lickety-Split Tip

A tasty whole-grain secret

In many of the recipes, you will see that I've called for whole-wheat pastry flour. This flour is different from the whole-wheat flour you commonly find in grocery stores. Whole-wheat pastry flour, sometimes called whole-grain pastry flour, is very nutritious because it is whole-grain flour, yet is very light and cakey in texture, similar to that of white flour. It can be used in equal amounts to replace all-purpose flour in any "non-yeast" recipe. It makes wonderfully light cookies, cakes, muffins and quick breads, and the best part is only you will know that you used "healthy" flour!

Yeast recipes, on the other hand, require gluten for structure and whole-wheat pastry flour has very little. This is where the common whole-wheat flour referred to as bread flour (that you find commonly in stores) is required. Just remember, if the recipe calls for baking powder or baking soda, it will work fine with whole-wheat pastry flour. If it uses yeast, it will not.

Now, where do you find it? Be aware that you may not find it in the standard flour section of your grocery store. It is considered specialty flour and may be found in the health food section among special brands like Hodgson Mill, Arrowhead Mills, or Bob's Red Mill. If you do not find it, request it from your grocer. I buy it in bulk quantities at natural food stores or co-ops. Please look for it. It really is worth the effort. Until you find it, you can substitute for each cup of whole-wheat pastry flour: 1/2 cup all-purpose flour and 1/2 cup whole-wheat flour, or (as a last resort) use 1 cup all-purpose flour.

Blueberry Buckle

Hands-on – 15 min. Oven – 35 min. **Serves 12**

This recipe, amazingly, contains no fat. It's super easy to make and delicious.
Don't feel guilty eating it for breakfast, either. It's just as nutritious as toast with jam and fruit!

Preheat oven to 375°.
Coat a 9" x 13" baking dish with cooking spray.

2 bags	(12 oz each) frozen blueberries, thawed or 2 pints fresh blueberries, washed, and drained	**Berry Bottom:** Spread blueberries in baking dish (allow frozen berries to thaw partially). Sprinkle sugar on top.
3 T	sugar	

1/2 cup	orange juice	**Cake Topping:**
1 cup	whole-wheat pastry flour*	Mix together in a medium bowl. Drop 12 equal spoonfuls on top of blueberries in 3 rows of 4.
1/4 cup	sugar	
1 tsp	baking powder	
3	egg whites	
1/4 tsp	lemon, orange, or almond extract (opt)	

1 T	sugar	Sprinkle sugar over dough. Bake for 35 minutes or until cake is lightly browned.

4 cups	fat-free vanilla ice cream	Take out of oven. Serve warm with 1/3 cup scoop of fat-free vanilla ice cream or yogurt. Yummm!

*To learn more about whole-wheat pastry flour see page 288. You can substitute 1/2 cup whole-wheat flour and 1/2 cup all-purpose flour.

Nutrition information for 1/12 recipe, with 1/3 cup ice cream

Exchanges/Choices: 2 1/2 Carbohydrate

Calories	166	Fat	0.5 g	Fiber	3 g	Sodium	77 mg	Total Carbohydrate	36 g
Calories from Fat	3%	Saturated Fat	0 g	Cholesterol	0 mg	Protein	3 g	Sugars	23 g

Lickety-Split Tip

True or False?

People with diabetes cannot eat foods containing sugar.

Answer: FALSE.

People with diabetes need to control the number of carbohydrates they consume at every meal and snack. Eating foods high in sugar makes this very difficult to do, since high-sugar foods contain high amounts of of carbohydrates. On the other hand, they can include foods containing sugar when done in the following way:

1. Know how many carbohydrates the serving of foods contains (by reading the nutrition facts).

2. Choose recipes using less sugar and more whole grains (like the ones in this book). The less sugar a dessert contains, the more generous a portion can be.

3. "Make room" for the dessert by cutting back equally on other carbohydrate-containing foods like bread, rice, potatoes, or pasta. Cutting back exactly 30 grams of carbohydrate to enjoy a 30-gram carbohydrate dessert means a controlled blood sugar level.

People with diabetes must remember that eating a diet that is low in fat and high in fiber is also of KEY importance to success in the control of their health.

Chocolate-Amaretto Cheesecake

Hands-on – 25 min. Oven – 45–50 min.

Serves 12

When invited over to friends for dinner, I love bringing this dessert. They can't believe a "dietitian" could bring anything so good. This is truly "crime without punishment"!

Preheat oven to 300°.

12	chocolate wafers or 6 graham cracker squares	8 hours or day before serving: Finely crush and sprinkle into bottom of 8" springform pan.*** Set aside.
1 tub	(8 oz) fat-free cream cheese	Position knife blade in food processor bowl. Add ingredients, processing until smooth.
1 cup	sugar	
1½ cups	nonfat cottage cheese	
6 T	unsweetened cocoa powder	
1/4 cup	all-purpose flour	
1/4 cup	Amaretto*	
1 tsp	vanilla extract	
1	egg	Add and process just until blended. Slowly pour mixture over crumbs in pan.
2 T	semi-sweet chocolate mini-morsels	Sprinkle on top of mixture. Bake 45 to 50 minutes or until cheesecake is set. Let cool in pan on wire rack. Once cheesecake is cool, cover and chill at least 8 hours. Remove sides of pan.
1 - 2 cups	raspberries or sliced strawberries (to taste)	Place in a bowl and serve alongside the cheesecake platter. Invite guests to top their cake as desired.

*Alcohol-free option: Substitute 2 T light corn syrup, 2 T water, and 1 tsp almond or peppermint extract. *Chocolate-Mint Cheesecake: Substitute 1/4 cup creme de menthe for the amaretto. ***An 8-inch round pan can be used, but it's more difficult to remove a slice neatly.

Nutrition information for 1 slice of alcohol-free option (1/12 of cake) topped with 6 raspberries

Exchanges/Choices: 2 Carbohydrate, 1/2 Fat

Calories	175	Fat	2.5 g	Fiber	2 g	Sodium	256 mg	Total Carbohydrate	31 g
Calories from Fat	12%	Saturated Fat	1 g	Cholesterol	20 mg	Protein	8 g	Sugars	24 g

Lickety-Split Diabetic Meals

Lickety-Split Tip

An argument **FOR** desserts

Many nutrition professionals suggest **NOT** getting in the habit of dessert every night. I have certainly worked with many clients who blame their "dessert after every meal" upbringing for their weight problems. On the other hand, clients who grew up never being allowed dessert now have the strong tendency to overeat them. Many studies clearly suggest that deprivation is a major contributor to overeating forbidden foods. The solution is to include something satisfyingly sweet in moderation.

Creamy Frosted Carrot Cake or Muffins

Hands-on – 25 min. Oven – 28–30 min.

1 cake or 18 muffins

Did you know traditional carrot cake uses 1 cup of oil? Add the cream cheese frosting and you're looking at 50 to 60 grams of fat per slice! Well, throw out that old recipe and replace it with this delicious treat. No one will know, I promise.

Preheat oven to 350°. Coat a 9" × 13" baking dish or 18 muffin cups with cooking spray.

3 cups	(10 oz bag) shredded carrots	Buy pre-shredded carrots or use a food processor to shred. Set aside 3 cups for this recipe. Use any leftovers in your next salad.
3/4 cup	firmly packed brown sugar	In a large bowl, mix well with a wire whisk.
3 T	canola oil	
1/2 cup	egg substitute	
2 tsp	vanilla extract	Add to brown sugar mixture and stir.
1 can	(8 oz) crushed pineapple, in its own juice (including the juice)	
1/2 cup	any of the following: skim milk, buttermilk, or soy milk	
1/2 cup	raisins	
2½ cups	whole-wheat pastry flour*	Mix together in a medium bowl. Add, a little at a time, to pineapple mixture and mix well. Stir in carrots.
2 tsp	baking soda	
1 tsp	ground cinnamon	Pour batter into pan(s). Bake 35 to 37 minutes (20 to 25 minutes for muffins) or until a toothpick inserted in center comes out clean.
1 tsp	pumpkin pie spice	
1/8 tsp	salt	
1 tub	(8 oz) light cream cheese	Allow the cream cheese to soften on the counter while cake is baking. When cake comes out of oven, mix ingredients together in a medium bowl. Once cake has cooled, frost it. (If using round pans, frosting will only cover tops of cakes, not the sides.)
1 tsp	vanilla extract	
1/2 cup	powdered sugar	

*To learn more about whole-wheat pastry flour, see page 288. You can substitute 1¼ cups whole-wheat flour and 1¼ cups all-purpose flour.

Nutrition information for 1 slice (1/18 of cake) with frosting or 1 muffin with frosting

Exchanges/Choices: 2 Carbohydrate, 1 Fat

Calories	185	Fat	4.5 g	Fiber	3 g	Sodium	245 mg	Total Carbohydrate	33 g
Calories from Fat	22%	Saturated Fat	1.4 g	Cholesterol	5 mg	Protein	4 g	Sugars	18 g

Lickety-Split Diabetic Meals

Lickety-Split Tip

How much dessert is TOO much?

First, take a look at the recommended serving size. Use this as a guide, but most importantly, listen to your body. It will tell you when you've had enough.

Unfortunately, we typically eat until full and then eat dessert. (After all, this is what our parents taught us to do.) This makes the dessert **COMPLETELY** fattening! Yes, even if it is fat or sugar free! Thin people and controlled diabetics eat dessert occasionally, but they "save room" for it. So, when you know you'll be having dessert, plan ahead by eating half of your potato or skipping the bread.

Never eat dessert when you are full. Always **SAVE ROOM FOR DESSERT.**

Chewy Multi-Grain Bars

Hands-on — 30 min. Oven — 23 min. **Makes 24 bars**

These mock Kellogg® NutriGrain Bars make a fabulous snack, dessert, or lunchbox treat. They're even nutritious enough for breakfast along with a glass of milk or yogurt and a piece of fruit. You can freeze half of the bars in resealable bags for future use.

Preheat oven to 350°.

1 cup	raisins	Measure raisins into a glass measuring cup. Add water and microwave for 1 minute on HIGH. Allow to soak.
1 T	water	

1/4 cup	firmly packed brown sugar	Place in large bowl and mix thoroughly.
2 T	canola oil	Purée the soaking raisins in a food processor or blender. Add to large bowl and mix thoroughly. (People who don't care for raisins will tolerate them better puréed. Puréeing increases sweetness and moisture. Raisins can be added without puréeing if you prefer.)
1 cup	unsweetened applesauce	
4	egg whites	
2 T	skim milk or soy milk	
2 tsp	vanilla extract	

1½ cups	whole-wheat pastry flour*	Measure and sift into the large bowl (or combine in another bowl using a fork to evenly distribute soda and cinnamon). Stir well into wet ingredients.
1 tsp	baking soda	
1½ tsp	ground cinnamon	

3 cups	Multi-Grain Oats or quick or old-fashioned oatmeal	Add and mix. Spread dough into an ungreased 9" x 13" baking dish. Bake 23 minutes. Cool and cut into 24 bars.
1/3 cup	walnuts, coarsely chopped	

Icing

1/2 cup	powdered sugar	Mix together in a small bowl. Drizzle over cooled bars before or after cutting.
1/4 tsp	vanilla extract	
1 T	skim milk	

*To learn more about whole-wheat pastry flour, see page 288. You can substitute 3/4 cup whole-wheat flour and 3/4 cup all-purpose flour.

Nutrition information for 1 bar with icing

Exchanges/Choices: 1 1/2 Carbohydrate, 1/2 Fat

Calories	125	Fat	2.5 g	Fiber	3 g	Sodium	65 mg	Total Carbohydrate	24 g
Calories from Fat	18%	Saturated Fat	<1 g	Cholesterol	0 mg	Protein	3 g	Sugars	9 g

Lickety-Split Diabetic Meals

Lickety-Split Tip

Preventing Portion Distortion

Remember, if the recipe says it makes 36 cookies and you don't pay attention while you're scooping them out (or slicing them as in these bar cookies) and end up with only 24 cookies, then the calories and carbs (etc.) will be 1/3 more than what's listed for each recipe. And you wondered what was happening to your blood sugar!

While one cookie or two may be perfectly fine for you, numbers 3 and 4 are the ones that play havoc with your blood sugar. It all boils down to moderation! And you can do it!

Chocolate Chip Bar Cookies

My thanks to Registered Dietitian Lori Hunt for this delicious guilt-free chocolate chip cookie recipe. The instant pudding and applesauce replace the shortening entirely. (Use chocolate pudding for chocolate chocolate chip cookies.) Since these cookies are so moist, I suggest storing them in the refrigerator or freezer. They freeze wonderfully.

Preheat oven to 350°. Coat one or two 9" × 13" baking dishes with cooking spray.

2 Doz.	4 Doz.		
1 cup	2 cup	unsweetened applesauce	Using a fork, mix well in a large bowl.
3/4 cup	1½ cups	firmly packed brown sugar	
2 tsp	1 T+1 tsp	vanilla	
4	8	egg whites	
1 lg pkg	2 lg pkg	(5.1 oz) instant vanilla or (5.9 oz) chocolate pudding	In a medium-sized bowl, mix with a fork. Then add to the liquid ingredients. Using a large wooden spoon, stir well.
1 tsp	2 tsp	baking soda	
1 tsp	2 tsp	baking powder	
2 cups	4 cups	whole-wheat pastry flour*	
1 cup	2 cups	oats (quick-cooking or old-fashioned)	Add and mix.
1/2 bag	1 bag	(12 oz) semi-sweet chocolate chips	Add and mix. Let dough sit about 10 min. Place dough in baking dishes. Lay a sheet of wax paper on top. Press dough out. Remove wax paper.

Bake 25 minutes. When you take the cookies out of the oven, they will look lightly browned on top and be soft to the touch. They will firm up as they cool. Then cut each pan into 24 equal-size bars. If keeping past 2 days, store cookies in refrigerator or freezer.

*To learn more about whole-wheat pastry flour, see page 288. You can substitute 1 cup whole-wheat flour and 1 cup all-purpose flour, or for the large recipe, 2 cups whole-wheat flour and 2 cups all-purpose flour.

Nutrition information for 1 bar cookie

Exchanges/Choices: 2 Carbohydrate

Calories	135	Fat	2 g	Fiber	2 g	Sodium	165 mg	Total Carbohydrate	28 g
Calories from Fat	14%	Saturated Fat	1 g	Cholesterol	0 mg	Protein	3 g	Sugars	16 g

Lickety-Split Diabetic Meals

Lickety-Split Tip

Can I substitute Splenda for these recipes?

Yes, you can. The carbohydrate and calorie contents will decrease by approximately 1/3. But be aware of the "sugar-free health halo." Without realizing it, many people think, "Since it's sugar free, I can eat it in addition to what I usually have for dinner, or I can have twice as much." And guess what? Your blood sugar and weight ends up worse.

Therefore, portion control trumps artificial sweeteners in baked goods every time.

Oatmeal Cookies

Hands-on – 30 min. Oven – 10 min.   **Makes 36 cookies**

This recipe was inspired by one of Evelyn Tribole's recipe makeovers in Shape magazine. I found that the sugar could come down further. The cream cheese works nicely for both flavor and moistness. As I love to say, 3 of these with milk and an orange are nutritious enough for breakfast!

Preheat oven to 350°.

4 oz	fat-free cream cheese	In a large mixing bowl, use an electric mixer to beat together. Set aside.
3/4 cup	firmly packed brown sugar	
1/4 cup	light corn syrup or molasses	
3 T	canola oil	
2	egg whites	
1 tsp	vanilla extract	

2 cups	oats (quick-cooking or old-fashioned)	In a medium bowl, mix together with a fork until soda and salt are well distributed. Add to liquid mixture and mix well.
2 cups	whole-wheat pastry flour*	
1 tsp	ground cinnamon	
1/2 tsp	ground nutmeg	
1/4 tsp	baking soda	
1/4 tsp	salt	

1 cup	raisins	Mix in.
1/2 cup	chopped walnuts	With a knife, cut dough into 3 equal sections. (Use this as a guide to make 3 dozen cookies.) Drop by slightly heaping tablespoons onto an ungreased nonstick baking sheet. Flatten each cookie with the back of your spoon. (Option: A reader tells me she places 3 chocolate chips firmly on top of each cookie. This doesn't add too much fat and calories, and her family raves!)

*To learn more about whole-wheat pastry flour, see page 288. You can substitute 1 cup whole-wheat flour and 1 cup all-purpose flour.

Bake 10 minutes or until lightly brown.

Nutrition information for 1 cookie

Exchanges/Choices: 1 Carbohydrate, 1/2 Fat

Calories	100	Fat	2.7 g	Fiber	1.5 g	Sodium	50 mg	Total Carbohydrate	18 g
Calories from Fat	24%	Saturated Fat	0 g	Cholesterol	0 mg	Protein	2.5 g	Sugars	9 g

Lickety-Split Diabetic Meals

Lickety-Split Tip

Chocoholics unite!

The following are a few of my favorite "healthier" ways to lick a chocolate craving:

• Cup of hot cocoa

• 1 oz dark chocolate-savored slowly

• Glass of chocolate milk (bottle of chocolate syrup comes in handy)

• Sliced 1/2 banana drizzled with chocolate syrup and topped with 1 tablespoon of chopped walnuts

• Frozen cherries (defrosted slightly) drizzled with chocolate syrup

• Low-fat chocolate chip granola bar

• Chocolate No-Bakes (page 301)

• Cocoa Lava Kisses (page 303)

• Chocolate Chip Bar Cookies (page 297)

Chocolate No-Bakes

Hands-on – 20 min.   **Makes 36 cookies**

The same wonderful cookie from my childhood, using no margarine and 1/2 the sugar!

1/3 cup	unsweetened cocoa powder	Bring to a boil in a medium saucepan and continue to boil 1 to 2 minutes. Remove from heat.
1/4 cup	nonfat dry milk	
3/4 cup	sugar	
1/4 cup	light corn syrup	
1/2 cup	skim milk	
1/2 cup	peanut butter (natural, crunchy)	
1 T	vanilla	Stir in.
3½ cups	oats (quick-cooking or old-fashioned)	Measure into a medium bowl. Pour hot mixture over oats and mix well.

Drop by spoonfuls onto waxed paper and allow to cool. Be sure to make 36 cookies if you want the nutrition information to be accurate.

Transfer to an airtight container and refrigerate. (Because these have less saturated fat, they do not set up "solid" at room temperature like the traditional No-Bakes. Expect them to be gooey and good.)

Nutrition information for 1 cookie

Exchanges/Choices: 1 Carbohydrate, 1/2 Fat

Calories	75	Fat	2.5 g	Fiber	1 g	Sodium	25 mg	Total Carbohydrate	12 g
Calories from Fat	30%	Saturated Fat	0.5 g	Cholesterol	0 mg	Protein	2.5 g	Sugars	7 g

Lickety-Split Diabetic Meals

Lickety-Split Tip

Chocolate facts: Did you know?

Chocolate is basically a creamy mixture of 3 ingredients: cocoa, sugar, and fat. Studies have shown that this combination of ingredients creates impulsive, addictive, "lack of control" behavior, with fat being the key culprit. The fat provides the creamy smoothness, dulling the sweetness slightly, so you don't tire of the teaspoons upon teaspoons of sugar that you are consuming. The fat combined with the sugar makes the calories soar.

But say you get smart and use the cocoa and sugar, but not the fat? Could you gain chocolate satisfaction with fewer calories and more control to stop at a few? Try this strategy in these Cocoa Lava Kisses. You'll be surprised at the satisfaction you'll feel with fewer bites. While a little sugar is fine, a lot is not. So exercise restraint!

Cocoa Lava Kisses

Hands-on — 30 min. Oven — 30 min.   **Makes 40 cookies**

These heavenly clouds of sweet chocolate work great to take care of a chocolate craving. Unbelievably, they're fat-free! They are intensely sweet, which will make it easier to stop at 3, which is only 60 calories!

These freeze well, making them convenient for future chocolate cravings!

Preheat oven to 250°.
Line 2 cookie sheets with wax paper.

3	egg whites	Place in medium bowl. Whip with an electric mixer until soft peaks form.
1/8 tsp	salt	

1 cup	sugar	Gradually add 1/2 cup of the sugar to egg whites while constantly whipping.

2 tsp	water	Combine in a cup. Add to mix, a few drops at a time, alternating with the remaining 1/2 cup sugar while constantly whipping.
1 tsp	vanilla extract	

3 T	unsweetened cocoa powder	Flake cocoa with a fork to break clumps. Sift if necessary. Fold completely into mix.

Place bite-size rounded teaspoons (not tablespoons) of batter onto the wax paper-lined sheets.

Bake approximately 30 minutes. They will be dry on the outside, but moist and lava-like on the inside. They will retain their shape. (If they become completely dry like styrofoam, they are overbaked.)

While kisses are still hot, remove from wax paper and place on a wire rack so they will not stick.

After cooling, store kisses in an airtight container.

Nutrition information for 1 cookie

Exchanges/Choices: Free Food (2 kisses equals 1/2 Carbohydrate)

Calories	20	Fat	0 g	Fiber	0 g	Sodium	12 mg	Total Carbohydrate	5 g
Calories from Fat	0%	Saturated Fat	0 g	Cholesterol	0 mg	Protein	0 g	Sugars	5 g

Lickety-Split Diabetic Meals

Lickety-Split Tip

Banana buying and ripening tips

1. Buy a few yellow and a few green, for "just in time" bananas all week.

2. Once your bananas reach their desired ripeness, place them in the refrigerator to halt the ripening process for a few days. Don't be alarmed when the skins turn black. They will still be perfect on the inside.

3. If your bananas have reached the banana bread stage, but you don't have the 30 minutes to mix this up, simply peel them and slip them into sealable baggies for the freezer. They can be thawed and used another time for 'Nana Bread (page 305), Banana Nut Cake (page 313), or Smoothies (page 11).

'Nana Bread

Hands-on – 15 min. Oven – 45 min.

2 loaves, 12 servings each

Who doesn't love banana bread? Every household needs a banana bread recipe for those bananas that get too ripe before the family can get around to eating them all. And the recipe needs to be without all the fat and sugar, yet so moist and sweet that each slice can be eaten as is! Ask no more, it's all right here!

In this recipe, mashed bananas completely replace the shortening or margarine!

Preheat oven to 350°.
Coat 2 loaf pans with cooking spray.

1/2 cup	firmly packed brown sugar	Mix together in a large mixing bowl.
2	egg whites	
2 T	vanilla extract	
3 cups	bananas (about 5)	Mash. (I use a food processor.) Stir into mixture.
2 T	canola oil	Add to mix and stir.
3 cups	whole-wheat pastry flour*	Place in a sifter and sift over mixture (or place in a separate bowl and use a fork to equally distribute the salt and soda). Stir together thoroughly with the wet ingredients.
2 tsp	baking soda	
1/2 tsp	salt	
2/3 cup	coarsely chopped walnuts (opt)	Stir into batter.
1/2 cup	ground flax seed (opt)	Divide batter evenly between the pans (loaves will not be high).

Bake 45 minutes, or until a toothpick inserted in center comes out clean.

*To learn more about whole-wheat pastry flour, see page 288. You can substitute 1½ cups whole-wheat and 1½ cups all-purpose flour.

Nutrition information for 1 slice including ground flax seed (1/12 of loaf)

Exchanges/Choices: 1 1/2 Carbohydrate, 1 Fat

Calories	137	Fat	4 g	Fiber	3.5 g	Sodium	160 mg	Total Carbohydrate	23 g
Calories from Fat	27%	Saturated Fat	0 g	Cholesterol	0 mg	Protein	3 g	Sugars	7 g

Lickety-Split Diabetic Meals

Lickety-Split Tip

I wish I could stop at one cookie or one brownie....but they "talk" to me, and sure enough, my blood sugar and weight soar. What can I do?

I know you want me to tell you that you can bake with artificial sweeteners and everything will be okay. But the fact is, artificial sweeteners still contain carbohydrates and calories, too. Sweets (natural or artificial) mean comfort, happiness, entertainment, and relief from boredom for us. But so does stepping outside for a breath of fresh air, going for a walk, calling a friend, or listening to music! So first, make your environment conducive to success by not having lots of tempting sweets around (don't forget to create that inviting fresh fruit bowl), and be sure to have lots of other resources handy like an MP3 player with all your favorite music. Keep a list of your favorite "non-food joys" posted on your computer or refrigerator. Every time you successfully choose a non-food joy put a marble in a jar. Once you reach 100 marbles, book a trip to Cancun. Hey! You'll deserve it. Besides, won't you look great in that swimsuit after making all those better choices?

Enlightened Zucchini Bread

Hands-on – 30 min. Oven – 45–55 min.

1 or 2 loaves, 12 slices per loaf

Toss out that old recipe that called for 1 cup of oil, because now you have a much healthier alternative, without sacrificing taste! My thanks to Ann Jones, MS, RD, and her daughter for this great find.

Preheat oven at 350°.
Coat 1 or 2 loaf pans with cooking spray.

1 loaf	2 loaves		
1½ cup	3 cups	whole-wheat pastry flour*	Mix together in a small or medium bowl.
1/2 tsp	1 tsp	baking soda	
1/4 tsp	1/2 tsp	baking powder	
1 tsp	2 tsp	ground cinnamon	
1/4 tsp	1/2 tsp	each, ground cloves and nutmeg	
3/4 cup	1½ cups	sugar	Beat together in a large bowl.
2	4	egg whites	
1/4 cup	1/2 cup	skim milk or nonfat plain yogurt	
1 tsp	2 tsp	vanilla extract	
1 T	2 T	lemon juice	
1/4 tsp	1/2 tsp	lemon extract	
1 cup	2 cups	shredded zucchini, unpeeled	Stir into wet ingredients. Stir in the dry ingredients just until combined.
1/2 cup	1 cup	nuts	Stir in nuts.

Divide batter evenly between pan(s). Bake 45 to 55 minutes or until a toothpick inserted in center comes out clean.

*To learn more about whole-wheat pastry flour, see page 288. You can substitute 3/4 cup whole-wheat flour and 3/4 cup all-purpose flour, or for the large recipe, 1½ cups whole-wheat flour and 1½ cups all-purpose flour.

Nutrition information for 1 slice (1/12 of loaf)

Exchanges/Choices: 1 1/2 Carbohydrate, 1/2 Fat

Calories	140	Fat	3 g	Fiber	2.5 g	Sodium	73 mg	Total Carbohydrate	25 g
Calories from Fat	22%	Saturated Fat	0 g	Cholesterol	0 mg	Protein	3.5 g	Sugars	13 g

Lickety-Split Tip

Halloween Survival Tips for KIDS

1. Don't let kids hide their candy underneath their beds. They just might snack unsupervised late into the night, playing havoc with their blood sugar (if they have diabetes) and leaving their teeth exposed to the sugar all night.

2. Gently remind kids that candy is not a "grow food." This is why you are asking them to limit themselves to 2 or 3 pieces a day, in order to leave room for plenty of "grow" food.

3. Have them count out 30 (or so) pieces they want to keep and give the rest to families less fortunate.

Surprise Pumpkin Pie

Hands-on – 10 min. Oven – 50–60 min.   **1 pie, 8 servings**

"Surprise" because it makes its own crust. What a time and fat saver! This pie is so fast that you can have it in the oven in less than 10 minutes. It's delicious and beta-carotene rich. Why not serve it all year round?

Preheat the oven to 350°.
Coat a 9" pie plate (preferably glass) with cooking spray.

2	eggs or 4 egg whites or 1/2 cup egg substitute
3/4 cup	sugar
1/2 cup	Hodgson Mill Insta-Bake or reduced-fat Bisquick mix
1 can	(15 oz) pumpkin
2 tsp	pumpkin pie spice (or 1 tsp cinnamon, 1/2 tsp ginger, 1/4 tsp cloves, and 1/4 tsp nutmeg)
1/4 tsp	salt
1 can	(13 oz) evaporated skim milk

Process together in a blender or food processor for 2 minutes.

Pour batter into prepared pie plate.

Bake 50 to 60 minutes, or until firm.

Cool completely before cutting. Serve with fat-free ice cream or yogurt, if desired.

*This recipe makes either (1) 9" deep-dish (4-cup volume) or (2) shallow dish (2-cup volume) pies. If making the (2) shallow pies, adjust baking time to 35 to 45 minutes. Nutrition information per slice will be 1/2 of what is listed below.

Nutrition information for 1 slice (1/8 of pie)

Exchanges/Choices: 2 Carbohydrate

Calories	167	Fat	2 g	Fiber	2 g	Sodium	197 mg	Total Carbohydrate	33 g
Calories from Fat	11%	Saturated Fat	<1 g	Cholesterol	55 mg	Protein	6.5 g	Sugars	25 g

Lickety-Split Diabetic Meals

Lickety-Split Tip

Halloween Survival Tips for ADULTS

1. If you have the tendency to eat most of your Halloween candy before October 31, then refrain from buying until the day before.

2. Buy candy you don't like (if there is such a thing!).

3. Increase your exercise during this period.

4. Use positive self-talk. If you've nibbled a bit more than you wanted to, say, "No big deal." Make a decision to end the "haunting" and give the candy away!

5. My favorite non-candy gifts include pencils, erasers, and plastic spiders. Kids love these, and leftovers can be tucked away and stored for the next year. (See the next page for more non-candy ideas.)

Pumpkin Oat Bran Bread or Muffins

A super way to eat beta-carotene-loaded pumpkin. This makes a large batch, so freeze the muffins for another busy time, especially breakfast!

Preheat oven to 350°. Coat 3 loaf pans or 1 loaf pan and 24 muffin cups with cooking spray.

2½ cups	whole-wheat pastry flour*	Mix together in a large bowl.
2½ cups	oat bran (dry, uncooked)	Make a well in center of mixture.
1½ cups	sugar	
1½ tsp	ground cinnamon	
1/2 tsp	ground cloves	
1 T	baking soda	

4	egg whites	Add to well in dry mixture. Stir just until moistened.
2 cans	(15 oz each) pumpkin	
1/2 cup	unsweetened applesauce	

| 1/2 cup | chopped nuts (opt) | Stir in. |
| 1 cup | raisins (opt) | Pour batter evenly into pans. |

Bake 45 minutes (30–35 minutes for muffins) or until toothpick inserted in center comes out clean.

*To learn more about whole-wheat pastry flour see page 288. You can substitute 1¼ cups whole-wheat flour and 1¼ cups all-purpose flour.

Nutrition information for 1 slice (1/12 of loaf) or 1 muffin with optional nuts and raisins

Exchanges/Choices: 1 1/2 Carbohydrate

| Calories | 111 | Fat | 2 g | Fiber | 3 g | Sodium | 110 mg | Total Carbohydrate | 24 g |
| Calories from Fat | 16% | Saturated Fat | 0 g | Cholesterol | 0 mg | Protein | 3 g | Sugars | 12 g |

Lickety-Split Diabetic Meals

Lickety-Split Tip

Halloween Survival: "Boo"tiful Alternatives to Candy

• Stickers

• Hand stamps and removable tattoos

• Dimes or nickels (You can actually "save" money this way!)

• Barrettes and ponytail holders for the fairy princesses

• Cool pencils, erasers, and crayons for the ghouls and goblins

• Fun plastic rings and jewelry with glitter, gems, and even spiders and bugs

• Sugar-free gum

• Granola bars

• Raisins (small boxes)

• Juice boxes (a refreshing treat for hard-working witches and warriors)

Banana Nut Cake or Muffins

This is a fruity, refreshing change from the standard cake mixes and is nutritionally superior. It's whole-grain and delicious without added fats.

Preheat oven to 350°. Coat one 9" x 13" baking dish, two 9" round cake pans or 18 muffin cups with cooking spray

2¹⁄₃ cups	whole-wheat pastry flour*	Using a fork, mix together in a large bowl.
1 cup	sugar	Be certain baking powder and soda are well distributed.
1½ tsp	baking powder	
1 tsp	baking soda	
1/2 tsp	salt	
1²⁄₃ cups	mashed bananas (about 3)	Mash bananas in a food processor or in a separate bowl by hand.
3	eggs	Add liquids and bananas to dry ingredients and mix.
2/3 cup	skim or buttermilk (reconstituted from powdered)	
2/3 cup	unsweetened applesauce	
1/2 cup	chopped nuts (opt)	Mix in.
1/4 cup	semi-sweet chocolate chips	Pour batter evenly into prepared pan(s). Bake until toothpick inserted in center comes out clean; rectangle 40 minutes, rounds 35 minutes, muffins 22 to 25 minutes.

Cool and cut into 18 squares and serve as a snacking cake.

If it's someone's birthday, I'll dust the entire cake with 1 T sprinkling of powdered sugar (adds negligible sugar and calories).

Nutrition information for 1 piece (1/18 of cake) or 1 muffin including optional nuts

*To learn more about whole-wheat pastry flour, see page 288. You can substitute 1 cup whole-wheat flour and 1¹⁄₃ cups all-purpose flour.

Exchanges/Choices: 2 Carbohydrate, 1 Fat

Calories	175	Fat	4 g	Fiber	3 g	Sodium	185 mg	Total Carbohydrate	31 g
Calories from Fat	20%	Saturated Fat	1 g	Cholesterol	35 mg	Protein	4 g	Sugars	16 g

Lickety-Split Diabetic Meals

Lickety-Split Tip

Flaming tips

• Use caution. The flames may rise 2 feet. Keep dangling hair and sleeves safely out of the way. Use long matches and keep a fire extinguisher handy.

• Turn lights down to enjoy the flame.

• Try this recipe outdoors, using your grill as your heat source.

• Try it after dark.

• Be aware that flaming does not remove all the alcohol.

Flaming Bananas Foster

Hands-on — 15 min. **Serves 6 (petite)**

I learned to make this when I was 15 years old, after dining at Brennans in New Orleans. It's my absolute favorite dessert for entertaining. Talk about fun, fast, tasty, and impressive!

Delegate someone to: Find the matches and scoop the ice cream (1/2 cup each serving)

3 T	light margarine	Melt brown sugar and margarine in a medium nonstick sauté pan over medium heat.
1/3 cup	firmly packed brown sugar	
3	bananas, peeled and diagonally sliced 1/4" thick	Add bananas and cinnamon, and sauté until tender, stirring occasionally.
6 dashes	ground cinnamon	(Use this time to find your matches!)
1/3 cup	white rum	With matches ready, pour separately over bananas, stand back and attempt to "touch" the liquid (particularly the rum, which is most flammable) with your lit match. Be sure to yell, "Everybody now… OOPA!" as it lights. (The louder the OOPAs, the better it will taste!)
3 T	banana liqueur	
		Continue to simmer dish over medium heat throughout flaming process (about 20 seconds).
3 cups	fat-free vanilla ice cream or yogurt	Once flame goes out on its own, serve immediately over 1/2 cup single servings of ice cream.

Nutrition information for scant 1/2 cup of banana topping over 1/2 cup ice cream

Exchanges/Choices: 3 Carbohydrate

Calories	257	Fat	1 g	Fiber	1.5 g	Sodium	108 mg	Total Carbohydrate	48 g
Calories from Fat	4%	Saturated Fat	0 g	Cholesterol	0 mg	Protein	4 g	Sugars	26 g

Lickety-Split Diabetic Meals

Lickety-Split Tip

Master the FATS of Life

Choose foods that are as low in fat as possible then add back limited amounts of the omega-3 good fat found in nuts, seeds, olive oil and salmon. By limiting the amount of saturated animal fat and partially hydrogenated trans fat, you can:

1. Lower your risk of heart disease

2. Lower your risk of cancer

3. Control your weight

4. Have **MORE** energy!

Hot Fudge Brownie Cake

Hands-on — 15 min. Oven — 35–40 min.　　　**Serves 9**

A quick way to bake up a super chocolate treat. The hot water poured over the top will turn into a yummy hot fudge.

Preheat oven to 350°.

1 cup	all-purpose flour	In a medium-sized bowl, combine with a fork until well distributed.
1/2 cup	sugar	
2 T	unsweetened cocoa powder	
2 tsp	baking powder	
1/4 tsp	salt	
1/2 cup	skim milk	Stir in until smooth. Spread batter in an ungreased 9" × 9" baking dish.
2 T	oil (canola)	
1 tsp	vanilla extract	
1/2 cup	firmly packed brown sugar	Sprinkle each evenly over batter.
3/4 cup	chopped nuts	
1/4 cup	unsweetened cocoa powder	
1½ cup	hot water	Pour over top and do not stir. (This is not a mistake!) Bake 35 to 40 minutes. Allow to stand for 10 minutes.
4½ cups	fat-free vanilla ice cream or frozen yogurt (opt)	Cut into 9 squares and serve warm with 1/2 cup scoop of fat-free ice cream or frozen yogurt, if desired.

Nutrition information for 1/9 of recipe, without ice cream

Exchanges/Choices: 2 1/2 Carbohydrate, 1 1/2 Fat

Calories	241	Fat	9.5 g	Fiber	2 g	Sodium	340 mg
Calories from Fat	34%	Saturated Fat	<1 g	Cholesterol	<1 mg	Protein	5 g

Total Carbohydrate	37 g
Sugars	23 g

Lickety-Split Diabetic Meals

Lickety-Split Tip

Tips on sugar

My recipes contain somewhere around 1/2 the sugar of other dessert recipes. The nutrition information provided in this book includes grams of sugar. Every 4 grams of sugar you see equal 1 teaspoon of sugar. Up to 3 teaspoons (or 12 grams) of sugar is an acceptable amount for a dessert. You can easily flip through the recipes and see which recipes have the most and least amounts of sugar.

P.S. Understanding "grams of sugar" also helps you evaluate breakfast cereals, telling you which ones have a lot of sugar and which ones don't. Check it out!

Applesauce Dumplings

Hands-on – 22 min.   **Serves 8**

Hungry for something sweet and there's nothing in the house? Try this simple-to-whip-up apple dessert that requires no apple peeling! My thanks to Grandma Minnie for this neat find.

3 cups	unsweetened applesauce	Place in a medium nonstick saucepan over medium heat.
1/2 cup	water	
1 tsp	ground cinnamon	

1 cup	reduced-fat Bisquick mix	In a medium bowl, combine just until moistened.
1/4 c	sugar	Applesauce should be boiling by now. Remove from heat and drop 6 even-size dumplings onto applesauce.
1/2 cup	skim milk	Cover and return to heat. Simmer 12 minutes. Serve warm.

2 cups	fat-free vanilla ice cream or frozen yogurt	Top each serving with 1/4 cup scoop of fat-free ice cream or frozen yogurt.

Nutrition information for 1 dumpling, 1/3 cup sauce, 1/4 cup frozen yogurt

Exchanges/Choices: 2 1/2 Carbohydrate

Calories	162	Fat	1.5 g	Fiber	2 g	Sodium	135 mg	Total Carbohydrate	37 g
Calories from Fat	8%	Saturated Fat	0 g	Cholesterol	0 mg	Protein	4 g	Sugars	9 g

Lickety-Split Diabetic Meals

Lickety-Split Tip

Isn't fruit high in sugar and, therefore, a person with diabetes should avoid it?

No. Since fruit is high in fiber, water, and valuable vitamins and minerals, it's one of the best-spent carbohydrates all day. Just be aware of the portion size. (Don't be eating an entire half of watermelon!) Besides, consuming at least two pieces of fruit will help curb sweet cravings the rest of the day. Fruit is nature's candy, so ask your diabetes educator how to best plan for the ideal number of fruits you would like to include each day.

Brownie Banana Split

Hands-on — 30 min.   **Serves 24**

This recipe utilizes the convenience of a brownie mix, and adds nutrition via flax seed and fresh fruit! This simple dessert ends up with nutritional value to go along with the sugar. Its heavenly appearance makes it a favorite for entertaining.

Preheat oven according to package directions.
Coat a 9" × 13" baking dish well with cooking spray.

1 pkg	low-fat brownie mix	Pour brownie mix in a large bowl. Add water as listed on package. Add flax seed, if desired. Mix well. Pour batter into prepared pan and bake as directed.
1/3 cup	ground flax seed or toasted wheat-germ (opt)	When finished baking, invert entire brownie cake onto a serving platter. Let cake cool.*
4 oz	fat-free cream cheese	Mix together in a medium bowl. Warm in microwave 30 seconds. Drizzle over the cooled brownie cake.
1/2 cup	powdered sugar	
1 can	(8 oz) pineapple tidbits, in its own juice	**Just before serving:** Drain pineapple well, reserving juice for another use. Sprinkle pineapple on top of cream cheese frosting.
2	fresh bananas, peeled	Slice, then place on top of pineapple.
12 to 15	fresh strawberries, hulled	
1/4 cup	chocolate syrup (squeeze bottle kind) (opt)	Just before serving, drizzle 1/2 teaspoon of syrup over each brownie, if desired. Enjoy!

*If you have 12 or fewer guests, cut cake in 1/2 and only top 1/2 now. Do the other 1/2 another day, since the fresh appearance does not keep overnight.

Nutrition information for 1 slice (with ground flax seed and chocolate syrup)

Exchanges/Choices: 2 Carbohydrate

Calories	130	Fat	2 g	Fiber	1.5 g	Sodium	105 mg	Total Carbohydrate	27 g
Calories from Fat	19%	Saturated Fat	<1 g	Cholesterol	0 mg	Protein	2.5 g	Sugars	18 g

Lickety-Split Diabetic Meals

Grocery List

Welcome to your Lickety-Split Shopping Solution!

The Lickety-Split Grocery List includes every ingredient necessary to make any recipe in *Lickety-Split Diabetic Meals*. This list is designed to: (1) Guide you in stocking your pantry so you can make any Lickety-Split recipe you wish and (2) Make weekly re-stocking a snap.

Gone are the days of not having everything you need when you need it. And NO more tedious list making! Each week your list is organized, neatly typed with brand name recommendations.

Here's how it works:

Step #1 Inventory Your Kitchen
& Customize Your List

While at home, use the list to guide you through your refrigerator, freezer, and all your cupboards. Using a pencil, check-mark any item that you don't already have or is so old it needs replacing. (This is a good time to "clean and toss" to make space for all the new items you'll be bringing home.)

The "par stock" column is the number I suggest you keep on hand for each item. This number is based on a family of four. You will need to adjust for your family size and preferences. The "re-stock" column is for marking the quantity you need in order to achieve the "par stock" level.

For an ingredient that you question you will ever use, look at the "for use in" column to see what recipe(s) the item is used in. If the item is perishable and used in a recipe that you don't plan to make this week, skip it. If it's an ingredient for a recipe that doesn't sound like one you may ever make, skip it. In fact, for any item that you know you will never use, simply draw a line through it.

Finally, use the blank lines in the back to write in items you commonly use that aren't on the list. (Every family has their own favorites!) Now your list is customized and ready for your first big "stocking" trip!

Step #2 Embark on Your First Big "Stocking" Trip

This initial trip will require extra time, energy and money. But I promise, you will enjoy having everything you need, and each subsequent trip will be super quick, easy, and much less expensive!

Pick a time when you are fresh and energized. Eat before you go. Consider enlisting someone to go with you for help. Find child care for small children. Be prepared to read some labels; however, you'll be glad to know that many times I've given you brand name recommendations.

Step #3 Organize and Train the Family

Once you're home with your fresh supply of ingredients, try to refrain from shoving stuff any old place. Take time to group all the like canned items together, like freezer items together, and so on. The minutes you spend now will save you hours in the coming weeks! Consider cleaning and cutting raw vegetables before putting them away for quick and easy snacking during the week.

Now, erase the "re-stock" column of your Lickety-Split Grocery List and return the book to its countertop position. Next, call all family members into the kitchen. Explain the shopping you have done. Point out the newly organized cupboards and brainstorm for simple strategies to keep them that way. And, most importantly, explain that whenever someone discovers an item is almost used up or all used up, they should mark it on the list. Point out how the list is organized and how to use it. Be prepared to spend the next few weeks reminding family members of this important new habit.

Assuming your education session is successful, when it's time to go shopping again, your list will be already made! All neatly typed and organized according to store sections and with brand name recommendations. Even Dad won't mind picking up the groceries once in a while! Now, this is living!

Abbreviations

opt	Optional item. Not required, but recommended.
0-1	Some weeks you will buy 0, some weeks you will buy 1 (or whatever quantity is stated) according to your menu choices for that week.
1+	Buy 1 or more, depending on your family's needs.
pkg	package
oz	ounce
lb	pound
qt	quart
sm	small
med	medium
lg	large

Lickety-Split Tip

How to calculate your "Family FRUIT Quota" for 1 WEEK

Decide if your goal is 1, 2, 3, or 4 pieces per person each day. Keep in mind that the American Institute for Cancer Research says that 2 servings is the minimum and if you have sweet cravings, a few more is better!

Yes, canned fruit in its own juice, applesauce and dried fruit can be substituted! (See page 260 to find out why juice is not recommended as one of your minimum servings.)

Number in family		1	2	3	4	5	6
Pieces per person per day	1	7	14	21	28	35	42
	2	14	28	42	56	70	84
	3	21	42	63	84	105	126
	4	28	56	84	112	140	168

I see your eyes popping out!!! I know this seems like WAY too much, but the facts are the FACTS!

Tips: If you have a large family, to prevent spoilage:

- Buy half now and shop for the rest mid-week
- Buy some bananas green and some yellow for "just in time" bananas all week
- Buy some hard and some soft peaches, pears and kiwis
- Store ripe, ready-to-eat fruit in the refrigerator and the rest at room temperature
- Place a fruit bowl on your kitchen counter to help everyone remember to snack on fruit!

What about the cost?

To generate "fruit" money, spend LESS in other departments:

1. Refrain from buying soda and beer. It's amazing how much more affordable water is!

2. Instead of buying products like instant scalloped potatoes and Rice-a-Roni, stick with the less expensive versions: raw potatoes and rice.

3. Serve smaller portions of meat and serve more vegetarian meals like beans and rice or pasta. Examples include: Veggie Sghetti, 3-Bean Chili, meatless stir-fry, and bean burritos.

Presto! Money to fuel your new stepped-up fruit habit!

What equals a fruit/vegetable serving?

1	small apple, pear, orange, nectarine, kiwi, etc.
2	plums
4	apricots
1 cup	berries or melon
15	grapes
2 T	raisins
4	dried apricots
1/2 cup	applesauce (unsweetened)
1/2 cup	canned fruit (in own juice, drained)
1/2 cup	cooked vegetables
1 cup	raw vegetables
6	baby carrots

Grocery List

Restock	Par stock	Item and size	For use in...

Fresh Fruit

(Choose from seasonal selections. Adjust the amount your family needs using the chart above. The par-stock numbers below are a guide for 2 people for one week.)

Restock	Par stock	Item and size	For use in...
_____	8	**Bananas (med)**	Breakfasts & snacking Smoothies Banana Nut Cake or Muffins Banana-Oat Pancakes Summer Fresh Fruit Pie Flaming Bananas Foster
_____	8	**Oranges**	Breakfasts & snacking
_____	8	**Apples (sm)**	Snacking Scrumptious Swiss Oats ... Crunchy Apple Salad
_____	1	**Grapes (bunch)**	Snacking Ambrosia Rice Almond Chicken Salad
_____	1	**Cantaloupe or Honeydew**	Breakfasts & snacking
_____	0-1	**Strawberries (qt)**	Breakfasts & snacking Scrumptious Swiss Oats ... Summer Fresh Fruit Pie
_____	0-1	**Blueberries (pt)**	Breakfasts & snacking Scrumptious Swiss Oats ... Summer Fresh Fruit Pie
_____	0-1	**Raspberries (pt)**	Breakfasts & snacking Scrumptious Swiss Oats ... Summer Fresh Fruit Pie Chocolate-Amaretto Cheesecake
_____	0-8	**Nectarines (sm)**	Breakfasts & snacking Summer Fresh Fruit Pie
_____	0-8	**Peaches (sm)**	Breakfasts & snacking Summer Fresh Fruit Pie
_____	4-8	**Pears (sm)**	Breakfasts & snacking
_____	4-6	**Grapefruit**	Breakfasts & snacking
_____	4	**Kiwi**	Breakfasts & snacking Scrumptious Swiss Oats ...
_____	1-2	**Lemon**	Flavoring ice water Recipes with fish Pasta Slaw Lentil Spinach Soup Curried Chickpeas ... Broiled Orange Roughy Tzatziki
_____	opt	**Pineapple**	Snacking Marinated Sesame Chicken ...
_____	opt	**Coconut**	Sunshine Carrot-Raisin Salad

Lickety-Split Diabetic Meals

Lickety-Split Tip

How to get your "Family Veggie Quota" for 1 WEEK

Do this math:

____# of people in your family x 3 servings per day (minimum) x 7 days a week = ____

For a family of 4 multiplied by 7 days, that equals 84 servings!

Here's an example of how to fuel your family for 1 week. Adjust according to your preferences:

Produce	Servings
2 bunches broccoli	16
1/2 head cauliflower (buy 1 head and serve 1/2 this week and 1/2 the next)	5
2 lb baby carrots	12
2 cucumbers	4
5 tomatoes	5
6 green/red bell peppers	12
8 small potatoes (4 oz each)	8
2 small sweet potatoes (8 oz each)	4
2 cans vegetable soup, green beans or beets	4
2 bags (1 lb each) frozen veggies	10
Total servings per week!!!	**84**

Tips

1. If your cart doesn't look anything like this, increase gradually!

2. If you have a large family, to prevent spoilage, buy half now and shop for the rest mid-week.

3. Instruct the whole family to think of "vegetables" for snacks.

4. Use your fresh produce early in the week and use frozen or canned later in the week.

5. Double the "token spoonful" of vegetables you may have grown up with.

6. Consider single-serving cans of V-8 juice for lunches and snacks.

7. Try vegetable soup and a weekly stir-fry to help meet your weekly quota.

Grocery List

Restock	Par stock	Item and size	For use in...
		Fresh Veggies	

Each week purchase as needed to have on hand:

Restock	Par stock	Item and size	For use in...
_____	1	**Potatoes (bag)** baking or red	Baked potatoes Oven Fries Potato Salad Pizzucchini with Redskins
_____	4+	**Sweet potatoes or yams** Don't forget these!	Baked sweet potatoes Gypsy Stew
_____	1	**Onions (bag)**	Used regularly
_____	opt	**Green onions (bunch)**	Salads South of the Border Roll-ups Herbed Salmon Spread Oklahoma Bean Dip 7-Layer Bean Dip Benito Bean Dip and Burritos Great Northern Tuna Salad ... Chicken Dijon Stuffed ... Caribbean Black Beans ... Oriental Noodle Toss
_____	1+	**Broccoli** 2 heads are better than 1!	Used regularly
_____	1+	**Cauliflower (heads)**	Used regularly

Restock	Par stock	Item and size	For use in...
_____	1+	**Baby carrots (lg bag)**	Used regularly
_____	1	**Celery (bunch)**	Snacking Salads Miracle Soup Potato Salad
_____	3+	**Green bell peppers**	Used regularly
_____	1+	**Red bell peppers**	Used regularly
_____	1+	**Yellow bell peppers**	Used regularly
_____	4+	**Tomatoes**	Used regularly
_____	1+	**Cucumbers**	Snacking Salad Tzatziki
_____	1+	**Lettuce (dark greens)** If desired, pre-bagged, ready to eat	Instant tossed salads 1-Minute Mini-Meals
_____	opt	**Shredded carrots (bag)**	Creamy Frosted Carrot Cake... Sunshine Carrot-Raisin Salad Pasta Slaw
_____	0-2	**Shredded cabbage (bags)**	Miracle Soup Pasta Slaw

Lickety-Split Tip

Tofu Buying Tips

You will find tofu in the produce section of your grocery store. Here's a summary of your options:

Fresh: Packed in a small tub of water, must be refrigerated (usually a 7–10-day shelf life).

Vacuum packaged: Does not require refrigeration and offers the luxury of a 6 month or more shelf life (looks like juice boxes).

Low-fat tofu: Available in the vacuum packaged varieties.

Soft, firm, extra firm, and silken: Refers to the texture and will have a huge effect on your recipe.

My recommendations:

The vacuum packaged is definitely the most convenient, but I've found even the "firm" variety is more "silken" and does not provide the meaty texture my recipes need. I therefore buy fresh tofu.

Tip: Changing the water every day will extend the freshness of the product a week or two past the stamped date.

While you might assume low-fat is the best choice, I've only found it available in the "silken" variety, which does not provide the meaty texture my recipes seek. Don't worry, regular tofu has only a small amount of soybean oil (healthy) and when balanced against the rest of the meal (potatoes, corn, bread, etc.), it calculates to a healthy percent of calories from fat. Because of this natural soybean oil, I use a nonstick cooking spray with tofu recipes rather than the oil I usually call for with dishes using chicken breast and ground turkey meat.

Grocery List

Restock	Par stock	Item and size	For use in...

Fresh Veggies (continued)

Each week choose 2 or 3 for variety:

Restock	Par stock	Item and size	For use in...
_____	0–1	**Green beans (1 lb)**	*Crispy Chicken Dijon* *Hungarian Chicken Paprikash*
_____	0–1	**Asparagus (bunch)** Buy frozen if you prefer	*Salmon Patties* *Chicken Dijon Stuffed ...* *Creamy Chicken Dijon*
_____	0–4	**Zucchini (sm)**	*Ratatouille* *Chicken Cacciatore* *Veggie Sghetti* *Southwest Chicken Pizza* *Easy Pepper Steak Stir-Fry* *Pizzucchini with Redskins*
_____	0–2	**Yellow crooked neck squash (sm)**	*Ratatouille* *Easy Pepper Steak Stir-Fry*
_____	0–20	**Mushrooms**	*Ratatouille* *Marinated Sesame Chicken ...*
_____	0–1	**Eggplant (med)**	*Ratatouille*
_____	0–2	**Butternut squash**	*Cinnamon Butternut Squash*
_____	opt	**Alfalfa sprouts**	*Salads* *Mediterranean Lavash Roll-ups* *Turkey & Hot Mustard Roll-ups*
_____	0–20	**Cherry tomatoes**	*Marinated Sesame Chicken ...* *1-Minute Mini-Meals*

Miscellaneous Produce

Restock	Par stock	Item and size	For use in...
_____	1	**Garlic, minced in a jar or head of fresh cloves**	Basic supply
_____	1	**Ginger root, minced in a jar, or a 4" fresh root**	Basic supply
_____	opt	**Parsley (bunch)** Will keep 3 wks. in fridge	*Curried Chickpeas & Gingered Black Beans*
_____	opt	**Cilantro (bunch)** Will keep 3 wks. in fridge	*Tofu Fiesta* *7-Layer Bean Dip* *Benito Bean Dip*
_____	0–2	**Tofu, firm (12-oz)**	*Scrambled Tofu* *Tofu Bites* *Tofu Fiesta* *Fajitas* *Sweet & Sour Stir-Fry* *Eggless Salad Stuffer*
_____	0–2	**Tofu, soft (12-oz)**	*Quick Creamy Tomato Soup*
_____	0–1	**Fresh salsa**	Snacking *Black Bean & Corn Salad* *Mexican LaZonya* *Spanish Red Beans & Rice*
_____	0–2	**Cranberries (12-oz bag)** Fresh are available in the fall. Buy several and freeze to have on hand.	*Cranberry Salad*

Lickety-Split Tip

Won't buying everything on this list cost me a fortune?

True, you will be writing a big check and going home with a car full of groceries on your first "stock-up" trip. But this is "bringing the grocery store to you," so you will ALWAYS have what you need. How much is that worth to you? To ALWAYS have what you need. (Listen to the sound of that word again!) You're not really spending more; you're just spending it earlier. And think, with all the time you'll be saving by not making extra trips to the store mid-week, and making your own pizza instead of having it delivered, you will recover that up-front investment in no time at all!

What are hummus and tabouli?

For information see page 76.

Grocery List

Restock	Par stock	Item and size	For use in...
		Miscellaneous Produce (continued)	
_____	0-1	**Tabouli**	*Mediterranean Lavash Roll-ups*
_____	0-1	**Pumpkin (med)** A special autumn treat!	*Jack in the Pumpkin*
_____	0-1	**Hummus** I recommend the roasted red pepper or hummus with spinach	Snacking *1-Minute Mini-Meals* *Mediterranean Lavash Roll-ups*
		Dried Fruit	
_____	1	**Raisins (box)**	Cereal Baking *Chewy Multi-Grain Bars* *Creamy Frosted Carrot Cake* *Breakfast in a Cookie* *Oatmeal Cookies* *Sunshine Carrot-Raisin Salad*
_____	0-1	**Dried cherries (tub)**	*Broccoli & Dried Cherry Salad* *Scrumptious Swiss Oats ...*
_____	opt	**Dried cranberries**	Salad toppings *Scrumptious Swiss Oats ...*
_____	0-1	**Dried apricots (box)**	Snacking Office pick-me-up *Scrumptious Swiss Oats ...*

Restock	Par stock	Item and size	For use in...
		Dried Beans and Grains	
_____	1	**Lentils, dried (16-oz bag)**	*Lentil Spinach Soup* *Baked Lentils & Rice*
_____	1	**Black beans, dried (16-oz bag)**	*Mexican Black Beans*
_____	1	**Split peas, dried (16-oz bag)**	*Split Pea Soup*
_____	2	**Uncle Ben's whole-grain instant brown rice**	Numerous meals
_____	1	**Brown rice** I highly recommend	*Baked Lentils & Rice* *Jack in the Pumpkin* *Spinach Veal Roll*
_____	opt	**Wild rice**	*Jack in the Pumpkin*
_____	1	**Barley, quick-cooking**	*Beef Barley Soup*

Lickety-Split Diabetic Meals

Misc. Produce (cont.)/Dried Fruit/Dried Beans & Grains

Grocery List
331

Lickety-Split Tip

Try to buy whole-grain pasta whenever possible

If you do not find whole-grain pasta in the pasta section, try the natural or health food section, or better yet, a natural food store. Remember, the nutritional benefit is worth the extra effort!

A brand of pasta I highly recommend is Eden. They make high-quality whole-grain pasta, including an ingenious alternative that is 60% whole-grain, making it lighter in texture. This is a great way for kids (or anyone) to warm up slowly to whole-grain pasta.

Storage tip

I store my pasta in clear decorative jars on top of my cupboards.
This saves me space INSIDE my cupboards and reminds me to cook pasta weekly.

Grocery List

Restock	Par stock	Item and size	For use in...

Pasta

The following is a recommended selection of pasta shapes to keep on hand. Look for whole-grain versions for more fiber and nutrition. My favorite brand is Eden Organic. Visit *www.EdenFoods.com*.

Restock	Par stock	Item and size	For use in...
_____	2	Spaghetti	*Veggie Sghetti*
_____	1	Angel hair	*Parmesan Turkey Cutlets* *Oriental Noodle Toss*
_____	1	Corkscrews	*Southwest Chili Pasta* *Chicken Cacciatore*
_____	1	Macaroni	*Herbed Italian Sausage*
_____	1	Shells, small	*Hearty Bean & Pasta Stew* *Tuna Noodle Casserole*
_____	1	Penne	*White Beans & Penne Pasta*
_____	2	Lasagna noodles	*LaZonya*
_____	1	Egg noodles	*Creamy Chicken Dijon* *Hungarian Chicken Paprikash* *Cranberry Pork Roast*
_____	1	Linguine	*Pasta Primavera*

Soups

Restock	Par stock	Item and size	For use in...
_____	opt	Chicken bouillon granules, low-sodium (sm)	Basic supply
_____	opt	Beef bouillon granules, low-sodium (sm)	Basic supply
_____	4	Chicken broth, 1/3 less sodium (14½-oz can)	Basic supply
_____	2	Beef broth (14½-oz can) reduced-sodium, if available	Basic supply
_____	3	Cream of mushroom soup, Campbell's Healthy Request (10½-oz can)	*Tuna Noodle Casserole* *Beef Stroganoff* *Simple Baked Chicken & Rice*
_____	2	Cream of chicken soup, Campbell's Healthy Request (10½-oz can)	*Creamy Chicken Enchiladas* *Simple Baked Chicken & Rice*
_____	2	Dry vegetable soup mix, Knorr or Mrs. Grass (pkg)	*Spinach Dip* *Miracle Soup*

Canned Fruit

Lickety-Split Tip

Do you know about Eden beans?

I highly recommend them! These are absolutely delicious, supreme quality, low-sodium, and organic beans. They come both plain and flavored, and taste great straight from the can. (Perfect for a 1-minute mini-meal!)

This is THE marriage of convenience, health, and taste that we've all been waiting for!

My favorites:

Eden Spicy Pintos

Eden Lentils with Sweet Onion and Bay Leaf

Eden Baked Beans with Sorghum & Mustard

Eden Chili Beans (great for my Chili Cornbread Pie, page 163)

Eden Garbanzo Beans (your new "croutons," perfect for topping a salad)

Eden Caribbean Black Beans

Find these at finer food stores like Whole Foods Market.

You can also order direct from Eden Foods at 888-424-EDEN or online at *www.EdenFoods.com*.

Grocery List

Restock	Par stock	Item and size	For use in...
_____	2	**Peaches, lite (16-oz can)**	Serve with meals
_____	2	**Pears, lite (16-oz can)**	Serve with meals
_____	1	**Apricots, lite (16-oz can)**	Serve with meals
_____	1	**Fruit cocktail, lite (16-oz can)**	Serve with meals
_____	1	**Mandarin oranges (15-oz can)**	*Ambrosia Rice* *Almond Chicken Salad*
_____	6	**Pineapple tidbits, packed in own juice (8-oz can)**	*Crunchy Apple Salad* *Sunshine Carrot-Raisin Salad* *Cranberry Salad* *Ambrosia Rice* *Sweet & Sour Stir-Fry* *Polynesian Pizza* *Brownie Banana Split* *Chicken Chutney Pizza*
_____	1	**Pineapple crushed, packed in own juice (8-oz can)**	*Creamy Frosted Carrot Cake*
_____	2	**Applesauce, unsweetened (large jar)**	Numerous recipes Serve with meals
_____	1	**Cranberry sauce, jellied (16-oz can)**	*Cranberry Pork Roast*

Canned Vegetables and Beans

Restock	Par stock	Item and size	For use in...
_____	2	**Corn, no salt added (16-oz can)**	*Black Bean & Corn Salad* 1-Minute Mini-Meals
_____	1	**Wax beans (15-oz can)**	*5-Bean Salad*
_____	1	**Green beans (15-oz can)**	*5-Bean Salad*
_____	1	**Butter beans (15-oz can)**	*5-Bean Salad*
_____	3	**Pumpkin (15-oz can)**	*Surprise Pumpkin Pie* *Pumpkin Oat Bran Bread . . .*
_____	4	**Mushrooms, sliced (8-oz can)**	Numerous main dishes
_____	2	**Beets, sliced (15-oz can)**	Serve with meals Great in salads
_____	6	**Diced tomatoes, no salt added (14½ oz can)**	Numerous entrees
_____	1	**Tomato purée (16-oz can)**	*Mexican LaZonya*
_____	2	**Eden Diced Tomatoes with Chiles**	*Chili Cornbread Pie*

Lickety-Split Diabetic Meals

Lickety-Split Tip

Hitting the Sauce

As you know, I love using ready-made spaghetti sauce to help speed my time in the kitchen. The following brands are selected samples of spaghetti sauces that meet the recommended criteria of 350 mg or less of sodium per ½ cup.

Recommended Sauce................................**Sodium (mg) per ½ cup**

Eden Organic, no salt added*.. 20

Eden Organic, with salt added.. 320

Classico (average of 5 selections)....................................... 345

Muir Glen Organic (average of 3 selections) 350

Healthy Choice Garlic & Herb... 320

Healthy Choice Super Chunky Tomato, Mushroom & Garlic 340

*This is my preference. For one, I love the fact that all the spaghetti sauce my family consumes is organic because it's a consistent way to help reduce our potential exposure to pesticides. Second, this sauce is "salt to YOUR taste." It works perfectly in all recipes including LaZonya.

For Comparison ....**Sodium (mg) per ½ cup**

Newman's Own (average of 9 selections) 557

Barilla (average of 5 selections) 572

Hunts (average of 9 selections) 570

Delallo (average of 4 selections) 520

Prego (average of 7 selections) 530

Ragu (average of 11 selections).. 552

Ragu, organic... 490

(Thirsty yet? For every 500 mg you consume, you've just swallowed ¼ tsp of salt!)

Grocery List

Restock	Par stock	Item and size	For use in...

Canned Vegetables and Beans (continued)

Restock	Par stock	Item and size	For use in...
_____	2	Black beans (15-oz can)	Black Bean & Corn Salad, Curried Chickpeas ..., 3-Bean Chili, Mexican 5-Bean Soup, Oriental Noodle Toss
_____	6	Pinto beans (15-oz can)	Benito Bean Dip, 7-Layer Bean Dip, Benito Bean Burritos
_____	1	Navy beans (15-oz can)	Mexican 5-Bean Soup
_____	6	Great Northern beans (15-oz can)	Great Northern Tuna ..., White Beans & Penne Pasta, White Beans w/Tomato, Basil
_____	2	Kidney beans (15-oz can)	3-Bean Chili, Mexican 5-Bean Soup, Crock-Pot Fajitas
_____	2	Garbanzo beans (15-oz can)	Curried Chickpeas & ..., Oklahoma Bean Dip, Gypsy Stew
_____	1	Black-eyed peas (15-oz can)	Oklahoma Bean Dip

Restock	Par stock	Item and size	For use in...
_____	2	Baked beans (15-oz can) (vegetarian if possible)	1-Minute Mini-Meals
_____	2	Eden Chili Beans (15-oz can)	Chili Cornbread Pie
_____	2	Eden Seasoned Beans (15-oz can)	1-Minute Mini-Meals
_____	2	Eden Pinto or Black Beans (15-oz can)	Guiltless Nachos Supreme
_____	2	Eden Organic Caribbean Black Beans (15-oz can)	Caribbean Black Beans ...

Canned Sauces

Restock	Par stock	Item and size	For use in...
_____	4	Spaghetti sauce (26-oz) My favorite brand: Eden Organic (see 336)	Numerous pastas, Numerous pizzas, Numerous stews
_____	2	Sloppy Joe sauce (16-oz)	Turkey Joes

Lickety-Split Tip

Sodium Savvy to the Max!

While my recipes are already healthfully low in sodium by staying below 800 mg of sodium per entrée, some people may wish to lower their sodium intake even further.

Simple steps to reduce your sodium intake further:

• Always use no-salt-added canned beans instead of the conventional brands. While rinsing and draining beans reduces sodium by about 1/3, this can still leave a recipe too high in sodium. (Use the Eden brand, which has no salt added, and you'll save 700 to 800 mg of sodium per can. And all their products are organic to boot!)

• Use no-salt-added canned chicken broth. Instead of the 1/3 less sodium and you'll save about 400 to 700 mg of sodium per can.)

• Buy reduced-sodium salsa. Often fresh salsa is lower in sodium than salsa in a jar. Check the label for less than 120 mg per 2 T. (Use Gourmet Jose® Fresh Salsa instead of Pace Picante from a jar, and you'll save 280 mg per 1/4 cup.)

• My recipes do not call for salt unless the recipe is particularly low in sodium and needs it for flavor. However, you can use a reduced-sodium salt (for instance, Morton's Lite-Salt) or complete salt substitute (like No-Salt) or eliminate the salt I've called for altogether.

Grocery List

Restock	Par stock	Item and size	For use in...

Canned Meat

Restock	Par stock	Item and size	For use in...
_____	4	**Tuna, water-packed (6 oz)**	*Great Northern Tuna...* *Tuna Noodle Casserole* *Creamy Tuna Twist*
_____	1	**Tuna, water-packed 3-oz single-serve cans**	*Desk drawer lunches* *1-Minute Mini-Meals*
_____	2	**Salmon, red or pink (15+ oz)**	*Salmon Burgers* *Herbed Salmon Spread*
_____	4	**Chicken, white meat (10 oz)**	*1-Minute Mini-Meals* *Simple Baked Chicken...* *Almond Chicken Salad* *Chicken Dijon Stuffed...* *Eggless Salad Stuffer*
_____	opt	**Sardines in mustard sauce (3+ oz)**	*1-Minute Mini-Meals*
_____	1	**Crab meat (6 oz)**	*Holiday Crab Dip*

Condiments

Restock	Par stock	Item and size	For use in...
_____	1	**Ketchup**	Basic supply
_____	1	**Mustard, regular**	Basic supply
_____	1	**Dijon mustard**	*Chicken Dijon Stuffed...* *Creamy Chicken Dijon* *Crispy Chicken Dijon* *Kickin' Chicken w/Fries* *Potato Salad*
_____	1	**Honeycup mustard or other spicy flavor of your choice**	*Turkey & tuna sandwiches* *Turkey & Hot Mustard ...*
_____	opt	**Pimentos, chopped (2-oz jar)**	*Salmon Burgers* *Oven-Baked Lentils & Rice*
_____ _____	2	**Black olives, sliced (2.25-oz can)**	*Creamy Chicken Enchiladas* *Mexican Pizza*
_____ _____	1	**Hot pepper rings or jalapeño rings (12-oz jar)**	*Mexican Black Beans* *Hot & Spicy Pizza* *3-Bean Chili* *Crock-Pot Fajitas*
_____	1	**Tabasco sauce**	Basic supply

Lickety-Split Tip

Miracle Whip Light

While I'm aware that fat-free Miracle Whip and mayonnaise are available, I've found that for taste, many people prefer the light versions instead of completely fat-free. I have called for and calculated the nutrition information using Miracle Whip Light for all recipes throughout the book. You are welcome to substitute fat-free if you prefer and you'll save a few more fat grams if you do.

Grocery List

Restock	Par stock	Item and size	For use in...
		Condiments (continued)	
_____	1	**Miracle Whip Light**	Basic supply
_____	1	**Thousand Island dressing, light or fat-free**	Basic supply
_____	1	**Italian dressing, light or fat-free**	*Oklahoma Bean Dip* *Chicken & Vegetables in Foil* *Marinated Vegetable Salad*
_____	1	**Light coleslaw dressing, or low-fat creamy Italian**	Pasta & potato salads
_____	1	**Chutney, mango, peach or pineapple (8-oz jar) (gourmet specialty section)**	*Chicken Chutney Pizza*
_____	1	**Barbecue sauce**	*Chicken & Vegetables in Foil* *Polynesian Pizza*
_____	1	**Heinz Seafood cocktail sauce (8-oz jar)**	*Shrimp Pizza* *Holiday Crab Dip*
_____	1	**Vinegar, balsamic**	Basic supply
_____	1	**Vinegar, cider**	Basic supply
_____	1	**Vinegar, red wine**	Basic supply

Restock	Par stock	Item and size	For use in...
		Cooking Oils	

You can get by with cooking spray and canola oil for everything if you wish.

Restock	Par stock	Item and size	For use in...
_____	1	**Cooking spray**	Basic supply
_____	1	**Canola oil (small bottle)**	Basic supply Desserts
_____	1	**Olive oil (small bottle)**	Italian dishes
_____	1	**Sesame oil (very small bottle)** Toasted tastes best	Stir-fry dinners Marinade *Oriental Noodle Toss* *Marinated Sesame Chicken*

Restock	Par stock	Item and size	For use in...
		Baking Supplies	
_____	1	**Granulated sugar (5–10 lb bag)**	Basic supply
_____	1	**Brown sugar (2-lb box)**	Basic supply
_____	1	**Powdered sugar (2 lb box)**	*Creamy Frosted Carrot Cake* *Brownie Banana Split* *Chewy Multi-Grain Bars*
_____	2	**Honey (1 honey-bear and 1 re-fill jar)**	*Breakfast in a Cookie* *Scrumptious Swiss Oats*

Lickety-Split Diabetic Meals

Lickety-Split Tip

What is whole-wheat pastry flour?

Whole-wheat pastry flour, sometimes called whole-grain pastry flour, is very nutritious because it is whole-grain flour, yet very light and cakey in texture, similar to that of white flour. It can be used in equal amounts to replace all-purpose flour in any non-yeast recipe. It makes wonderfully light cookies, cakes, muffins, and quick breads, and the best part is, only you will know that you used "healthy" flour!

Where do you find it?

Be aware that you may not find it in the standard flour section of your grocery store. It is considered specialty flour and may be found in the health food section among special brands like Arrowhead Mills, Bob's Red Mill, or Hodgson Mill. If you do not find it, request it from your grocer. I buy it in bulk quantities at finer food stores or co-ops. Please look for it. It really is worth the effort!

Grocery List

Restock	Par stock	Item and size	For use in...

Baking Supplies (continued)

Restock	Par stock	Item and size	For use in...
_____	1	**Corn syrup (light, not dark)**	*Glazed Cinnamon Nut Buns* *Oatmeal Cookies* *Chocolate No-Bakes*
_____	1	**Pancake syrup (light)**	Basic supply
_____	opt	**Molasses**	Basic supply
_____	1	**Unbleached all-purpose flour (5-lb bag)**	Basic supply
_____	1	**Whole-wheat pastry flour (10-lb bag)**	Basic supply
_____	1	**Cornmeal, yellow, whole-grain (sm. canister)**	*Cornbread* *Chili Cornbread Pie*
_____	1	**Hodgson Mill Insta-Bake or Bisquick, reduced-fat**	*Surprise Pumpkin Pie* *Applesauce Dumplings*
_____	1	**Brownie mix, reduced-fat**	*Brownie Banana Split*
_____	1	**Oat bran (1-lb box) Similar to the way you buy Cream of Wheat®**	*Breakfast in a Cookie* *Ambrosia Rice* *Pumpkin Oat Bran Bread or Muffins*
_____	1	**Ground Flax Seed**	Basic supply

Restock	Par stock	Item and size	For use in...
_____	1	**Wheat Germ** Tastes best toasted	*Whole-Grain Pancakes* *Over cereal*
_____	1	**Oats, quick-cooking or old-fashioned (lg. canister)**	*Scrumptious Swiss Oats...* *Banana-Oat Pancakes* *Breakfast in a Cookie* *Chocolate No-Bakes* *Oatmeal Cookies* *Chocolate Chip Bar Cookies*
_____	opt	**Multi-grain oats (sm. canister)**	*Chewy Multi-Grain Bars*
_____	1	**Nonfat dry milk (sm. box)**	*Breakfast in a Cookie* *Chocolate No-Bakes*
_____	opt	**Nonfat dry buttermilk**	*Banana Nut Cake or Muffins*
_____	1	**Evaporated skim milk (12-oz can)**	*Pasta Primavera* *Surprise Pumpkin Pie*
_____	1	**Baking powder (sm. canister)**	Basic supply
_____	1	**Baking soda (sm. box)**	Basic supply
_____	1	**Cornstarch**	Basic supply
_____	1	**Cocoa, unsweetened powder for baking**	*Chocolate No-Bakes* *Choc. Amaretto Cheesecake* *Cocoa Lava Kisses* *Hot Fudge Brownie Cake*

Lickety-Split Tip

Will I need to add on a second kitchen?
This Lickety-Split list is HUGE!

Negative on the second kitchen, but you will need to do some cupboard cleaning. For instance, throw out the 5-year-old pudding boxes and cake decorating icing that you know are ready to toss. Bingo, a new shelf.

You may even want to open up a couple of shelves in your laundry room to store extra canned items. What good is that broken flashlight, anyway? Can't half of this stuff go in the garage? There's two more new shelves.

And yes, give up that junk drawer full of pens that don't write, old glasses you will never wear, and keys to unknown locks. I'm sure you can find another place for these precious items—like the dumpster.

If the thought of this is too much to bear, simply transfer the gems to a cardboard box and place them in the basement as a safe purgatory.

And lastly, what about that drawer full of the kids' crayons, coloring books, shoestrings, and a yo-yo? If it doesn't help you cook, get it out of the kitchen! Presto! You now have two open drawers and three open pantry shelves for the extra *Lickety-Split* cooking supplies you will need!

Grocery List

Restock	Par stock	Item and size	For use in...

Restock	Par stock	Item and size	For use in...

Baking Supplies (continued)

Restock	Par stock	Item and size	For use in...
_____	2	Vanilla pudding, instant (5.1-oz box)	*Summer Fresh Fruit Pie* *Chocolate Chip Bar Cookies*
_____	2	Chocolate pudding, instant (5.9-oz box)	*Chocolate Chip Bar Cookies*
_____	2	Strawberry gelatin, sugar-free (0.6-oz box)	*Summer Fresh Fruit Pie* *Cranberry Salad*
_____	1	Semi-sweet chocolate chips (6-oz bag) store in freezer	*Chocolate Chip Bar Cookies* *Banana Nut Cake*
_____	1	Chocolate chips mini-morsels (6-oz bag) Store in freezer	*Choc. Amaretto Cheesecake*
_____	2	Graham cracker crusts, regular or chocolate (9-oz deep-dish size)	*Summer Fresh Fruit Pie*

Peanut Butter & Nuts

(store nuts in freezer)

Restock	Par stock	Item and size	For use in...
_____	1	Peanut butter, preferably natural (sm or lg jar)	Snacking *Chocolate No-Bakes*
_____	1	Chopped walnuts (8 oz)	Cookies Stir-fry Pancakes *Banana Nut Cake or Muffins* *Scrumptious Swiss Oats*
_____	1	Chopped pecans (8 oz)	*Ambrosia Rice* *Glazed Cinnamon Nut Buns* *Dried Cherry & Broccoli Salad* *Scrumptious Swiss Oats*
_____	1	Slivered almonds (8 oz)	Stir-fry dinners *Almond Chicken Salad* *Scrumptious Swiss Oats*

Lickety-Split Tip

Money-saving tip for buying spices

If your spices are over 5 years old, empty out the jars and head to your local bulk food store, health food store or co-op, where you can purchase spices by the ounce (the staff will show you how). You can purchase as little as 1 tablespoon if that's all you want to try. This would cost you less than 10 cents. You buy only what you know you'll need and replenish your supply with fresh after that. No more paying $3 for a jar of spice that you'll only use a little of!

Grocery List

Restock	Par stock	Item and size	For use in...
		Spices, Dried Herbs, and Flavorings	
_____	1	**Vanilla extract (lg)**	Basic supply
_____	1	**Lemon extract (sm)**	Basic supply
_____	1	**Almond extract (sm)**	Basic supply
_____	1	**Basil**	Basic supply
_____	1	**Cayenne**	Basic supply
_____	1	**Chili powder (lg)**	Basic supply
_____	opt	**Chinese Five Spice**	*Crunchy Apple Salad*
_____	1	**Cinnamon (lg)**	Basic supply
_____	1	**Cloves, ground**	Basic supply
_____	1	**Red pepper flakes**	Basic supply
_____	1	**Cumin, ground (lg)**	Basic supply
_____	opt	**Cumin seeds**	*Mexican Black Beans*
_____	1	**Curry powder**	*Curried Chickpeas & Gingered Black Beans*
_____	1	**Dill weed**	Basic supply
_____	1	**Garlic powder**	Basic supply
_____	1	**Italian seasoning**	Basic supply
_____	1	**Lemon Pepper, salt-free**	*Spinach Veal Roll*
_____	1	**Marjoram**	*Creamy Cauliflower Soup*

Restock	Par stock	Item and size	For use in...
_____	1	**Dry mustard**	Basic supply
_____	1	**Orange rind (grated) or extract**	*Breakfast in a Cookie*
_____	1	**Oregano (lg)**	Basic supply
_____	1	**Onion flakes**	Basic supply
_____	1	**Paprika (lg)**	Basic supply
_____	1	**Peppercorns, whole black**	Basic supply
_____	1	**Poultry seasoning**	Basic supply
_____	1	**Pumpkin Pie Spice**	Basic supply
_____	1	**Red Pepper flakes**	Basic supply
_____	1	**Rosemary**	Basic supply
_____	1	**Sage**	Basic supply
_____	1	**Savory**	*Creamy Cauliflower Soup*
_____	1	**Sesame seeds**	*Marinated Sesame Chicken*
_____	1	**Salt (consider lite or salt substitute)**	Basic supply
_____	1	**Thyme**	Basic supply
_____	1	**True Lemon (1 box)**	Basic supply
_____	1	**True Lime (1 box)**	*Crock-Pot Fajitas*
_____	1	**Mrs. Dash or Spike Salt-Free**	Basic supply

Lickety-Split Tip

Cereal Selection Tips

For healthy cereal, follow these label-reading criteria:

Fat: 2 grams of fat or less per serving. (Keep in mind that whole grains, including oats, have up to 2 grams of naturally occurring fat. The goal is to avoid cereals with added fats.)

Fiber: 4 or more grams of fiber per serving is ideal.

Sugar: Less than 6 grams of sugar. (The lower the better.) Every 4 grams equal 1 teaspoon of sugar. And don't you think 1 1/2 teapoons is enough?

Iron-Fortified Cereals: The good and not so good

While 100% fortification of the RDA of iron is great for people who run low in iron (like heavily menstruating women or recent blood donors), it may not be so good for others who are not low in iron. Recent concerns are based on the understanding that iron is a pro-oxidant, which can be harmful in excess. Many health professionals suggest iron only be supplemented when a person is in need of it. Therefore, you may prefer to choose cereals that have been fortified with no more than 25% of iron.

P.S. It's smart to use iron-fortified cereals or iron supplements for 4 weeks after donating blood.

Grocery List

Cereal

The following are a few of my favorite cereals, meeting my criteria for fat, fiber and taste.

Restock		Item and size	For use in...
_____		**Kashi Go Lean**	Breakfast
_____		**Grape-Nuts**	Breakfast
_____		**Shredded wheat with bran**	Breakfast
_____		**Frosted shredded wheat**	Breakfast & snacking
_____		**Quaker Oat Bran** (cold, ready-to-eat hexagon chex)	Breakfast & snacking
_____		**Quaker Oat Squares**	Breakfast & snacking
_____		**Corn bran**	Breakfast & snacking
_____		**Wheaties**	Breakfast
_____		**Bran flakes**	Breakfast
_____		**Low-fat granola**	Breakfast
_____		**Cheerios**	Breakfast & snacking

Ethnic Foods

Restock	Par stock	Item and size	For use in...
_____	2	**Refried beans, fat-free (16-oz can)**	*Quick Nachos* / *Chicken & Bean Enchiladas* / *Fiesta Bean Burrito*
_____	1	**Enchilada sauce (10-oz can)**	*Chicken & Bean Enchiladas*
_____	2	**Green chilies, chopped (4-oz can)**	*Creamy Chicken Enchiladas* / *Southwest Pizza* / *South of the Border Roll-ups* / *Mexican 5-Bean Soup*
_____	2	**Water chestnuts, sliced (8-oz can)**	*Spinach Dip* / *Saucy Almond Chicken...*
_____	3	**Salsa, hot, medium or mild** (fresh salsa may have less sodium, look in your deli)	Numerous entrees / Snacking
_____	1	**Soy sauce, reduced-sodium (lg)**	Numerous entrees / "Appeteasers"
_____	opt	**Tamari sauce, reduced-sodium (sm)**	*Marinated Sesame Chicken Kabobs* / *Simple Tofu Bites*
_____	3	**Sweet & sour sauce LaChoy (10-oz jar)**	*Easiest Stir-Fry Ever* / *Sweet & Sour Chicken*

Lickety-Split Diabetic Meals

Lickety-Split Tip

Nutrients lost when whole wheat is refined

86%.......................................Vitamin E

81%.......................................Niacin*

80%.......................................Riboflavin*

77%.......................................Thiamin*

75%.......................................Fiber

70%.......................................Vitamin B-6

67%.......................................Folic acid

50% ....Pantothenic acid

* Replaced commercially after refinement, as required by law.

Now you know WHY I make all the fuss about whole-wheat flour!

Grocery List

Restock	Par stock	Item and size	For use in...
		Bread Products	

Buy according to your family's needs & all breads freeze well!

Restock	Par stock	Item and size	For use in...
_____	1–4	**100% whole-wheat bread** (preferably with ground flax seed and no hydrogenated fats)	Sandwiches Toast
_____	0–1	**Rye or pumpernickel bread, round loaf**	*Spinach Dip in Pumpernickel*
_____	0–6	**Pita bread, whole-wheat**	Pita sandwiches *Pita Pizza* *Herbed Salmon Spread*
_____	0–6	**Hamburger buns, whole-wheat**	*Salmon Burgers*
_____	0–12	**Rolls, whole-wheat or 9-grain**	Serve with meals
_____	0–6	**English muffins, whole-grain**	Breakfasts

Restock	Par stock	Item and size	For use in...
_____	1–12	**Bagels, whole-grain (3 oz each)**	Breakfasts Snacking 1-Minute Mini-Meals
_____	1	**Flour tortillas, 6" fat-free (pkg of 10)**	*South of the Border Roll-ups* *Benito Bean Burritos* *Creamy Chicken Enchiladas* *Crockpot Fajitas* *Mexican LaZonya*
_____	1	**Corn tortillas 6" (pkg of 10)** These freeze well.	*Mexican LaZonya* *Southwest Chicken Pizza*
_____	1–2	**Lavash, flat breads (pkg of 6)**	Roll-up sandwiches *"Appeteasers"*
_____	1–4	**Pizza crusts, ready-made whole-wheat**	Friday night pizzas
_____	1–4	**Rice cakes, popcorn cakes (pkg)**	Snacking 1-Minute Mini-Meals
_____	1	**Bread crumbs, unseasoned (canister)**	*Tantalizing Turkey Loaf* *Crispy Chicken Dijon*

Lickety-Split Tip

Tips for selecting a "healthy" commercial stir-fry sauce

Comparing the labels for stir-fry sauces can be quite confusing. Sometimes the serving size is 1 T, sometimes it's 1/2 cup! What should be the appropriate serving size? I find 1/4 cup works nicely, and an 8-ounce jar serves 4 very well. In the sweet-and-sour type sauces, fat is not an issue but sodium is. Take a look at the following to get an idea of what's out there. I've adjusted all the portions to 1/4 cup (that's 4 tablespoons).

Sodium per 1/4 cup

LaChoy Sweet and Sour Sauce ....210 mg

Kraft Sweet 'n Sour Sauce ....250 mg

Kikkoman Sweet & Sour Sauce ....380 mg

LaChoy Stir-Fry Vegetables 'n Sauce ....410 mg

Lawry's Stir-Fry Oriental Style Cooking Sauce........................1,320 mg

Kame Szechuan Sauce...1,640 mg

As you can see, some are salt mines!

Your goal is 250 mg or less per 1/4 cup.

What about sugar? It's darn near impossible to make a stir-fry sauce out of just protein or fat (ok, butter). So a sweet and sour sauce is going to have some sort of carbohydrate/sweetener. Just remember that you are using it on VEGETABLES. Healthy, low-calorie, disease-fighting vegetables. I always say that the best place to spend some sugar on is vegetables! Besides, all the recipes in this book are analyzed, so you know just how many carbohydrates you are consuming!

Grocery List

Restock	Par stock	Item and size	For use in...
Snacks			
_____	1	**Chocolate syrup (squeeze bottle kind)**	*Chocolate milk* *Drizzling over fruit* *Brownie Banana Split*
_____	1	**Hot cocoa mix**	Snacking
_____	1–2	**Baked tortilla chips Tostitos®**	*Guiltless Nachos Supreme* *7-Layer Bean Dip* *Oklahoma Bean Dip* *Crockpot Fajitas* *Mexican Black Beans* *Mexican 5-Bean Soup*
_____	1–2	**Baked potato chips**	Snacking Sandwiches Soups
_____	0–1	**Fig Newtons, regular or fat-free**	Snacking Desserts Lunchbox treat
_____	1	**Chocolate wafers**	*Chocolate Amaretto Cheescake*

Restock	Par stock	Item and size	For use in...
_____	0–1	**Gingersnaps**	Snacking Desserts "Ice cream" sandwiches Lunchbox treat
_____	0–12	**Fortune cookies** (only 30 calories each, fat-free, and fun)	Stir-fry dinners
_____	1	**Crackers, saltine-type**	*Salmon Burgers*
_____	1	**Crackers, low-fat whole-wheat**	Snacking Soups
_____	1–2	**Triscuits, reduced-fat**	Snacking 1-Minute Mini-Meals
_____	1	**Graham crackers, low-fat**	Snacking Desserts "Ice cream" sandwiches
_____	1–2	**Popcorn, microwave, Orville Redenbacher Smart Pop or Pop Secret by Request**	Snacking Soups 1-Minute Meals

Lickety-Split Tip

Should we give eggs a break?

Egg yolks certainly do have a lot of cholesterol (a full day's allowance in just one egg) AND 5 grams of fat. Egg whites, on the other hand, are fat- and cholesterol-free. The recommendation is to consume fewer than 4 egg yolks a week and fewer (or none) if you have high cholesterol.

I choose to limit egg yolks by diluting them with egg whites, as called for in these recipes. I find this convenient and economical. This provides some of the color and texture of whole eggs, while staying within the weekly recommendation. However, to completely omit egg yolks from your diet, replace each egg yolk with 2 whites. You can also use egg substitutes: 1/4 cup replaces 1 large egg.

What about fat-free cream cheese and sour cream?

See my important message about both of these Recommended Ingredients in the Introduction on page viii.

Grocery List

Restock	Par stock	Item and size	For use in...

Eggs & Dairy

Restock	Par stock	Item and size	For use in...
_____	2	**Dozen eggs (or egg substitute)**	Various uses
_____	1–2	**Skim or 1/2% milk (gal)**	Various uses
_____	opt	**Soy milk**	Pancakes Baking Cereals *Scrumptious Swiss Oats* *Smoothies*
_____	1	**Margarine, light (tub)**	Used in 1 recipe only: *Flaming Bananas Foster*
_____	1	**Spray butter, I Can't Believe It's Not Butter**	Variety of uses
_____	1	**Sour cream, fat-free (16-oz container)**	*Creamy Chicken Enchiladas* *Chicken & Bean Enchiladas* *Hungarian Chicken Paprikash* *Simple Baked Chicken...* *Creamy Chicken Dijon* *Chicken Dijon Stuffed...* *Guiltless Nachos Supreme* *Beef Stroganoff* *Spinach Dip* *South of the Border Roll-ups*

Restock	Par stock	Item and size	For use in...
_____	1	**Cream cheese, fat-free (8-oz pkg)**	*Holiday Crab Dip* *Turkey & Hot Mustard...* *South of the Border...* *Chocolate Amaretto Cheesecake* *Brownie Banana Split* *Oatmeal Cookies*
_____	1	**Cream cheese, light (8-oz pkg)**	*Creamy Frosted Carrot Cake*
_____	1	**Cottage cheese, nonfat (16-oz container)**	*1-Minute Mini-Meals* *Spinach Veal Roll* *Chocolate-Amaretto Cheesecake*
_____	1	**Ricotta cheese, fat-free (15-oz container)**	*LaZonya*
_____	1	**Feta cheese, reduced-fat (4-oz)**	*Spinach Veal Roll*
_____	1	**String cheese, part-skim mozzarella**	*1-Minute Mini-Meals*
_____	1	**Sliced cheese, low-fat**	*1-Minute Mini-Meals*
_____	1	**Nonfat plain yogurt (16-oz container)**	*Baking* *Mixing with Miracle Whip Light 50-50* *Smoothies*
_____	6	**Nonfat fruit yogurts (8-oz container)**	*Snacking* *Ambrosia Rice* *1-Minute Mini-Meals*

Lickety-Split Diabetic Meals

Lickety-Split Tip

How does cheese fit into a healthy diet?

I would really miss cheese if I had to give it up, wouldn't you? And thanks to so many low-fat and fat-free cheeses on the market, we don't have to!

The ideal is to use fat-free cheese. But what about taste? There are great-tasting low-fat cheeses available, but they run 5–7 grams of fat per ounce, which is TOO MUCH. So, when it comes to shredded cheese, why not mix fat-free with reduced-fat for a great compromise? I recommend Sharp 2% Milk by Kraft and I mix it 50–50 with the fat-free cheese by Kraft or Healthy Choice. This produces a wonderful, tasty, and evenly melting cheese for only 3 grams of fat per ounce. I do this with both cheddar and mozzarella. This is the "reduced-fat shredded cheese" I am referring to in all recipes. If you prefer to use the fat-free exclusively, please do!

The next trick is to keep your portion to 1 ounce only (equal to 1/4 cup shredded cheese). This actually goes a long way melted across a serving of broccoli, pizza or nachos! Enjoy!

Parmesan cheese

Parmesan cheese is high in fat. However, the amounts called for in this book do not add unreasonable amounts of fat. I therefore suggest using regular Parmesan cheese and have calculated the recipes accordingly. If you would like to use fat-free instead, please do.

(I personally have had great results mixing regular and fat-free, 50–50.)

Grocery List

Restock	Par stock	Item and size	For use in...

Eggs & Dairy (continued)

Restock	Par stock	Item and size	For use in...
_____	1	**Parmesan cheese**	Numerous entrees
_____	1	**Mozzarella, shredded, fat-free, Kraft**	Numerous entrees
_____	1	**Mozzarella, shredded, 2% Milk by Kraft or reduced fat**	Numerous entrees
_____	1	**Cheddar cheese, shredded fat-free, Kraft**	Numerous entrees
_____	1	**Cheddar cheese, sharp, shredded, 2% Milk by Kraft**	Numerous entrees

Make your own reduced-fat cheese by mixing the 2 white cheeses and 2 cheddar cheeses together. Do this when putting groceries away so you don't forget. Freezes well!

Convenience Meats

Restock	Par stock	Item and size	For use in...
_____	1–2	**Turkey breast slices, 97% fat-free, deli thin (lb)**	1-Minute Mini-Meals Sandwiches
_____	1	**Ham, 98% fat-free chunk or slices (lb) (When putting groceries away, chop and divide ham into 8 2-oz portions. Freeze in airtight bags.)**	Pizza topping *Split Pea Soup* *Breakfast Casserole* *Scrambled Omelette*
_____	opt	**Canadian bacon**	
_____	opt	**Low-fat smoked sausage, Healthy Choice**	*Breakfast Casserole*

Seafood

Restock	Par stock	Item and size	For use in...
_____		**Orange roughy, fresh or frozen fillets (lg bag)**	**Broiled Orange Roughy**
_____		**Trout, cod, whitefish, perch, or snapper (2 lb)**	**Delicate Baked Fish**
_____	1	**Shrimp, frozen, cooked, ready to eat (12-oz bag)**	**Shrimp Pizza** **Pasta Primavera**

Lickety-Split Diabetic Meals

Lickety-Split Tip

Red meat. Where do you draw the line?

All you have to do is follow these 3 guidelines and you can enjoy red meat up to 3 times per week!

1. Choose lean. NOT prime rib, but tenderloin or filet mignon; NOT hamburger but ground sirloin. Whatever you do, don't worry about it costing more because guideline #3 will offset the cost. Besides, you either pay now or you pay later! (See page 124 for a list of the leanest cuts of beef.)

2. Trim well. Trim all meats meticulously of fat.

3. Think small. Keep your portion to 4 ounces. (This looks like the size of a deck of cards or the palm of your hand.) Fill the plate up with lots of vegetables and a baked potato. Of course, slicing the meat up for stir-fry or pepper steak works great. Try it!

What about pork?

See page 246 for good news about today's pork.

Grocery List

Restock	Par stock	Item and size	For use in...
		Poultry • Beef • Pork	
_____		**Chicken breasts, skinless, boneless (4 lb)** (Freeze in 4-oz size portions for convenience and portion control.)	*Marinated Sesame Chicken* *Creamy Chicken Dijon* *Skillet Chicken & Vegetables* *Chicken Marsala* *Hungarian Chicken Paprikash* *Southwest Chicken Pizza* *Chicken Chutney Pizza* *Saucy Almond Chicken...* *Sweet & Sour Stir-fry* *Kickin' Chicken w/Fries* *Chicken & Vegetables in Foil* *Creamy Chicken Enchiladas* *Crock-Pot Fajitas* *Chicken Cacciatore* *Sweet & Sour Chicken* *Ratatouille*
_____	1	**Chicken leg quarters, optional (thigh and drumstick, pkg of 4)**	*To accompany Oven Fries*
_____	2	**Chicken thighs, skinless, boneless (pkg of 6)**	*Ratatouille* *Chicken Cacciatore*
_____	4	**Turkey, extra-lean ground breast (20-oz pkgs)**	*Unstuffed Peppers* *Veggie Sghetti* *Tantalizing Turkey Loaf* *3-Bean Chili* *Turkey Joes*

Restock	Par stock	Item and size	For use in...
_____	1	**Turkey tenderloin, boneless (1 lb)**	*Turkey Vegetable Stew*
_____	1	**Jennie-O Turkey tenderloin, boneless slices or cutlets (1 lb)**	*Parmesan Turkey Cutlets...*
_____	1–2	**Lean top round or sirloin (1–2 lb)**	*Crock-Pot Fajitas* *Easy Pepper Steak Stir-Fry* *Beef Barley Soup* *Beef Stroganoff*
_____		**Pork tenderloin (2 lb)**	*Cranberry Pork Roast* *Sweet & Sour Stir-Fry* *Gypsy Stew* *Crockpot Fajitas*
_____	1	**Thin-sliced veal (scaloppini) (1 lb)**	*Spinach Veal Roll*

Alcohol for Cooking

Purchase small bottles.

Restock	Par stock	Item and size	For use in...
_____	1	**Marsala wine**	*Chicken Marsala*
_____ _____	1	**White wine**	*Skillet Chicken & Vegetables* *Oven-Baked Lentils & Rice*
_____	1	**Amaretto**	*Chocolate-Amaretto Cheesecake*
_____	1	**Banana liqueur**	*Flaming Bananas Foster*
_____	1	**White rum**	*Flaming Bananas Foster*
_____	opt	**Beer**	*Mexican 5-Bean Soup*

Lickety-Split Tip

Will I need to buy a deep freezer?

It's definitely a plus to own a deep freezer. But if you don't have one, simply plan on extra strict cleaning and organizing of your freezer to optimize capacity. Either way, be sure to reserve a separate area for vegetables, meats, juices, etc., so you can keep things rotated (first in, first out) and find things FAST.

Remember:

• Use your fresh produce early in the week and frozen later in the week.

• A full variety of frozen vegetables is nice to have on hand.

• A one-pound bag of vegetables should serve 3 to 4, not 5 to 6.

• Fruits are a delicious snack eaten frozen or just partially thawed.

• Try chocolate syrup drizzled over frozen cherries for "healthy" chocolate-covered cherries!

Grocery List

Restock	Par stock	Item and size	For use in...

Frozen Veggies

Yes, I do suggest having all these on hand, in addition to having a full drawer of fresh. Use the fresh early in the week and the frozen later in the week.

Restock	Par stock	Item and size	For use in...
_____	1	Corn (16-oz bag)	Various entrees
_____	1	Peas (16-oz bag)	Various entrees
_____	1	Lima beans (16-oz bag)	Various entrees
_____	1	Mixed vegetables (16-oz bag)	Various entrees
_____	1	Cut green beans (16 oz bag)	Various entrees
_____	1	Whole green beans (16-oz bag)	Various entrees
_____	1	California blend broccoli, cauliflower, and carrots (16-oz bag)	Various entrees
_____	1	Mixed stir-fry vegetables (16-oz bag)	*Easiest Stir-Fry Ever!* *Mexican LaZonya*
_____	4	Spinach, chopped (10-oz box)	*Veggie Sghetti* *Unstuffed Peppers* *Gypsy Stew* *Spinach Dip* *Spinach Veal Roll*
_____	1	Peas pods or snow peas (10-oz box)	Various entrees

Restock	Par stock	Item and size	For use in...
_____	1	Carrots, crinkle cut (10-oz box)	Various entrees
_____	1	Asparagus (10-oz box) use fresh if you prefer	*Chicken Dijon Stuffed...* *Creamy Chicken Dijon*
_____	1	Ore Ida Potatoes O'Brien (24-oz bag)	*Breakfast Casserole* *Scrambled Omelette* *Cheesy Potato Skillet* *Cheesy Scrambled Tofu*
_____	1	Potato wedges with skins, Ore Ida (24-oz bag)	*Kickin' Chicken w/Fries* *Delicate Baked Fish*
_____	opt	Broccoli	*Crispy Chicken Dijon*

Frozen or Bottled Juices

Restock	Par stock	Item and size	For use in...
_____	4	Orange juice	*Breakfast in a Cookie* *Cranberry Pork Roast ...*
_____	1	V-8 juice, low-sodium (46-oz jar)	*Miracle Soup* *3-Bean Chili* *1-Minute Mini-Meals*
_____	1	V-8 juice, low-sodium (6 pack of 6-oz cans)	Snacking
_____	4	100% fruit juice, your choice of flavors	Snacking
_____	1	Lemon juice (sm bottle)	Various entrees
_____	1	Lime juice (sm bottle)	*Crock-Pot Fajitas*

Lickety-Split Diabetic Meals

Lickety-Split Tip

Grocery Store Checkout 1-Minute Stress Buster

Whew! Aren't you glad you're done? Now for the torturous checkout. While waiting there (instead of musing about the slow line, reading tabloids, or drooling over the chocolate bars), refresh your body by doing some deep breathing, stretching, and strengthening exercises.

1. Lift your hands straight up over your head and stretch. Take a deep breath in. Exhale. (Care not what others think of you!) Repeat twice.

2. Raise up on one foot at a time and work each calf separately.

3. Looking first, lift your leg straight out behind you. Feel the muscle in your buttocks contract. Alternate legs.

4. Standing with feet shoulder-width apart, curl your foot up to almost kick your behind. Feel the muscle in the back of your leg contract. Alternate feet back and forth.

5. Before you know it, it will be time to start unloading your cart and you will hardly have noticed that the line was slow, or that the candy bars were a temptation.

P.S. No matter what you've been doing all day—chained to your computer, running errands, chasing children or flying from airport to airport—give these 1-minute stress busters a try.

Grocery List

Restock	Par stock	Item and size	For use in...

Frozen Fruit

Restock	Par stock	Item and size	For use in...
_____	1	**Strawberries, unsweetened (12-oz bag)**	*Snacking* *Smoothies*
_____	1	**Blueberries unsweetened (12-oz bag)**	*Snacking* *Smoothies* *Blueberry Buckle*
_____	1	**Cherries unsweetened (12-oz bag)**	*Snacking*

Frozen Miscellaneous

Restock	Par stock	Item and size	For use in...
_____	1	**Honey-wheat bread dough (pkg of 3)**	*Glazed Cinnamon Nut Buns*
_____	1	**Cheese tortellini (16-oz bag)**	*Tortellini Stew*

Choose 1 or 2 of the following:

Restock	Par stock	Item and size	For use in...
_____	1	**Vanilla ice cream or frozen yogurt, fat-free**	*Blueberry Buckle* *Flaming Bananas Foster* *Applesauce Dumplings* *Hot Fudge Brownie Cake*
_____	opt	**Lemon or raspberry sorbet**	*Dessert*
_____	opt	**Fudgesicles**	*Dessert*
_____	opt	**Frozen yogurt bars**	*Dessert*

Cleaning Supplies

_____ _____
_____ _____
_____ _____
_____ _____

Laundry Supplies

_____ _____
_____ _____
_____ _____

Personal Hygiene

_____ _____
_____ _____
_____ _____
_____ _____

Pet Supplies

_____ _____

Paper Goods

_____ _____
_____ _____
_____ _____
_____ _____

Optional Items

_____ _____
_____ _____
_____ _____
_____ _____

Lickety-Split Diabetic Meals

Recipe Index

Recipes by Topic

Recipe Index

Recipes by Topic

Recipe Index

Recipes Alphabetically

Recipes by Topic

Lickety-Split Diabetic Meals

Recipe Index

Recipes Alphabetically

Tip Index

Tip Index

Tip Index

Tip Index

OTHER TITLES FROM THE AMERICAN DIABETES ASSOCIATION

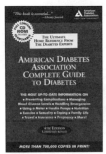

American Diabetes Association Complete Guide to Diabetes, 4th Edition
by American Diabetes Association

Have all the tips and information on diabetes that you need close at hand. The world's largest collection of diabetes self-care tips, techniques, and tricks for solving diabetes-related problems is back in its fourth edition, and it's bigger and better than ever before.
Order no. 4809-04; New low price $19.95

16 Myths of a Diabetic Diet, 2nd Edition
by Karen Hanson Chalmers, MS, RD, LDN, CDE, and Amy Peterson Campbell, MS, RD, LDN, CDE
16 Myths of a Diabetic Diet will tell you the truth about diabetes and how to eat when you have diabetes. Learn what the most common myths about diabetes meal plans are, where they came from, and how to overcome them. Diabetes doesn't have to be a life sentence of boring, dull meals. Let experts Karen Chalmers and Amy Campbell show you how to create and follow a healthy, enjoyable way of eating.
Order no. 4829-02; Price $14.95

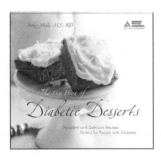

The Big Book of Diabetic Desserts
by Jackie Mills, MS, RD

This first-ever collection of guilty pleasures proves that people with diabetes never have to say no to dessert again. Packed with familiar favorites and some delicious new surprises, *The Big Book of Diabetic Desserts* has more than 150 tantalizing treats that will satisfy any sweet tooth.
Order no. 4664-01; Price $18.95

Mix 'n' Match Meals in Minutes, 2nd Edition
By Linda Gassenheimer

Designed for simplicity and diversity, *Mix 'n' Match Meals in Minutes*, 2nd edition, offers an assortment of breakfast, lunch, and dinner recipes for people who need entire meals planned in a snap. Let *Mix 'n' Match* take the stress out of planning your meals and help you have more time to enjoy other parts of your life.
Order no. 4644-02; Price $16.95